The
Blockchain Code

Decrypt the Jungle of Complexity to Win the Crypto-Anarchy Game

Dave Kinsey

Copyright © 2019 Modern Expert, LLC

All rights reserved.

No part of this book may be used or reproduced in any manner whatsoever without the prior written consent of the author, except as provided by the United States of America Copyright law.

Because of the dynamic nature of the Internet, any web addresses or links contained in this book may have changed since publication and may no longer be valid. The Wayback Machine (a.k.a. Internet Archive) may possibly be used to access snapshots of how these web pages looked at the time of publication. However, the author and publisher have no control over what any third party does (including the Wayback Machine). Information about the Wayback Machine is included in Chapter 22 of this book.

The Wired Magazine May/June 1993 cover image used in Chapter 4 of this book was provided by and permission granted for inclusion in this book by Larry Dyer (larrydyer.com).

Although the author has made every effort to ensure that the information in this book was correct at publication time, the author and publisher do not assume and hereby disclaim any liability to any party for any loss, damage, or disruption caused by errors or omissions, whether such errors or omissions result from negligence, accident, or any other cause.

ISBN 9781731014078

Independently published

Visit our website at modern.expert

The plan is to strike at the state from the jungle of complexity.
—*"James A. Donald", The Cypherpunk Program*

CONTENTS

Preface vii
Introduction 1
Part I.   **Crypto-Anarchy** 5
   Chapter 1 A Curious Revolution 7
   Chapter 2 1986-1988 9
   Chapter 3 Blockchain & Cryptocurrency 15
   Chapter 4 1992: The Cypherpunks' Crypto-Anarchy Game 19
   Chapter 5 Bitcoin 27
   Chapter 6 1993 31
   Chapter 7 Pseudonyms and Reputations 37
   Chapter 8 1994 41
   Chapter 9 Blocks 49
   Chapter 10 Blockchain 53
   Chapter 11 1995 57
   Chapter 12 Modern Money 61
   Chapter 13 1996 67
   Chapter 14 Decrypting Cryptography - The Art of Hiding 71
   Chapter 15 1997 73
   Chapter 16 1998 77
   Chapter 17 Follow the Money 81
   Chapter 18 2001 85

Chapter 19 Catch Me if You Can 89

Chapter 20 2003 95

Chapter 21 Peer-to-Peer (P2P) 101

Chapter 22 The Wayback Machine 105

Chapter 23 December 2005 Blockchain is Born 109

Chapter 24 A "Trustless" System 117

Chapter 25 Wallets 125

Chapter 26 2013 137

Part II.   **Decrypting Blockchain** 139

Chapter 27 "Mining" Decrypted 141

Chapter 28 Traditional & Social Media 149

Chapter 29 Great Stories 155

Chapter 30 Blockchain - Higher Education & Business 159

Chapter 31 The Blockchain Technology Story 167

Chapter 32 Who Can You Trust? 179

Chapter 33 A Fork in the Road 187

Chapter 34 Crypto-Coin Copying 189

Chapter 35 Exchanges 193

Chapter 36 Smart Contracts 203

Chapter 37 The Blockchain Preacher 211

Chapter 38 Wikileaks 217

Chapter 39 NOW 227

APPENDIX **The Crypto-Story of Meltdown** 235

Acknowledgments 251

PREFACE

Sometimes you choose to write a book, and apparently, sometimes the book chooses you.

The last thing I would have expected to do was to write a book about Blockchain. I serve on a technology advisory group for the State Bar of Arizona. In late 2017, I received a request to help the State Bar's continuing legal education (CLE) efforts by teaching a class about Blockchain. I provided some of my thoughts and suggested some potential resources for the CLE, though I declined to serve as a presenter.

A few months later, a staff member of the State Bar visited my office in person and requested that I write an article on the topic. She was very insistent and persuasive. She handed me a copy of the then hot-off-the-presses February 2018 edition of *Arizona Attorney*, the State Bar's magazine. The cover featured a single headline, "BLOCKCHAIN: What it means for clients, contracts-and law practice." We discussed the buzz around Blockchain, which was supposed to revolutionize legal and other professions. I explained how I declined an earlier opportunity to present a CLE on the topic, to which she replied, "Dave, what the heck are you doing? At least write an article!"

After she left, I read the *Arizona Attorney* Blockchain article, which I felt overlooked significant concerns with the technology. I was motivated to write a better, more accurate article!

From the outset of my research, I began to uncover some rather shocking details about what was going on with Blockchain. I also began to appreciate how a growing number of people were expressing a passion for this political-technical movement, which has some real potential power and danger for our society, but is relatively unknown and misunderstood. My article grew and grew to the point where I realized that the only way I could do justice to the subject of Blockchain was to write a book about it.

This book is nonfiction and educational, and it tells the tale of a true-life mystery. As I dug into the details to figure out the truth of what was going on, I found myself reading the software *code* that creates the Bitcoin blockchain. At that point, it became clear that this book had to be named *The Blockchain Code*. *The DaVinci Code* inspired the title of this book, but the connection goes deeper than that. Dan Brown's excellent mystery novel juggles intricate storylines, puzzles, and plot twists, yet never loses the reader. At one point in writing *The Blockchain Code*, I re-read *The DaVinci Code* to see what I could learn from Brown's approach. I have tried to include just enough detail throughout this book to decrypt this important mystery without overwhelming the reader.

Standing before us is the jungle of complexity that is Blockchain! There is nothing to pack for this expedition. You need only bring a curious and open mind.

INTRODUCTION

Hidden deep in a jungle of complexity, obscured by fancy words and misinformation, lies the fascinating story of Blockchain. Its proponents have hailed the technology as the solution for many problems they propose are plaguing humanity. Skeptics denounce Blockchain, Bitcoin, and cryptocurrency in terms ranging from hype to scam. So, what's the truth? Is there hype and scam surrounding Blockchain? Absolutely! Are there grandiose plans to change the world as well? Yes, there are. These plans are very real, and the scope is enormous.

The biggest problem with a fancy word like "Blockchain" is that it makes it hard to decipher **true meaning**. Fancy words, in turn, invite simple explanations that are often misleading, empty, or false. An *empty* explanation is when a fancy word is described with a bunch of other fancy words. Empty explanations sound great but explain nothing. Consider how magicians rely on misdirection to make their magic seem real. Similarly, word magicians use simple, pleasant-sounding explanations to misdirect audiences in magical ways.

As fancy words are clearly *defined*, this weakens their power to misdirect. Fancy words can confuse even those who are well versed in their use. Definitional confusion can be a real problem even among the most brilliant minds and "experts." Sometimes, *even more so* than among those who are less skilled. The less skilled must stop and ask the more fundamental questions in areas that "experts" already assume that they know.

Terms such as "consensus ledger" and "trustless" can seem magical and wonderful. But what do these terms really mean? And how are they used to build a blockchain? Exactly *how* will Blockchain change the world as many proclaim?

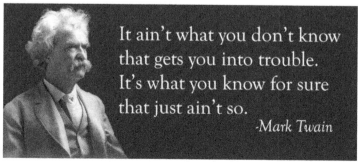

It ain't what you don't know that gets you into trouble. It's what you know for sure that just ain't so.
-Mark Twain

THE BLOCKCHAIN CODE

You may have seen this quote before. It was featured at the beginning of the movie *The Big Short*. The most interesting thing about this quote is that there appears to be no solid evidence that Mark Twain (a.k.a. Samuel Clemens) ever said these words. The fact that Mark Twain probably never said this is wonderful irony. It helps the quote make its own point! *The Big Short* book begins with an even better quote:

```
The most difficult subjects can be ex-
plained to the most slow-witted man if he
has not formed any idea of them already;
but the simplest thing cannot be made clear
to the most intelligent man if he is firmly
persuaded that he knows already, without a
shadow of a doubt what is laid before him.
     —Leo Tolstoy
```

False assumptions are *powerful*, particularly when they are based upon empty or misleading definitions. Misleading explanations like "blockchain is a distributed consensus ledger" may have been repeated often enough to become deeply held beliefs for some readers. Master explorers are always on the lookout for traps, dangerous animals, and falling rocks. The toughest obstacles in this jungle are "what you know for sure that just ain't so." Numerous myths surround Blockchain.

My first step into the jungle of complexity that is Blockchain began when I read the famous Bitcoin white paper written by the mysterious "Satoshi Nakamoto." The last page lists eight references and after reading the *first cited reference*[1], I was hooked. It drew me into the jungle. It begins:

```
I am fascinated by Tim May's crypto-anar-
chy. Unlike the communities traditionally
associated with the word "anarchy", in a
crypto-anarchy the government is not tem-
porarily destroyed but permanently forbid-
den and permanently unnecessary.[2]
```

What is *crypto-anarchy*? What does this have to do with Bitcoin? How does the system defined in the Bitcoin whitepaper relate to Blockchain? I had to know. The further I explored, the more I realized just how large the

---

[1] "Nakamoto, Satoshi." 2008. "Bitcoin: A Peer-to-Peer Electronic Cash System." Oct 31. https://bitcoin.org/bitcoin.pdf, p 9

[2] "Dai, Wei". Republished Dec 2006 (originally published 1998). "b-money." http://www.weidai.com/bmoney.txt

INTRODUCTION

jungle is. The story of Blockchain is larger, more complex, more intriguing, and more important than I had ever imagined.

There are considerations for investors, regulators, businesses, and governments, which this book will help make clear. These concerns are important, but the bigger picture is even more interesting and more important than the investment and regulatory story. Blockchain advocates proclaim a new way for the world, which deserves to be understood by everyone.

Anarchists like Julian Assange are the creators of Blockchain and cryptocurrency.[3] Assange is also a key figure in the 2016 US presidential election story. His WikiLeaks organization published Hillary Clinton's emails to the world, altering the trajectory of the election. This also set in motion a chain of events that led to an investigation of a sitting President of the United States of America. The Republicans, the Democrats, and the Russian government are all at cross-purposes with the anarchists. This book will help explain why this is so and just what anarchists are hoping to achieve.

Assange has repeatedly stated that the source of the emails was not the Russian government, though the popular story assumes that he is lying. The full extent of Assange's involvement in the DNC hack and the Mueller investigation should become more apparent over time. In addition to accurately explaining the Blockchain and cryptocurrency story, this book provides background information that can help decrypt some important, hidden details about this ongoing political circus.

The *Blockchain Code* is a true story about people, technology, and different visions for the future. The chapters of the book are intentionally short so that they are focused on a very specific topic and most easily understood. Part One provides a chronological narrative of the history of crypto-anarchy with intervening chapters explaining the important technical concepts. I got the idea for this approach from Michael Lewis' book *The Big Short*, which is story-driven and does an excellent job of explaining technical financial concepts along the way. This not only makes for a more engaging story, it seemed nearly the only way to present the foundations of the technology in context with the motivation of its creators.

---

[3] Bitcoin is a product of the anarchist community called the Cypherpunks, and Assange is arguably their most famous member. His 2012 book *Cypherpunks: Freedom and the Future of the Internet* describes the Cypherpunks' anarchist assessment of the ills of modern society and their vision for the future of the world.

Part Two breaks down detailed aspects of how Blockchain works, how it has been introduced into society, and its impact. It begins with a technical explanation of what "mining" is, since it is a source of great confusion and misinformation. The final four chapters (36-39) are minimally technical and highlight the impact and potential risks of the technology.

For the shortest and least technical possible read, one could theoretically read Part One, skipping Chapter 25 (Wallets – the most complex chapter – it begins with a warning to that effect), and then just read Chapters 36 – 39. However, I strongly encourage you to read the entire book in order as this is the best way to gain the deepest understanding of this complex subject that may one day affect all of us. The technical chapters are short and build upon previous ones. The narrative portion also generally follows chronologically throughout the book as well (though not strictly, particularly in Part Two – which is concept-driven, not story-driven).

Readers with varying levels of technical expertise should get different things from the various chapters. However, the book has been written so that all skill levels will receive value. Non-technical readers, do not fear if you find any of the detailed parts confusing, I would encourage you to simply press on and skim read any challenging sections. While absorbing all of the material will lead to the deepest understanding of the subject, it is not necessary for you to understand every detail. Focus on the story and the big picture. Cryptocurrency and Blockchain are, in a very real sense, part of a long-range attack against every nation on Earth. While speculative investors play "crypto Vegas", hardcore anarchist proponents of the technology seek a new way for the world. Their ultimate objective is to have all governments eventually collapse and become relics of the past so that a new world order, built upon cryptography, can arise.

May this book be your guide through unfamiliar and at times *intentionally* obscure, poorly defined territory. This expedition is designed to tell the real story and sharpen your machete of definitions. By the end of our journey, you should be able to hack through even the toughest vines of empty explanation.

PART I.

CRYPTO-ANARCHY

CHAPTER 1
A CURIOUS REVOLUTION

Something strange is going on.

Cryptocurrencies

Cryptocurrencies that were created to realize a crypto-anarchist ideal are going mainstream as speculative investments. Many people seem to understand that cryptocurrencies are anti-establishment, but few have a meaningful appreciation for what cryptocurrencies are, how they work, and what they mean for society.

Apart from the societal ramifications of cryptocurrency economies, the prices of cryptocurrencies have been, and continue to be, manipulated. The jungle of complexity may make it seem like it is a free market, but it is not.[4]

Blockchain

There is a second storyline about Blockchain, the technology behind cryptocurrencies. The approach that was taken to create cryptocurrencies is unique and clever. However, the popular story that is being told about Blockchain by the advocates of this technology is factually inaccurate.

The type of Blockchain used by most cryptocurrencies is something called public, *permissionless* Blockchain. You can think of permissionless Blockchain as *anonymous* Blockchain, and it is ideal for creating untraceable applications between anonymous parties. Few people seem to be asking if these applications are what we truly want in our society. Instead, vague, wonderful-sounding yet empty explanations dominate the Blockchain discussion.

---

[4] See Chapters 30 and 35

There is also something called *permissioned* (non-anonymous) Blockchain. Almost everything that has been proposed or implemented with permissioned Blockchain may likely be achieved with non-Blockchain approaches more simply, more securely, and far more efficiently.[5]

This book will cut through the jungle of complexity and explain what all of this means and why these obscure technical terms are important to you and to society.

Mass Confusion

Blockchain "experts" are presenting material with passion and conviction that is flat-out wrong regarding key details of both the technology and the movement behind the technology. What in the world is happening?

To make sense of it all, we must journey on into the jungle of complexity.

---

[5] See Chapters 31 and 32

CHAPTER 2
1986-1988

In February 2016, **Timothy C. May** spoke to an enthusiastic audience via video conference from his home in Santa Cruz, California. The audience gathered in Prague, the capital of the Czech Republic, at the annual Hackers Congress of the Institute of Cryptoanarchy. The group had gathered to hear May, the founder of cryptoanarchy, talk about the beginning of the movement.[6]

Flanked by signs advertising the Bitcoin-related companies General Bytes, Slush Pool, and Trezor, two Czech men huddled over a computer ensuring that the video conference was working. One of the men let Tim May know that he was about to introduce him, then turned around and addressed the crowd. "Paralelní Polis was a concept invented by one Czech dissident [Vaclav Benda]," the speaker began.[7]

"It was a dictatorship regime in Czechoslovakia at that time," the speaker continued. He described how there seemed to be little chance of realizing a political change in the late 1970s. In 1978, Benda authored the "Paralelní Polis Manifesto" as the speaker would describe it. This manifesto encouraged people to create an underground parallel society to escape the dictatorship communist regime that would continue to rule Czechoslovakia until 1993. The speaker hailed May as the visionary who wrote *The Crypto Anarchist Manifesto* and *The Cyphernomicon*. "These texts completely changed my life," declared the speaker.[8]

Following rousing applause, Tim May recounted the events that led to the creation of cryptoanarchy and Blockchain. "I left Intel in 1986, for various reasons, and then I spent about a year sitting on a beach here in Santa Cruz. Reading novels, reading technical papers, it took me about a

---

[6] May, Timothy C. 2016. *Timothy C. May – Thirty Years of Crypto Anarchy.* Video. Prague: Institute of Cryptoanarchy - Hackers Congress 2016, Feb 2. https://youtu.be/TdmpAy1hI8g (0:00-3:50)
[7] Ibid
[8] Ibid

complete year to get back into high gear on technical things," said Timothy C. May.[9]

May then described a December 1987 discussion with Phil Salin that got the ball rolling. "About a year after I moved out here, a friend of mine put me in touch with a guy [Salin] doing an information market... The idea was six or eight years before eBay... His idea was to sell information on the internet... He told me about his idea to buy and sell information. Things like the best surfboard to buy, the best sailboat, and whatnot," said May.[10]

May then indicated, "And being sort of a devious person, who just read *True Names* and was heavily immersed in a lot of the science fiction [of the time]," he explained to Salin how he misunderstood the information marketplace. May told Salin that the real market for selling information was not going to be which sailboat to buy. It would be "secret information, pharmaceutical information, corporate information... troop movement information - someone sitting in an apartment in San Francisco watching ships going in and out – classic spy stuff."[11]

Salin suggested ways he could avoid having his system used for espionage, but May had an answer for each of Salin's ideas. May told Salin how people would use pseudonyms and powerful methods of anonymization that had been pioneered by Dr. David Chaum. May's discussion with Phil Salin encouraged him to read up on Dr. Chaum's work, which got him "really fired up to investigate modern techniques of cryptography."[12] It appears that at this point in the story, if anyone was going to build an information black market, May was going to be a part of it!

May then recounted a second conversation that took place two months later, in February 1988. May's friend said, "You know, it's too bad that Ayn Rand's old ideas from 1955 [from Rand's book, *Atlas Shrugged*] were never properly implemented with technology." May described how Rand had a vision for "the anarcho-capitalists of the world" to rise up and rebel against the social order. He indicated that Rand "hated the term *anarcho-capitalist* because it suggested anarchy, which she did not like, but that's the origins of modern libertarianism... and many, many other political philosophies at the time."[13]

---

[9] Ibid (3:50 - 4:40)
[10] Ibid (4:40 - 6:40)
[11] Ibid (6:40 – 8:50)
[12] Ibid
[13] Ibid (10:30 - 11:45)

CHAPTER 2
1986-1988

Galt's Gulch in Cyberspace

In Atlas Shrugged, the anarcho-capitalists, as May described them, literally withdraw from society and move to a place called Galt's Gulch. The world spectacularly crumbles in their absence. "It occurred to my friend and I that we could use modern technology. And I was telling him about cryptography techniques and saying essentially Galt's Gulch. This idea of this valley in Colorado..., which was somehow covered over with some electronic shield. She [Rand] didn't describe how it worked, but basically, it stopped planes from seeing what was happening in the valley. It was called Galt's Gulch after John Galt, one of the main characters in *Atlas Shrugged*," said May.[14]

May explained, "It still shows up in the ideas of creating islands someplace. Bruce Sterling's [science fiction novel] *Islands in the Net*. Data havens in Polynesia, for example, down near Indonesia. And it shows up in people doing seasteading projects, that is creating floating platforms. Even former World War II gunnery platforms off the coast of England. A project to move there and create a new nation happened."[15] At this point, May's idea for an information black market expanded into a vision to create an entire hidden society. The dream of an online hidden corner of cyberspace was born.

A Global, Hidden Anti-State

"To me, the idea of moving to a state or a platform or an oil rig, or even a ship, just wasn't very interesting. I like it here in California, despite its problems. And the idea of living in a very attackable region where a single torpedo could sink a ship or a blockade could stop the flow of supplies to a region; it wasn't very appealing," May explained. However, "moving into Cyberspace" could be accomplished through cryptography. "Digital money, remailers, data havens, timestamping services, were all very much implementable," said May.[16]

---

[14] Ibid (11:45 - 12:18)
[15] Ibid (12:18 - 12:45)
[16] Ibid (12:57 - 14:06)

The Crypto Anarchist Manifesto

Tim May created a concept using the ideas from these two conversations and named it "Crypto Anarchy." In August 1988, in Santa Barbara, California, May created and distributed *The Crypto Anarchist Manifesto* to, as May would describe it, "some like-minded techno-anarchists." This meeting of the minds at the Crypto '88 Conference was the beginning of a movement.

The manifesto reads:

The Crypto Anarchist Manifesto
Timothy C. May <tcmay@netcom.com>
A specter is haunting the modern world, the specter of crypto anarchy.
Computer technology is on the verge of providing **the ability for individuals and groups to communicate and interact with each other in a totally anonymous manner. Two persons may exchange messages, conduct business, and negotiate electronic contracts without ever knowing the True Name, or legal identity, of the other. Interactions over networks will be untraceable,** [*emphasis added*] via extensive re-routing of encrypted packets and tamper-proof boxes which implement cryptographic protocols with nearly perfect assurance against any tampering. Reputations will be of central importance, far more important in dealings than even the credit ratings of today. These developments will alter completely the nature of government regulation, the ability to tax and control economic interactions, the ability to keep information secret, and will even alter the nature of trust and reputation.
The technology for this revolution--and **it surely will be both a social and economic revolution** [*emphasis added*]--has existed in theory for the past decade. The methods are based upon public-key encryption, zero-knowledge interactive proof systems, and various software protocols for interaction, authentication, and verification. The focus has until now been on academic conferences in Europe and the U.S., conferences monitored closely by the National Security Agency. But only recently have computer networks and personal computers attained sufficient speed to make the ideas practically realizable. And the next ten years will bring enough

CHAPTER 2
1986-1988

additional speed to make the ideas economically feasible and essentially unstoppable. High-speed networks, ISDN, tamper-proof boxes, smart cards, satellites, Ku-band transmitters, multi-MIPS personal computers, and encryption chips now under development will be some of the enabling technologies.

The State will of course try to slow or halt the spread of this technology, citing **national security concerns, use of the technology by drug dealers and tax evaders, and fears of societal disintegration. Many of these concerns will be valid; crypto anarchy will allow national secrets to be trade** [sic] **freely and will allow illicit and stolen materials to be traded. An anonymous computerized market will even make possible abhorrent markets for assassinations and extortion. Various criminal and foreign elements will be active users of CryptoNet. But this will not halt the spread of crypto anarchy.** [emphasis added]

Just as the technology of printing altered and reduced the power of medieval guilds and the social power structure, so too will cryptologic methods fundamentally alter the nature of corporations and of government interference in economic transactions. Combined with emerging information markets, crypto anarchy will create a liquid market for any and all material which can be put into words and pictures. And just as a seemingly minor invention like barbed wire made possible the fencing-off of vast ranches and farms, thus altering forever the concepts of land and property rights in the frontier West, so too will the seemingly minor discovery out of an arcane branch of mathematics come to be the wire clippers which **dismantle the barbed wire around intellectual property**. [emphasis added]

Arise, you have nothing to lose but your barbed wire fences!

....

Timothy C. May | Crypto Anarchy: encryption, digital money,
tcmay@netcom.com | anonymous networks, digital pseudonyms, zero
408-688-5409 | knowledge, reputations, information markets,
W.A.S.T.E.: Aptos, CA | black markets, collapse of governments.
Higher Power: 2^756839| PGP Public Key: by arrangement. [17]

---

[17] May, Timothy C. "The Crypto Anarchist Manifesto." Email from May. 11/22/92. https://www.activism.net/cypherpunk/crypto-anarchy.html

Crypto-Anarchists Unite

May went on to speak at the "Hackers Conference" in 1989 and 1990, proclaiming a vision of cryptoanarchy.[18] In May's words, the manifesto calls for a return to the "frontier West" of the United States and lawless freedom. This movement led to the creation of the Cypherpunks, the techno-activist community that would eventually create and launch Bitcoin.

---

[18] Ibid

CHAPTER 3
BLOCKCHAIN & CRYPTOCURRENCY

Cryptocurrencies, like Bitcoin, create a separate economic system powered by Blockchain. Let's walk through a basic example of how this separate economic system might work.

Imagine that you and a friend, Bob, want to create an economic system to trade services like babysitting. Bob might want to go out all the time, but you go out only infrequently. Neither of you wants to pay the other in traditional money, like dollars, because date nights are "priceless." You want to ensure that your babysitting services are returned in kind and want to ensure that the arrangement is equitable. Imagine that you and Bob have separate pieces of paper where you record every babysitting transaction. Theoretically, both pieces of paper should be identical. However, one of you might forget to log some of the transactions or might make some other error, and disputes over the accounting are inevitable.

Option 1: One Authoritative Ledger

The simplest answer to resolve the accounting problem for your babysitting co-op might be to perhaps find a website that manages this or possibly set up a shared online spreadsheet with a good audit trail like a Google Sheet.

Option 2: Everyone Keeps Their Own Ledger

Let's compare this to how Bitcoin accomplishes the same basic concept of creating a separate economic system, but with no centralized custodian of the ledger. This system works in a fashion similar to the different pieces of paper but is computerized.

THE BLOCKCHAIN CODE

Blockchain = Option 2

Suppose your friend, Bob, creates a computer program to handle the accounting and creates a new currency, let's call it bobcoin. Bob tells you that this software will fix the problem where your manual paper ledgers get out of sync, plus it's a digital cash system that you could theoretically use anywhere you might use traditional money like dollars. He tells you it could revolutionize everything and you can get rich off of all the newly made money. He provides you with instructions on how to download the software and install it, which you do. You use the program to create a wallet with the *address* 183kf8kR284hU982be4591dkh3kh32.

PO Boxes, Collisions, and Wallets

Bob tells you that you can think of the address like a Post Office Box with a combination lock that opens the box. He says that while there is no official registration or reservation to ensure that you are the *only* owner of that address (PO Box), it is extremely unlikely that someone else might end up with a combination (private key) to the *same* PO Box (address). If they did, that would be called an **address collision**, and you would both be able to spend any bobcoins at that address, but don't worry about it, because this doesn't happen very often. Bob tells you the important thing is to keep your wallet backed up and *private*, so nobody steals your coins.

Your wallet has the combination (key) to PO Boxes (addresses). You are supposed to be the only person in the world who knows the magic numbers (keys) that unlock these specific addresses. If anybody else learns the combination, they can open the PO Box and spend all the coins inside.

If your wallet file gets corrupted, overwritten, or deleted, you will lose the key (the lock combination) to the PO Box (address), and you will lose all coins inside the PO Box. There are no do-overs in bobcoin. You ask again about collisions, he tells you not to worry, that almost never happens.

Transaction Blocks

You launch the software and see many transaction blocks. These blocks have timestamps that seem somewhat random but indicate the creation of a new block **about every 10 minutes**. In each of these blocks, you notice that someone received 50 new bobcoins (presumably Bob). Bob explains that the software uses these coins as currency, and new coins are created by running the software. He says that you will receive coins as well. So, you check the software to see for yourself. Sure enough, you just received

50 coins at address 13f45c4de12345sk3nmx3393k3ks9k (a different address than the one we talked about earlier).

Bob tells you that you can be the most **anonymous** and keep the network the most anonymous for everybody else as well if you use a different random address for every bobcoin transaction. Bob shows you how to use the software to pay him the next time he babysits your kids. The application makes it kind of like emailing money, but the "from" and "to" addresses are an awful lot longer and more complicated than email addresses!

The Need for Critical Thinking

You thank Bob for explaining this, but ask him, "Since each computer keeps its own copy of the ledger, and neither one is the official record... this is still like having separate pieces of paper, only now it's computerized. So, exactly how does this fix the problem where our pieces of paper had a different record of our babysitting services? And why aren't the collisions important?" By the end of this book, you should be able to answer these questions and much, much more.

Welcome to the Jungle

Blockchain introduces a jungle of complexity while seeking to support a crypto-anarchist way of thinking. *The Blockchain Code* will walk through these details in a way that should help you understand not only how they work, but also why these different solutions exist in the first place.

CHAPTER 4
1992: THE CYPHERPUNKS' CRYPTO-ANARCHY GAME

Participants can be anonymous.
— *"Satoshi Nakamoto" from the email announcing Bitcoin (October 31, 2008)*[19]

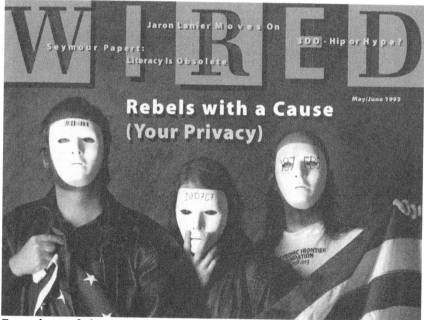

Founders of the Cypherpunks: Timothy C. May, Eric Hughes, and John Gilmore (*Wired Magazine* Cover - May/June 1993.)

---

[19] "Nakamoto, Satoshi". Email from "Satoshi" to The Cryptography Mailing List. "Bitcoin P2P e-cash paper." Oct 31, 2008.
http://www.metzdowd.com/pipermail/cryptography/2008-October/014810.html

In September 1992, Tim May recalls, "about 20-25 of us met in his [Eric Hughes] unfurnished house, and we sat on the floor... Probably one or more of them were founders of Bitcoin, were in the room at the time." In recalling this inaugural meeting of the Cypherpunks, May explains, "In the afternoon, we played a primitive game called **Crypto-Anarchy Game**."[20] [*emphasis added*]

Crypto War Game

May described the Crypto-Anarchy Game as follows:

> We played as if we were simulating a war game. We simulated things like anonymous remailers by using envelopes within envelopes within envelopes so that people could get a feel for how this might work in a future economy. A future system. People invented things like weapons-trading systems, like drug-trading systems. Obviously, this was long before Silk Road, the drug-trading platform and information-trading platform developed. So, we played with the ideas and saw what was needed.[21]

Silk Road was an online black market where customers bought illegal drugs or stolen information like credit card numbers. The coin of the realm on Silk Road was bitcoin. The stated goal of Silk Road was, "To grow into a force to be reckoned with that can challenge the powers that be and at last give people the option to choose freedom over tyranny."[22]

The weapons-trading system invented by the Cypherpunks' Crypto-Anarchy war game has also been built. *Gawker* journalist Adrian Chen wrote in 2012, "It's been eight months since we exposed Silk Road, the underground online marketplace where you can anonymously buy any drug imaginable. After our article, a couple U.S. senators declared war on Silk Road. But it hasn't been shut down. It's bigger than ever, and now you can buy a Glock with your LSD. Yesterday, Betabeat pointed out that Silk

---

[20] May. *Thirty Years of Crypto Anarchy*. (20:30-22:40)
[21] Ibid (22:00-22:40)
[22] Anderson and Farivar. "How the feds took down the Dread Pirate Roberts." *Ars Technica*. Oct 2, 2013. https://arstechnica.com/tech-policy/2013/10/how-the-feds-took-down-the-dread-pirate-roberts/

CHAPTER 4
1992: THE CYPHERPUNKS' CRYPTO-ANARCHY GAME

Road still exists, and is still home to hundreds of users openly trading illegal drugs using the nearly-untraceable hacker currency Bitcoins."[23]

The FBI was eventually able to shut down Silk Road. However, this was twenty months after Chen's article referenced above. Taking Chen's *first* article as the starting point, it took nearly two and a half years. The concepts pioneered by the Cypherpunks had been well thought out through war game planning. Tremendous time and careful consideration went into the development of this technology. As Anderson and Farivar of *Ars Technica* put it, "encryption, Tor, and 'tumbled' Bitcoins were a potent combination to crack."[24] Other underground marketplaces took Silk Road's place after it was shut down.

Cypherpunk

The name of the group is a play on words combining *cipher* (an encryption term) and *cyberpunk* (the dystopian science fiction literature/movie genre). One novel that was particularly influential with the Cypherpunks was *True Names*, by Vernor Vinge. The book tells the story of a computer hacker group whose members call each other "warlocks." The warlocks connect to a full-immersion virtual reality called the "Other Plane." Warlocks keep their identities (their "True Names") unknown to each other and to the "Great Adversary" (the United States government). If anyone learns a warlock's True Name, it could mean enslavement or "True Death" (death in the real world).

The September 1992 meeting was the first gathering of this collection of brilliant technical minds from the San Francisco Bay Area. From the first meeting, they were already hard at work overcoming the technical challenges that needed to be solved in order to implement cryptoanarchy. An email distribution list was created shortly after the group's initial meeting. This email list would be crucial to keep the Cypherpunks organized. They would continue monthly meetings in the Bay Area and maintain active discussions on the email list. This distribution list also helped the group grow and gain an international following.

---

[23] Chen, Adrian. "Now You Can Buy Guns on the Online Underground Marketplace." *Gawker*. Jan 27, 2012. http://gawker.com/5879924/now-you-can-buy-guns-on-the-online-underground-marketplace

[24] Anderson and Farivar. "How the feds took down the Dread Pirate Roberts."

The Cypherpunk Mailing List

Messages sent to cypherpunks@toad.com would be distributed to the growing group. On Monday, September 21, 1992, Russell Whitaker sent the first message to the Cypherpunks email list. He forwarded the text of the speech "From Crossbows to Cryptography: Thwarting the State via Technology" by mathematician Chuck Hammill to launch the distribution list.

In the speech, Hammill asserts that "...technology represents one of the most promising avenues available for recapturing our freedoms from those who have stolen them."[25] This first email sent to the Cypherpunks mailing list made a statement. It actually proclaimed *two* statements. First, the Cypherpunks are much smarter than "the State" (every government). Second, cryptography, an important technology in every military conflict, would be their means to defeat all governments on earth.

Later that day, Eric Hughes authored the second email sent to the distribution list where he announced that he would be the official list maintainer. He also announced the second meeting and offered the following assessment:

> The crypto-anarchy game we tried out at the first meeting was as good a success as we could have hoped for from an untested idea. The game seems useful and fun enough to warrant continued play and play testing, so we'll be playing again at this and future meetings.[26]

The Cypherpunks are deep thinkers, creators, and long-range planners. Thought experiments and role-playing games have been popular with the Cypherpunks since the group's inception. In these initial meetings, the Cypherpunks began to figure out how to implement Tim May's vision of cryptoanarchy. Over time, the group gained an international following of technologist intellectuals.

The discussions were spirited and often heated, including a moment in December 1992 involving Perry Metzger. Later, in 2001, Metzger would create The Cryptography Mailing List, a successor to the Cypherpunks mailing list (and the list to which Bitcoin was announced).[27]

---

[25] Cypherpunks Email Archive (1992).
http://cypherpunks.venona.com/raw/cyp-1992.txt
[26] Ibid
[27] See Chapter 18

CHAPTER 4
1992: THE CYPHERPUNKS' CRYPTO-ANARCHY GAME

Responding to an email from *treason@gnu.ai.mit.edu*, Metzger demanded, "Put up or shut up, Mr. 'Treason'. Give us one lick of evidence that you know what you are talking about." Treason@gnu.ai.mit.edu shot back at Metzger with information attempting to support his viewpoint and then requested that Metzger now shut up.[28]

While the group sought to bring about anarchy, it was not entirely chaotic. Many brilliant minds participated in this email list, along with a few agitators. In response to the Metzger versus "Treason" email melee, Tim May interjected, "And could I suggest to all of us that we be very careful in the language we use when disagreeing with others? 'Treason's' demand that Perry now 'SHUT UP' is intemperate and counterproductive. Our list is not moderated, that is, there is no censor or moderator holding people back when they feel the temptation to spew bile all over the list. With hundred [sic] of folks now on this list, great care must be taken."[29]

Anonymous

Anonymous is a "hacktivist" group known for attacks against governments and corporations. In 2008, Anonymous claimed responsibility for attacks against the Church of Scientology, taking down their website and protesting outside their offices wearing Guy Fawkes masks.[30] [31]

In 2010, Anonymous claimed responsibility for attacking a company that was contracted to stop copyright infringement. They also attacked the

---

[28] Cypherpunks Email Archive (1992)
[29] Ibid
[30] Vamosi, Robert. "Anonymous hackers take on the Church of Scientology." *Cnet*. Jan 25, 2008. https://www.cnet.com/news/anonymous-hackers-take-on-the-church-of-scientology/
[31] Neuman, Scott. "Anonymous Comes Out In The Open." *National Public Radio*. Sep 16, 2011. https://www.npr.org/2011/09/16/140539560/anonymous-comes-out-in-the-open

Recording Industry Association of America and the Motion Picture Association of America, the organizations that hired this contractor.[32]

In 2010, Panda Security spoke with some Anonymous organizers for a Q&A session. The first question was "Who is Anonymous?" The answer was:

> I believe it is just a description of what we are. Anonymous is not an organization with hierarchy and leaders. **We manifest as Anarchy.** [*emphasis added*] We are comprised of people from all walks of life. In short, we feel strongly motivated to do what we can to fight back against things which are morally questionable.[33]

In that interview, the Anonymous organizers indicated that they "will keep going until we stop being angry."[34] In subsequent years, Anonymous has claimed responsibility for numerous attacks against government and corporate entities.[35]

Are the Cypherpunks also this "hacktivist" group known as Anonymous? The thing about anarchy is that it is literally the *avoidance* of formal hierarchy. **Are *some* members of the Cypherpunks involved in Anonymous?** Substantial evidence suggests that there may be shared membership between these two groups:

1. *Anarchy:* The Cypherpunks were founded to implement Crypto-Anarchy. The first meeting of the group was spent playing The Crypto-Anarchy Game. Organizers of Anonymous have proclaimed: "We manifest as Anarchy."
2. *Against Intellectual Property:* Tim May, a co-founder of the Cypherpunks, has issued a call to "dismantle the barbed wire around intellectual property." The targets of the 2010 Anonymous attacks highlighted above were groups working to enforce their intellectual property rights.

---

[32] Vaughan-Nichols, Steven J. "How Anonymous took down the DoJ, RIAA, MPAA and Universal Music Website." *ZDNet*. Jan 20, 2012. https://www.zdnet.com/article/how-anonymous-took-down-the-doj-riaa-mpaa-and-universal-music-websites/

[33] "An Interview with Anonymous." Panda Security. Sep 29, 2010. https://www.pandasecurity.com/mediacenter/interviews/an-interview-with-anonymous/?ref=mc_bloglabs_en

[34] Ibid

[35] CBS News. *Anonymous: the hacking collective that inherited WikiLeaks legacy.* https://www.cbsnews.com/pictures/anonymous-most-memorable-hacks/

3. ***Anonymity***: Cypherpunks co-founder Eric Hughes has declared, "We must come together and create systems which allow anonymous transactions to take place... We the Cypherpunks are dedicated to building anonymous systems."[36] Anonymous is, well, anonymous.
4. ***Shared WikiLeaks Ties***: The most famous Cypherpunk, Julian Assange, is the head of WikiLeaks.[37] In 2010, when the US government forced companies to shut off payment sources to WikiLeaks, Anonymous fought back with "Operation Avenge Assange" taking down the websites of PayPal, Visa, and MasterCard.[38] [39]

The Cypherpunks and Anonymous share an anarchist mission. This shared mission may have led to shared affiliations between these groups, though it's hard to definitively prove who anybody is when they are anonymous. It is at least safe to say that Anonymous and clearly at least *some* of the Cypherpunks are extremely invested in *remaining* anonymous.

Typos & History

In November 1992, Tim May emailed *The Crypto Anarchist Manifesto* to the Cypherpunks:

```
From: tcmay@netcom.com (Timothy C. May)
Subject: The Crypto Anarchist Manifesto
Date: Sun, 22 Nov 92 12:11:24 PST

Cypherpunks of the World,

Several of you at the "physical Cypherpunks"
gathering yesterday in Silicon Valley requested
that more of the material passed out in meet-
ings be available electronically to the entire
```

---

[36] Hughes, Eric. 1993. *A Cypherpunk's Manifesto.* Mar 9. https://www.activism.net/cypherpunk/manifesto.html

[37] See Chapter 38

[38] "Operation: Payback broadens to 'Operation Avenge Assange.'" Panda Security. Dec 8, 2010. https://www.pandasecurity.com/mediacenter/news/operation-payback-broadens-to-operation-avenge-assange/

[39] Leyden, John. "Anonymous attacks Paypal in 'Operation Avenge Assange.'" *The Register.* Dec 6, 2010. https://www.theregister.co.uk/2010/12/06/anonymous_launches_pro_wikileaks_campaign/

> readership of the Cypherpunks list, spooks,
> eavesdroppers, and all. <Gulp>
>
> Here's the "Crypto Anarchist Manifesto" I read
> at the September 1992 founding meeting. It
> dates back to mid-1988 and was distributed to
> some like-minded techno-anarchists at the
> "Crypto '88" conference and then again at the
> "Hackers Conference" that year. I later gave
> talks at Hackers on this in 1989 and 1990.
>
> **There are a few things I'd change, but for historical reasons I'll just leave it as is.**[*emphasis added*] Some of the terms may be unfamiliar to you...I hope the Crypto Glossary I just distributed will help.
>
>   (This should explain all those cryptic terms in my .signature!)
>
>   --Tim May[40]

There is a typographical error in *The Crypto Anarchist Manifesto*, which I did not correct when including it in Chapter 2. Instead, I noted [*sic*], which denotes "spelling is correct." This designation indicates that the source of the typo is the author of the quote, not me.

By 1992, May's manifesto had become a historical document for the cryptoanarchy movement. To this movement, this document might be akin to the Declaration of Independence or Lenin's *What is to Be Done?* pamphlet. One does not alter such important historical documents, which is perhaps what May meant when he said that there are a few things he would change, but did not for historical reasons.

I mention this also because, throughout this book, I have not fixed similar typos in documents that I will reference later, such as Tim May's *The Cyphernomicon*. Similarly, I have not fixed typos from "James A. Donald's" *The Cypherpunk Program* document, which will be referenced later in this book. "James A. Donald" is likely a pseudonym and may possibly have been an alias for Tim May, himself.

---

[40] Cypherpunks Email Archive (1992)

CHAPTER 5
BITCOIN

First, we must clarify the *multiple definitions* of bitcoin. Bitcoin is the name of a software program. It is also the name of an economic system that this software created. It is also a unit of measure in this system. For example, "an anonymous software developer or software development team created Bitcoin" and "Bob sent Alice one bitcoin."

Bitcoin versus bitcoin

To help ensure that we are talking about the same thing, we will use the following conventions:

- **Bitcoin (big 'B'):** We will use Bitcoin to describe the software and the system that the software created.
- **bitcoin (little 'b'):** We will use bitcoin to describe the unit of measure within the system (a.k.a. the "coins"). These "coins" are merely numbers within a computer program. There are no gold coins. You may have seen pictures of gold coins with a Bitcoin logo on it, but that's just marketing.

Anonymous Developer & Initial Lottery

Chapter 3 described the high-level details of Bitcoin. Instead of Bob, an anonymous software developer or software development team known by the pseudonym "Satoshi Nakamoto" created Bitcoin. A lottery system distributes newly manufactured Bitcoins. The probability assumptions inherent in this lottery results in a new block "about" every ten minutes. Immediately following the launch of Bitcoin, it is reasonable to assume that "Satoshi" received the first collection of bitcoins. For a significant portion of time, "Satoshi" would likely have been the only participant in the initial lottery receiving 50 bitcoins about every 10 minutes.

Anonymity via Digital Pseudonymity

Bitcoin has been described as pseudonymous, which means that it uses "fictitious names." These names are called bitcoin addresses and look like 183kf8kR284hU982b4591dkh3kh3. They are unlikely to be used as anyone's pen name; pseudonyms like Mark Twain and Satoshi Nakamoto are far easier to recognize and pronounce. These randomly-generated bitcoin addresses are *digital pseudonyms*. A single person may have thousands of these random-looking bitcoin addresses. These addresses form the foundation of how Bitcoin facilitates transactions between **anonymous** parties.

By default, bitcoin addresses are designed to be completely anonymous. However, you are free to reveal your identity along with any of your bitcoin addresses if you choose to do so. For example, WikiLeaks has published 36EEHh9ME3kU7AZ3rUxBCyKR5FhR3RbqVo as an address where you can donate bitcoins if you wish to support their cause. By reviewing the Bitcoin blockchain, it is clear when WikiLeaks receives bitcoins at that address, though donors are free to remain anonymous.

No system is flawlessly anonymous, but Bitcoin achieves an extremely high degree of anonymity. No party is required to reveal their identity at any time during a bitcoin transaction. A best practice is to use a different bitcoin address for every bitcoin transaction to maximize anonymity.

Enabling Private Sales

In Chapter 3, we used the example of a babysitting co-op as a separate economic system. In that example, the idea was that the participants did not want to be paid in dollars. They wanted their services returned in kind, so there was some motivation for a separate economic or accounting system. Now, let's consider an example where the *privacy* of cryptocurrency offers a real benefit to both parties involved in a financial transaction.

Let's say you find a site on the dark web offering one kilogram of high-grade cocaine and an RPG-7 (a rocket-propelled grenade launcher) with a dozen anti-tank grenades. Through a limited-time special offer on the website, you purchase the drugs and weaponry for ten bitcoins. Using your Bitcoin software, you enter the bitcoin address specified by the seller along with a bitcoin address holding some of your bitcoins. Voilà! Payment has been handled.

CHAPTER 5
BITCOIN

In this transaction, it is almost certainly best for both parties if they can remain anonymous. Because there are physical items involved, there are delivery logistics that need to be worked out (possibly with the help of a separate anonymizing Blockchain application), but the financial portion of the transaction can be handled anonymously via Bitcoin. Bitcoin allows individuals to transact with each other in a completely **anonymous** manner where nobody ever needs to know another person's true name.

CHAPTER 6
1993

> We must come together and create systems which allow **anonymous** transactions to take place. ... We the Cypherpunks are dedicated to building **anonymous** systems. We are defending our privacy with cryptography, with **anonymous** mail forwarding systems, with digital signatures, and with **electronic money**.
> — Eric Hughes (March 9, 1993) [emphasis added][41]

Eric Hughes, co-founder of the Cypherpunks, and fellow Cypherpunk **Nick Szabo,** are both former software developers at *DigiCash*. DigiCash was a company created by David Chaum that sought to develop a privacy-focused payment alternative to credit cards. Szabo's first email contribution to the Cypherpunks mailing list was in April 1993.[42]

Szabo Inspired by Tim May

In a 2017 interview discussing the origins of Bitcoin, Szabo recalled, "Tim May had a vision of Galt's Gulch in cyberspace."[43] Galt's Gulch, also known as Mulligan's Valley or Atlantis, is a fictional hidden community in Ayn Rand's novel *Atlas Shrugged*. In the book, Midas Mulligan established Galt's Gulch following the "Strike of the Men of the Mind" (a revolution against societal injustice).

Szabo describes Galt's Gulch as, "a place where you could go to get away from things and do your business without outside interference. In the book, that was like a physics fantasy. But Tim said, well we have strong

---

[41] Hughes. *A Cypherpunk's Manifesto*
[42] Cypherpunks Email Archive (1993).
 http://cypherpunks.venona.com/raw/cyp-1993.txt
[43] *"Nick Szabo Interview."* Video. The Tim Ferriss Show. Aug 11, 2017. https://youtu.be/3FA3UjA0igY, (11:50 - 12:45)

cryptography now so we can do that. And I thought 'well yes, but you still want to do things like enforce contracts, protect property and so forth.' So, I started thinking about, and to some extent, others started thinking about, how do you protect your business in cyberspace."[44]

Szabo's Smart Contracts

Mr. Szabo was inspired to help realize Tim May's cryptoanarchy vision and he specifically began thinking about ideas that would come to be known as *smart contracts*. Smart contracts are bits of computer code recorded on a blockchain. A *blockchain* is commonly described as shared ledger where transactions are recorded. I will provide a more complete explanation of Blockchain in the coming chapters.

The goal of smart contracts is to create rules managed by mutually agreed upon computer code to support transactions between anonymous parties. We will explain smart contracts in more detail at various points throughout this book. Chapter 36 is devoted entirely to the topic of smart contracts.

April 16, 1993: Clipper Chip

On April 16, the US government announced a plan to implement the Clipper Chip, a controversial NSA-promoted technology that would allow government officials to decode intercepted voice and data transmissions.

Tim May was the first to notice the announcement and forward this email to the Cypherpunks mailing list:

```
From: tcmay@netcom.com (Timothy C. May)
Date: Fri, 16 Apr 93 09:38:00 PDT
To: cypherpunks@toad.com
Subject: White House announcement on encryption--FORWARDED

Cypherpunks,

Here's a message from sci.crypt that's of relevance to us in several ways. I assume from its length, seriousness, and wording that it's not a spoof...I can't check the White House's signature!
```

---

[44] Ibid

CHAPTER 6
1993

Some messages:
1. It tells us what Denning and Rivest were probably actually working on when they floated their "trial balloons" last summer and fall.
2. A goverment-sanctioned [sic] phone encryption technique has implications for the phone encryption topics we've discussed at the Cypherpunks meetings (notably with Paul Rubin and Whit Diffie).
3. As always, end-to-end encryption, bypassing such schemes as this, is looking better and better.
4. It is not clear if the government scheme will legally preclude other encryption schemes.
5. I expect a lively debate will soon take place in sci.crypt.

Newsgroups: sci.crypt
From: clipper@csrc.ncsl.nist.gov (Clipper Chip Announcement)
Subject: text of White House announcement and Q&As on clipper chip encryption
Sender: news@dove.nist.gov
Organization: National Institute of Standards & Technology
Date: Fri, 16 Apr 1993 15:19:06 GMT

THE WHITE HOUSE

Office of the Press Secretary

For Immediate Release
April 16, 1993

STATEMENT BY THE PRESS SECRETARY

The President today announced a new initiative that will bring the Federal Government together with industry in a voluntary program to improve the security and privacy of telephone communications while meeting the legitimate needs of law enforcement.

The initiative will involve the creation of new

```
products to accelerate the development and use
of advanced and secure telecommunications net-
works and wireless communications links. ...⁴⁵
```

Two Days Later: "James A. Donald"

Two days later, on Sunday, April 18, "James A. Donald" subscribed to the Cypherpunks mailing list:

```
From: "James A. Donald" <jamesdon@infoserv.com>
Date: Sun, 18 Apr 93 23:27:00 PDT
To: cypherpunks@toad.com
Subject: subscribe

subscribe James A. Donald

In case a human is reading this, I wish to sub-
scribe to the cypherpunks mailing list.
```

```
                     ---------------------------------------------------------
                                     |
     James A. Donald | Joseph Stalin said: "Ideas are more powerful
                     | than guns.  We would not let our enemies have
                     | guns, why should we let them have ideas."
jamesdon@infoserv.com⁴⁶
```

As an aside, there appears to be no reliable source attributing the quote in the signature of "James. A Donald" to Stalin. Wikiquote lists this as a frequently misattributed quote.⁴⁷ As another aside, I have taken some minor formatting liberties with the email signatures of "James A. Donald" and Tim May. The email signatures of "James" and May are lengthy and do not fit without a more compact font and occasionally other minor formatting adjustments. Without these adjustments, the email signatures would be extremely difficult to read. For example, this misattributed Stalin quote covers multiple lines in the signature and would not make much sense if it were simply word-wrapped to fit.

---

⁴⁵ Cypherpunks Email Archive (1993)
⁴⁶ Ibid
⁴⁷ "Joseph Stalin." *Wikiquote.* https://en.wikiquote.org/wiki/Joseph_Stalin

CHAPTER 6
1993

"James" is an important character in the Bitcoin and Blockchain story. This email would be the only email sent in 1993 by "James" to the Cypherpunks mailing list. This email was sent from jamesdon@infoserv.com[48], indicating that "James" was using the Santa Cruz County, California based Internet Service Provider, Infoserv Connections.[49] As coincidence would have it, Santa Cruz, California is also where Tim May lived from 1986 until his death in December 2018. However, it is reasonable to expect that other Cypherpunks might have lived in Santa Cruz as well or might have otherwise had infoserv.com email addresses at that time. The next time we would see "James" on the Cypherpunks mailing list, in 1994, he would use the email address jamesd@netcom.com.[50]

"James" sent his 1993 subscription request directly to the list rather than the proper email address that was designed to handle subscription requests. This mistake in protocol occurred frequently and had, in this case, the side effect of broadcasting this subscription request to the entire list.[51]

It also had the side effect of portraying that "James" was unfamiliar with the proper list subscription procedure. "James A. Donald" is likely a pseudonym and may even have been an alias for Tim May.[52]

---

[48] Cypherpunks Email Archive (1994). http://cypherpunks.venona.com/raw/cyp-1994.txt

[49] Wayback Machine Archive for www.infoserv.com, https://web.archive.org/web/19961103200815/http://www.infoserv.com:80/ (beginning Nov 3, 1996)

[50] Cypherpunks Email Archive (1994)

[51] Cypherpunks Email Archive (1993)

[52] Evidence that suggests that "James" was a pseudonym for Tim May is detailed in Chapter 8

CHAPTER 7
PSEUDONYMS AND REPUTATIONS

Mark Twain is a pen name, a famous alias that was used by Samuel Clemens. The Mark Twain pseudonym developed a reputation that endures to this day. Rather than using the term *nom de plume* (French for "pen name"), Twain preferred the term *nom de guerre* ("war name") when referring to his pseudonym.

Importance of Pseudonyms

Vladimir Ilyich Ulyanov is far better known by the pseudonym *Lenin*, a name he adopted sometime around 1901 as his revolutionary nom de guerre. The pseudonym Lenin developed an enormous reputation before, during, and after the Russian Revolution. As with the famous Mark Twain pseudonym, Lenin was eventually known only by his famous pseudonym. Early on, however, Lenin risked severe, potentially fatal, consequences for his activities, so the use of his famous pseudonym was essential.

The creators of Bitcoin faced serious risks as well. Nick Szabo lamented how the US government shut down a precursor of Bitcoin in his 2006 article, "E-gold challenges forfeiture." Governments were likely to do the same thing and shut down Bitcoin if they could identify the source. Public opinion was generally with the government on these matters. The first comment on Szabo's pro-E-Gold article begins, "Why do I have the feeling that these statements could have been made by Ponzi? Or by Enron? Or Long Term Capital Management? Or the savings and loan industry?"[53]

For Bitcoin to have any chance of success, it virtually required the use of pseudonyms. The pseudonymous "Satoshi Nakamoto" and the likely

---

[53] Szabo, Nick. 2006. "E-gold challenges forfeiture." *Unenumerated (Szabo's Blog)*. Jan 26. http://unenumerated.blogspot.com/2006/01/e-gold-challenges-forfeiture.html

pseudonymous "James A. Donald" launched Bitcoin.[54] The "Satoshi" pseudonym/persona developed a reputation as the mysterious creator of Bitcoin. "Wei Dai" was also involved.[55]

There is evidence that Wei Dai is the true name of a person involved with cryptography.[56] However, it is possible that the "Wei Dai" involved with the Cypherpunks is not the same Wei Dai. "Wei" and "James" are nearly as mysterious as "Satoshi", and they played important supporting roles. These may be additional aliases for "Satoshi" or separate, distinct individuals.

Reputations and Crypto-Anarchy

Tim May's Crypto Anarchist Manifesto states, "Reputations will be of central importance, far more important in dealings than even the credit ratings of today." May's email signature, as listed in Chapter 2, refers to "digital pseudonyms, zero knowledge, reputations." Tim May and Eric Hughes co-authored "Crypto Glossary" in 1992, which states, "In crypto anarchy, reputations... will be of paramount importance."[57]

The basic idea is that you cannot create a fully functional hidden corner of cyberspace if everybody is simply 100% anonymous. Pseudonyms must develop personas and reputations if you want to build a true online hidden community. Pseudonyms and reputations allow a persistent identity in what would otherwise be a completely random, anonymous online hiding place. People may begin to have reasons to trust a certain pseudonym even though they may never know that person's true name.

Anonymity through Bitcoin Addresses

Similarly, your bitcoin addresses can serve as pseudonyms for you. You can be the anonymous 183kf8kRhe284hU982be4591dkh3kh32 and send a bitcoin to an anonymous 13f45c4de12345sk3nmx3393k3ks9k for drugs,

---

[54] See Chapter 23
[55] Ibid
[56] U.S. Patent 6,081,598. "Cryptographic system and method with fast decryption". Inventor: Wei Dai.
[57] May, Tim and Hughes, Eric. 1992. "Crypto Glossary." https://nakamotoinstitute.org/static/docs/crypto-glossary.txt

CHAPTER 7
PSEUDONYMS AND REPUTATIONS

guns, or perhaps secret information. You may intentionally have thousands of these addresses to maximize your anonymity. Alternatively, you might reuse a particular bitcoin address and possibly develop a reputation.

CHAPTER 8
1994

Public policy on encryption was a matter of national debate. The Cypherpunks discussed the political, philosophical, and technical aspects of these matters on the mailing list. One of the hottest topics in 1994 was the NSA promoted Clipper Chip. This proposed standard bit of hardware would allow government officials to decode intercepted voice and data transmissions.[58]

Sinking the Clipper Chip

Matt Blaze, an active contributor to the Cypherpunks mailing list, identified a vulnerability that could be exploited to circumvent government surveillance. Blaze's 1994 findings and published paper helped speed the demise of the already very controversial project.[59]

Mosaic - Emergence of the World Wide Web

Another popular discussion topic in early 1994 was Mosaic, the world's first popular web browser. The web was in its infancy, and the Cypherpunks were discussing how encryption might be used to facilitate electronic commerce using this new thing called a Web Browser.[60]

---

[58] Cypherpunks Email Archive (1994)

[59] Blaze, Matt. 1994. "Protocol Failure in the Escrowed Encryption Standard." Aug 20, http://www.mattblaze.org/papers/eesproto.pdf

[60] Cypherpunks Email Archive (1994)

May 9, 1994

Technical difficulties were encountered with the Cypherpunks mailing list on Sunday, May 8, 1994. This prompted the following email from Tim May the next day:

```
From: tcmay@netcom.com (Timothy C. May)
Date: Mon, 9 May 94 01:24:32 PDT
To: cypherpunks@toad.com
Subject: My form letter

Here's a form letter I expect to send to people
who I see asking about the status of the list.
If someone has better information than I have,
I'll be happy to use it, or to let someone else
handle responses.

THIS IS A FORM LETTER (to save me having to
type the same stuff)

You have asked what happened to the Cypherpunks
list.

I don't know, but as of Sunday night, 8 May,
there were only about a dozen or so subscrib-
ers. Apparently something happened to the list.
I have messages in to Eric Hughes and Hugh Dan-
iel.

The subscriber list may get restored. I don't
know.

You can also resubscribe by sending a message
to majordomo@toad.com with this as the body:

subscribe cypherpunks

If this is successful, you'll get a confirma-
tion message within a few minutes.

Volume is likely to be low, until things get
back to normal.

I hope this helps.

--Tim May, not acting officially on behalf of
```

CHAPTER 8
1994

```
the list.

--
```

```
..........................................................
Timothy C. May        | Crypto Anarchy: encryption, digital money,
tcmay@netcom.com      | anonymous networks, digital pseudonyms,
408-688-5409          | zero knowledge, reputations, information
W.A.S.T.E.: Aptos, CA | markets, black markets, collapse of
Higher Power: 2^859433| governments.
Public Key: PGP and MailSafe available.
"National borders are just speed bumps on the information su-
perhighway."⁶¹
```

"James A. Donald"

Also starting on May 9, 1994, "James A. Donald" proceeded to become an active contributor to the mailing list. Approximately one year earlier, "James" had sent an email asking to subscribe to the Cypherpunks mailing list. At the time of his subscription request, he used the email address jamesdon@infoserv.com. However, it was not until May 9, 1994 that "James" actually joined in on discussions and became an active contributor. As coincidence would have it, this change in behavior occurred on precisely the same day that May sent above email. The first email address that "James" used when he became an active contributor to the discussions was jamesd@netcom.com.

Evidence suggests that "James" might have been a pseudonym for Tim May. In the opinion of this author, the writing styles of "James" and May are similar. In addition, on May 19, 1994, in his fourth emailed contribution to the discussions, James offers the opinion, "The cypherpunks are experimenting with digital token based money. Digital token based money is damn inconvenient… I think decentralized account based digital money is the best hope." Less than a week earlier, Tim May had been similarly critical of a token-based money system called "Magic Money/Tacky Tokens."[62]

Additionally, a few weeks after "James" began contributing, "James" chided Perry Metzger, in a fashion similar to how Timothy C. May had chided Metzger in the past regarding email etiquette (see Chapter 4's 1992 interaction between Metzger and *treason@gnu.ai.mit.edu*). Additionally, "James" appeared to know quite a bit about Metzger on a personal level:

---

[61] Ibid

[62] Ibid

From: "Perry E. Metzger" <perry@imsi.com>
Date: Tue, 31 May 94 16:49:45 PDT
To: jamesd@netcom.com (James A. Donald)
Subject: Re: New MacPGP2.3a has arrived.

James A. Donald says:
> Perry E. Metzger writes
> > [offensive ranting deleted]
> > I know that many people assume that others
> > will drop everything and immediately start
> > doing whatever they ask, but frankly, why
> > should *I* care? I don't even own a Mac
> > ferchrissake.
>
> This little rant would sound better if it
> came from one of the cypherpunks that had
> actually written some code on some
> machine recently.

I love James Donald.

I'm probably one of the few people on this list who is actively involved in cryptography as a business, albeit in a startup capacity.

> I recommend that Perry eat a pizza supreme
> with double cheese and salami.

Most people wouldn't understand your reference, so I'll explain. I'm a vegan. James thinks that he's making himself sound more impressive by being personally insulting. Unfortunately, he doesn't understand that I don't insult easily -- certainly the suggestion that I eat meat and cheese isn't terribly stinging. I can take consolation in the fact that James is likely accumulating cholesterol plaques in his arteries as we speak, and I am thus likely to outlive him.

Perry[63]

---

[63] Ibid

CHAPTER 8
1994

"Wei Dai"

A few months later, on August 19, 1994, "Wei Dai" sent his first email to the Cypherpunk mailing list. "Wei's" email address weidai@eskimo.com indicates that "Wei" was using Eskimo North, a Washington State Internet Service Provider.[64]

When asked about "Wei" in a 2018 interview, Tim May indicated:

> ```
> I've never met Wei Dai. For a long time, we didn't
> know whether it was a female or a male. People
> would posit theories that Wei could be a female
> name, but we now believe it's a he. We believe he
> was a grad student at University of Washington
> Seattle, which Nick Szabo also went to. But to
> Nick's knowledge, they never intersect- never
> crossed paths with each other.[65]
> ```

"Wei" may be a pseudonym and is possibly an alias for Nick Szabo. However, as discussed in Chapter 7, the evidence on "Wei Dai" being a pseudonym is far from clear-cut. Is the "Wei Dai" on the Cypherpunks mailing list the same Wei Dai that is recorded as having a US patent?[66] I am assuming that Wei Dai is the true name of the patent holder since patents are supposed to only be registered to true names. However, there is nothing stopping anybody from using that name as a pseudonym.

This initial email from "Wei" provided computer code that "Wei" had created to implement time-stamping (something that is part of Bitcoin and Blockchain). Tim May reviewed the computer code supplied by "Wei" and offered the assessment that "the hard part is time stamper reliability, i.e. how does the world (and the courts) know that the time stamper(s) did not simply reset his clock and fake the times. "Wei" suggested using "a large number of time stamping services. This way, they must all have colluded or been subverted in order to forge your time stamp."[67]

This approach is consistent with what would become the Blockchain approach, created by Nick Szabo. The manner in which blocks are linked (or "chained") together is how the system performs time-stamping.

---

[64] Ibid

[65] Weatherman, JW. *Under the Microscope - Timothy C. May*. Video Interview. Apr 20, 2018. https://youtu.be/MgmTnRivwXw (25:45- 26:15)

[66] U.S. Patent 6,081,598. "Cryptographic system and method with fast decryption". Inventor: Wei Dai.

[67] Ibid

The Cyphernomicon

In 1994, Timothy C. May published objectives in *The Cyphernomicon*, a voluminous repository of Cypherpunk information that is roughly four times the size of *The Blockchain Code*.

Uses for Digital Cash

May's document lists the following use cases for digital cash: gambling, bribes, payoffs, assassinations and other contract crimes, fencing, purchases of goods, tax avoidance (income hiding, offshore funds transfers, illegal markets). [68]

There are numerous references in *The Cyphernomicon* to DigiCash, the former employer of two particularly noteworthy Cypherpunks, Nick Szabo and Eric Hughes.

Overthrow of Governments

The Cyphernomicon includes a Frequently Asked Questions (FAQ), which includes the following question:

```
10.3.11.   "Is it legal to advocate the over-
           throw of governments or the break-
           ing of laws?"
```
[69]

The response to this question is lengthy and fascinating. The *first* bullet item of the response to the above question is:

```
-  Although many Cypherpunks are not radicals,
   many others of us are, and we often advocate
   "collapse of governments" and other such
   things as money laundering schemes, tax eva-
   sion, new methods for espionage, information
   markets, data havens, etc. This rasises
   [sic] obvious concerns about legality.
```
[70]

---

[68] May, Timothy C. 1994. *The Cyphernomicon: Cypherpunks FAQ and More*, Version 0.666. Sep 10. https://nakamotoinstitute.org/static/docs/cyphernomicon.txt
[69] Ibid
[70] Ibid

CHAPTER 8
1994

Uses for Crypto Anarchy

The Cyphernomicon lists the following uses for Crypto Anarchy:

```
16.9. Uses of Crypto Anarchy
16.9.1. Markets unfettered by local laws
        (digital black markets, at least
        for items that can be moved
        through cyberspace)
16.9.2. Espionage[71]
```

---

[71] Ibid

CHAPTER 9
BLOCKS

A Bitcoin block is primarily a collection of transactions structured in the following format:
1. Input bitcoin address(es) and amounts
2. Output bitcoin address(es) and amounts

Bitcoin produces new blocks about every ten minutes, so you can think of each block as all the transactions that happened in the past ten minutes. In addition to the collection of transactions, there is also information that links (*chains*) multiple blocks together into a more complex data structure called a block*chain*. Chapter 10 is dedicated to the topic of Blockchain, but before we start chaining blocks together, we should be clear on what blocks are in the first place.

Bitcoin Transactions

A single transaction might look like this (the addresses have been vastly abbreviated):

Input Bitcoin Addresses	Output Bitcoin Addresses
1a3kg4kg... (0.025 BTC) →	14m0dk49... (0.045 BTC)
1k3k3yz4... (0.017 BTC)	14k3x4e3... (0.005 BTC)
18sk3hd7... (0.008 BTC)	

In this example, let's say someone took .050 bitcoins from three of their bitcoin addresses and sent 0.045 bitcoins to another person who has 14m0dk49... as one of their bitcoin addresses. Let's assume that this transaction emptied out (spent) all of the bitcoins at the three input addresses and kept the change (0.005) from the transaction. This 0.005 has been moved into a single new bitcoin address 14k3x4e3...

While Bitcoin achieves a high degree of anonymity, this example demonstrates how the Bitcoin ledger itself can provide some identity clues. This transaction record would be published on the blockchain for all to see and inferences can be made. Input addresses that are used together indicate that all addresses are the same party (though it is possible that an address could be a "joint account" with a spouse or business partner). Small output amounts will most likely be the same party as the input addresses to keep the change in a transaction.

An expert cryptographer (hider) might theoretically perform a transaction like this, where they owned the three input addresses, but not the 14k3x4e3... address. They could perhaps give a little bit of bitcoin to a random address to try to fool you into thinking that they owned that address, too. Or all five addresses could be the same person. Or there could be two separate payees. However, most of the time it should be a reasonable assumption that 14k3x4e3... is an address owned by the same party that owns the input addresses. To identify the true name behind those four bitcoin addresses, you would need some source of additional information or side-channel.[72]

The **first transaction of every Bitcoin block is special**, because there are **no inputs**,[73] like this example:

Input Bitcoin Addresses	Output Bitcoin Addresses
(none) →	149f1w3... (50 BTC)

In this case, there is nothing for the input. Fifty new bitcoins have been fabricated and placed into the address 149f1w3... By convention, these are called newly "mined" coins. Mining is a lottery process where one "miner" gets lucky and gets to create the next block that extends the blockchain. When this "miner" creates the block, it will specify an address that "wins" these newly created coins.[74] Chapter 27 explains "mining" in detail.

Anonymous Lottery Winners

Most Bitcoin blocks for the first couple of years had just the money creation transaction and no other transactions in the block. Via the Bitcoin lottery system:

- By July 2016, **15.75 million bitcoins** were won by the creators and early adopters of the system in the first two lotteries.

---

[72] Side channels will be discussed in detail in Chapter 19
[73] New coins will be manufactured out of nothingness until approximately the year 2140, assuming Bitcoin still exists and assuming the software is not updated to change the behavior.
[74] The lucky "miner" also collects any transaction fees.

CHAPTER 9
BLOCKS

This represents 75 percent of all of the bitcoins that should theoretically ever be mined. A sizable percentage would have been won by Cypherpunk anarchists.

- There is an opportunity to win **2.625 million bitcoins** <u>in the current (third) lottery</u>. By the time this book was published, the majority of these coins had already been won, and this lottery should end in mid-2020. At that time, nearly 88 percent of the theoretical twenty one million possible bitcoins will have been mined. When the third lottery completes, the fourth lottery will commence where there will be an opportunity to win 1.3125 million bitcoins.

Buying Bitcoin Winnings

Transactions recorded in blocks are how you can buy bitcoins. Through the use of a cryptocurrency exchange, existing bitcoin winners or receivers send bitcoins to one of *your* randomly created anonymous bitcoin addresses. In this manner, you get the bitcoins, and they get your dollars.

In the process of buying bitcoins, the exchange may likely learn your identity. You could use a sack or a briefcase containing a pile of hundred dollar bills and a piece of paper with a bitcoin address on it. If you arranged for this sack to be anonymously picked up and exchanged for bitcoins sent to the address in the sack, you could theoretically remain anonymous. Most exchanges will probably not work this way, so they are a point where some de-anonymization generally occurs. However, there are many ways to immediately re-anonymize (launder) any bitcoins that have been purchased.

Criminals and terrorists desire this anonymity and became early adopters of the system. More mainstream adoption was accomplished through bitcoin giveaways targeting college students, combined with price manipulation.[75] The recent addition of more mainstream money mixes cryptocurrency money further, increasing its anonymity.

---

[75] See Chapters 30 and 35

CHAPTER 10
BLOCKCHAIN

In Blockchain, blocks are linked (chained) together to form a data structure known as a block*chain*. As the name implies, it is a "chain of blocks." The many subtle, but very different, uses of the term blockchain are far more complicated than the multiple uses of the word bitcoin.

Blockchain is Bitcoin-*ish*

After Bitcoin was created, the term blockchain began to be used to describe not only the data structure that Bitcoin uses but also the general concept of Bitcoin. It has also been used to describe the algorithm that Bitcoin uses. Additionally, blockchain has been used to describe both the general idea of Bitcoin's data structure as well as specific implementations of the data structure. The word *blockchain* has been used to describe anything that is *Bitcoin-ish* as well as the various technical aspects of the things used to build something like Bitcoin. This can get terribly confusing very quickly!

Blockchain Naming Conventions

This book will use the following conventions:

- **Blockchain (big 'B'):** We will use *Blockchain* to describe the general concept of a collection of blocks that are chained together in the manner of Bitcoin or other cryptocurrencies. This will include general approaches, algorithms, and the *concept* of the Blockchain data structure (the concept of the Blockchain ledger).
- **blockchain (little 'b'):** We will use *blockchain* when are describing a *specific implementation* of the data structure (a specific collection of information). The lower-case blockchain may be used in a general sense for a particular cryptocurrency, such as "Bitcoin Cash, a hard fork of Bitcoin, created a copy of Bitcoin's blockchain. This hard fork gave the initial lottery winners of the Bitcoin blockchain duplicate

coins, but the copied coins are Bitcoin Cash bitcoins instead of Bitcoin bitcoins." Additionally, blockchain may be used to describe individual copies of the blockchain, such as "my copy of the Bitcoin blockchain has different transactions than the copy of the Bitcoin blockchain that Bob has."

Blockchain & the Jungle of Complexity

The proponents of Blockchain seek to use the general technical approach of Bitcoin to implement systems that may or may not have anything to do with economics. The visions are large, and the approaches required to achieve them are extremely complex.

Blockchain Domain Name Service (DNS)

Domain Name Service (DNS) maps names like google.com or amazon.com to IP addresses. It's easier and more natural for people to type "google.com" instead of a number like 172.217.8.14. This also allows maintenance work to be performed and DNS can magically redirect traffic to a different IP address in the background without anybody realizing what is going on. DNS is a universal directory service with three tiers of control:

1. Top-level domains (.com, .edu, .net, etc.) are managed by a central authority called the Internet Corporation for Assigned Names and Numbers (ICANN), which works with the various registrars.
2. Various registrars, such as GoDaddy, manage the next level down (i.e. google.com). The end-user domain owner (the registrant) reserves and registers the domain with the registrar. This registration is what stops someone from claiming the name amazon.com (that domain is already reserved and registered). A domain can be owned by a person or an organization.
3. The end-user domain owner is responsible for managing all of the IP address information for the domain.

Proponents of Blockchain DNS have expressed concerns about the power of ICANN and registrars to exert control over those that violate terms of service (criminal, terrorist, or other less dramatic violations). Additionally, as individuals browse the web, their systems perform DNS lookups to determine what IP address will connect them to microsoft.com, for example. These lookups potentially provide a means of tracking your online activity. Blockchain DNS is ostensibly used to provide access to domains that exist outside of ICANN (.onion, .bit, .lib, .emc, .coin, .bazar), however, once a PC is updated to use the Blockchain DNS, all names for that PC may theoretically be controlled by this software. Blockchain DNS seeks to make the "dark web" easier and more user-friendly to access.[76]

Anonymizing DNS helps allow individuals to act online in a more private, hidden manner. In countries that exercise substantial government censorship, this has the potential to simplify anonymous access to the internet, which could open floodgates of information, which might be a wonderful thing. However, as with most technology, there are at least two sides to every story. This technology should simplify access to the "dark web" where drugs, weapons, and other items are traded. This may be a very welcome feature for some. However, there is also an additional important risk facing any users of this service. By obfuscating DNS controls and creating an intentional lack of transparency, this additionally creates fertile ground for a hacker to seize control and covertly redirect web browsers to display altered information that can expose people to data theft.

Beyond just criminal or terrorist motives, anonymous actors could replace information with *political propaganda*. The anonymous nature of Blockchain might allow this to be accomplished where nobody, other than the hackers, realizes that this has happened. This is a significant threat, as it has been said, "when war comes, the first casualty is Truth."

---

[76] Amado, Rafael. "How Cybercriminals are using Blockchain DNS: From the Market to the Bazar." *Digital Shadows*. June 12, 2018. https://www.digitalshadows.com/blog-and-research/how-cybercriminals-are-using-blockchain-dns-from-the-market-to-the-bazar/

CHAPTER 11
1995

Dr. David Chaum established the theoretical foundation of cryptoanarchy technology (anonymous online transactions) in 1981 and 1982. In 1995, an additional concept would extend Chaum's work to advance the theoretical foundations of cryptoanarchy.

Anonymous Communication

Chaum's 1981 paper, "Untraceable Electronic Mail, Return Addresses, and Digital Pseudonyms", established the framework for the pseudonymous remailer. Remailers allow individuals to exchange secret messages with a high degree of anonymity.[77] This work was later expanded to eliminate the concept of pseudonyms, creating more thoroughly anonymizing remailers such as the cypherpunk remailer.

Anonymous Digital Cash

Chaum's 1982 paper, "Blind Signatures for Untraceable Payments",[78] led to the creation of DigiCash in 1989. DigiCash offered a privacy-focused payment alternative to credit cards. On Monday, October 23, 1995, Mark Twain Bank of St. Louis Missouri became the first bank to begin a trial of DigiCash.[79]

---

[77] Chaum, David. 1981. "Untraceable Electronic Mail, Return Addresses, and Digital Pseudonyms." https://www.freehaven.net/anonbib/cache/chaum-mix.pdf

[78] Chaum, David. "Blind Signatures for Untraceable Payments." Advances in Cryptology (1982). https://link.springer.com/chapter/10.1007/978-1-4757-0602-4_18

[79] DigiCash. "First Bank to Launch Electronic Cash." Press Release. Oct 23, 1995. https://chaum.com/ecash/articles/1995/10-23-95%20-%20First%20Bank%20to%20Launch%20Electronic%20Cash.pdf

Assassination Politics

Also in 1995, Cypherpunk James Dalton Bell published an essay that created a theoretical advance in realizing cryptoanarchy. Bell combined anonymous communication and anonymous digital cash in a dark, yet disturbingly logical manner. The article was titled **"Assassination Politics."**[80]

Bell said, "In 1995... I noticed a particular senator who was well known for bringing pork back to his district. And I said to myself that the people of 49 states would be better off if that guy woke up one day dead. That's a problem I thought, or it's a task." Bell worked out the mechanics required to accomplish this task, which became known in the Cypherpunk community as **AP**.[81]

Crowdfunded Murder

The concept is that anonymous individuals contribute anonymous digital cash into a pool designated to pay for the assassination of a hated politician, law enforcement official, or IRS agent. Anonymous individuals would then predict the target's time of death. The person who correctly predicts the time of death, presumably the assassin, wins the prize money. Effectively, this is crowdfunded murder where targets are "voted on" for elimination with anonymous cryptocurrency.[82]

In this manner, a crowd ordering the killing and the assassin(s) can remain completely anonymous. All identities other than the assassination target remain private. Additionally, the payment is untraceable. This system provides an efficient and untraceable means to coordinate assassinations of anybody, anywhere in the world.

Political Change

At the Institute of Cryptoanarchy 2017 annual Hackers Congress, Jim Bell described AP as a means of effecting political change. "Instead of 51% of people voting on which politicians to occupy the office, I proposed that a

---

[80] Bell, Jim. 1995. *Assassination Politics*, https://jimbellproject.org/assassination-politics-ap-essay/
[81] Berwick, Jeff. "World Exclusive: Assassination Politics -First Interview with Jim Bell Since Released From Jail." Video Interview. *TheAnarchast*. Aug 13, 2016. https://youtu.be/t0YfUGKlBIQ (2:40 - 2:55)
[82] Bell. *Assassination Politics*.

much smaller number of people could decide which politicians won't ever be in office again."[83]

AP - Making Anarchy Practical

This concept is considered by some, such as Mr. Bell, as the **solution to anarchy's hardest problem**: defending an anarchist region from another region that has a powerful, centrally coordinated army.[84] [85]

For Defense

"The upshot of this idea is that is that it makes Anarchism/Anarchy practical because it solves David Friedman's Hard Problem. His hard problem was how do you defend a region that is not centrally run," says Bell.[86]

And Offense

Bell describes how AP can be used as an *offensive* weapon to destroy all governments, by killing heads of state and other leaders:

> My solution Assassination Politics … not only provides that defense, it actually provides an unstoppable mechanism to tear down all governments wherever they may be. It won't stop in one region. It can't stop. It's like a tidal wave of bringing down centralized government. … It will take down whatever governments are there.[87]

The First Thing We Do, Kill all the Politicians

In a 1996 response on the Cypherpunks mailing list, "Re: Campaign Finance Reform", Bell advocated for an AP solution:

> Well, I have an even better and cheaper solution to the problem of government and politics. At an

---

[83] Bell, Jim. 2017. *Jim Bell – ASSASINATION POLITICS*. Video. Prague: Institute of Cryptoanarchy - Hackers Congress 2017. Jun 8. https://youtu.be/KcJdvQvzlNU (1:25-1:45)
[84] Ibid
[85] Berwick. "World Exclusive: Assassination Politics." (5:50 - 7:00)
[86] Ibid
[87] Ibid

```
            average of $20,000 per Congressman, we could
            clean up Washington for $10 million dollars.⁸⁸
```
In 1996, nearly untraceable cryptocurrency did not exist. Today AP is an alarmingly practical, implementable reality.

---

[88] Cypherpunks Email Archive (1996). http://cypherpunks.venona.com/raw/cyp-1996.txt

CHAPTER 12
MODERN MONEY

A popular criticism of bitcoin is that it has no intrinsic value, which does not seem entirely accurate. It is true that bitcoin is unlike stocks, bonds, or mutual funds. Stocks and stock funds have valuation standards like P/E ratios and dividend yields. Bonds have yields, par value, and maturity dates. If these types of things form the basis for your measuring stick, bitcoin clearly does not have *that* type of intrinsic value.

Is bitcoin useful for routine payments? No. Bitcoin payments take far too long to confirm for retail use. It takes about six blocks, or roughly one hour, for a payment to be considered reasonably confirmed. There is no FDIC/NCUA insurance, no fraud protection, and there are potentially sizable transaction fees that are paid by the spender.

Costs and/or Refunds

Modern options for electronic payment have varying fees (or refund in the case of credit cards):

Transaction Type	Seller Fee	Spender
Credit Card	~2 to 3.5%	~1% to 2% **kickback**
Debit Card - person-to-person	free	free
Debit Card - commercial	~1 to 2%	free
ACH	nominal	free
Bank/Financial Wire Transfer	free	possibly free
Western Union Wire Transfer	free	~2% to ~30% **fee**
Walmart Wire Transfer	free	~1% to ~10% **fee**
Bitcoin	free	varies extremely, ~$0.10 - $50/trans

Credit cards are unique in that it is the only payment type listed that actually refunds ("kicks back") money to the spender. Part of the variability of bitcoin fees stems from the fact that transaction fees are not generally set as a percentage of the amount of money moved. On a percentage basis, the fees for payment of a million dollars' worth of bitcoin will be far less than paying for a cup of coffee in bitcoins. Nobody should be willing to pay $50 in fees for a latte, but a $50 fee for a million dollar payment is inconsequential. Bitcoin fees reached an apex at the beginning of 2018.

For person-to-person payments, *debit* card payments using Google Pay, Apple Pay, Venmo, or Zelle are hard to beat. Once you set it up, you can simply email or text your friends and family, and the money can be instantly transferred for free. In Gmail, you can also email money using the $ icon. All of these solutions offer free, easy, person-to-person payments and include fraud protection.

Bitcoin Payments

While person-to-person electronic payments via debit cards win in many categories, they leave behind a clear money trail. If you email a payment, not only are there banking transaction records, there is an additional email record. Bitcoin transactions are completely anonymous. **Privacy is where Bitcoin outshines every other option listed**. Bitcoin payments avoid a money trail, and a buyer and seller never need to know the other's identity. Facilitating transactions with an extremely high degree of privacy is Bitcoin's intrinsic value. While Bitcoin is nearly untraceable, it is not perfect. There are alternative coins, sometimes called *altcoins*, like Monero and Zcash, that are trying to make cryptocurrency even more untraceable than Bitcoin.

Bitcoin transactions are also designed to be irreversible, which means that bank mediation/intervention is impossible. Bitcoin's proponents cite this as a feature, which it may be. The combination of anonymity and irreversibility may be desired for certain legitimate transactions. With credit and debit cards, no means exist for two parties to perform a transaction where "all sales are *absolutely* final," and a customer waives *all* recourse for *every* possible dispute including fraud. Reversing fraudulent transactions is more commonly called **fraud protection.** For those with less than honorable intentions, the anonymity and irreversibility of Bitcoin are clearly desirable features when committing fraud, extortion, and other crimes.

CHAPTER 12
MODERN MONEY

Fee and Delay Uncertainty

The fees associated with Bitcoin transactions are a little challenging to specify with a great deal of accuracy. This uncertainty can make using bitcoin a little tricky. The bitcoin spender chooses how much of a fee they wish to pay as part of the transaction. The fees are factored into a kind of auction to determine whose transactions will make it into the next block.

Bitcoin has a fixed block size, so if there are a lot of transactions at a particular point in time, there will be a transaction queue that can cause your transaction to be "in limbo" for hours or days before it is either processed or "times out." This variable potential delay is in addition to waiting an hour after a transaction is accepted for reasonable confirmation.

The general theory is that the higher the fee, the more likely your transaction will be included in any given block and therefore processed more quickly. Bitcoin transaction fees varied particularly wildly throughout 2018. These fees have been perhaps as little as 10 cents per transaction and as high as $50 per transaction.

Float

Bitcoin works the opposite of credit cards with respect to float (interest-free use of money). You must first purchase bitcoins in advance with your own money so that you have them on hand to spend. The float, transaction delays, lack of fraud protection, and unclear costs issues would generally make bitcoin a rather poor option for payments, but that is not why people are playing the Bitcoin game.

Casino Royale

People generally buy bitcoins to "roll the dice" and play "crypto-Vegas", where cryptocurrency exchanges act like global online casinos. Traditional casinos (the house) use alternative currency (chips) to control payout, and so that the house never needs to gamble with its own money (effectively, the house is always gambling using players' money). Similarly, cryptocurrency exchanges use cryptocurrencies, such as bitcoin, like chips or tokens. They also manage the primary game (the exchange rate), and while it may appear to be a free market, it is not. There are several ways in which the exchange rate has been (and continues to be) manipulated.[89]

---

[89] See Chapters 30 and 35

The Credit Card Reverse Casino

With credit cards, if you pay off your balance in full each month, credit card companies (banks) act as a sort of reverse casino. The bank lets you use their money and the bank bets on *you* (that you won't default), a good bet if you pay your credit card in full each month. You get a *float* from the bank (use of the bank's money for free) for, on average, perhaps forty-five days. When you pay by credit card, the vendors from whom you purchase pay fees to banks of up to 3.5% of your purchase price. This would be a typical fee for a *card not present* rate (common for online purchases); rates for retail purchases with card swipe might be closer to 2%. Credit card loyalty programs reward the bank's best customers with kickbacks (comps in casino parlance) in the form of airline miles or actual cash.

The sizable fees paid by merchants have been the subject of some contention. It is commonplace to have those paying by credit card, debit card, or cash to pay the same price, despite the substantial difference in the amount of money received by the seller. If a merchant charges $100 and is paid in cash, they receive $100, and if they are paid via a debit card, they might receive around $99. When paid by credit card, they only receive perhaps about $96.50. This is why some vendors charge a surcharge for customers paying by credit card. In the absence of such a surcharge, the argument is that those paying by cash or debit card are unfairly subsidizing those that pay by credit card.

In most of the United States, it is clearly legal for merchants to apply a surcharge to customers paying by credit card. However, some states have laws that require prices be communicated in reverse (a *discount* for paying with cash or debit card). The validity of those laws is in question after the March 2017 U.S. Supreme Court decision in *Expressions Hair Design v. Schneiderman*, where the court unanimously ruled that these laws were regulating speech and remanded the matter back to lower court for reconsideration.[90]

A Harvard Law Review (HLR) article opined that "The Court not only erred in refusing to address the parties' constitutional arguments, but given that the statute withheld commercial information for the purpose of manipulating consumer behavior, also missed an opportunity to answer definitively whether such a statute is per se illegitimate or whether it should undergo intermediate scrutiny..." The HLR article also takes a dim view

---

[90] *Oyez.* "Expressions Hair Design v. Schneiderman", https://www.oyez.org/cases/2016/15-1391

of the New York law saying, "As deceptive legislation, Section 518 violates both of these principles. First, it abridges the merchant's ability to describe any additional fee as a surcharge because credit card lobbyists, working through the state legislature, feared that the volume of credit card use would decline if surcharges were permitted. Second, instead of directly regulating credit card and cash use, the state legislature sought to abridge speech by shrouding Section 518 in language that seemed, on its face, to regulate conduct."[91]

The matter of credit card fees remains an area of active legal activity, including a 5-4 decision by the Supreme Court in June 2018 in *Ohio v. American Express* involving the matter of fees.[92]

Debit Cards

Apple Pay and Google Pay using a debit card generally costs merchants less than credit cards and **can be free** for person-to-person transactions. Debit cards are float-free, casino-free direct digital payment. Unlike Bitcoin, both debit cards and credit cards offer rapid confirmation and **fraud protection**.

ACH & Wire Transfers

Banks generally include the ability to send payments online via ACH **for free or nearly free**. Additionally, there are many bank account plans (especially business accounts and investment accounts) that offer **free wire transfers**. Banks have been increasingly adopting enhanced security protocols for wire transfers to limit *their* fraud risk liability. Unlike Bitcoin, your bank accounts have some fraud protection requiring the banks to validate your identity, though if you specifically authorize a payment to a party who is defrauding you, you have some risk of money loss.

Western Union, the original giant in the telegraph industry, began in the mid-19th century transmitting information (telegrams) and eventually added the ability to transmit money by telegraph (the origin of the Wire

---

[91] "Expressions Hair Design v. Schneiderman." *Harvard Law Review.* Nov 10, 2017. https://harvardlawreview.org/2017/11/expressions-hair-design-v-schneiderman/

[92] Klein, Aaron. "Why the Supreme Court's decision in Ohio v. AmEx will fatten the wealthy's wallet (at the expense of the middle class)." *Brookings.* June 25, 2018. https://www.brookings.edu/research/ohio-v-amex/

Transfer we know today). The original transfers were accomplished via passwords and codebooks that authorized fund transfers. Some countries still use the term telegraphic transfer to describe wire transfers. While Western Union no longer transmits telegraphs, it continues to provide wire transfer services for those wishing to conduct transfers outside of banking and investment institutions.

Since these services are already available inexpensively or for free through banking and investment institutions, Western Union's services have been a magnet for criminal and terrorist activity. In January 2017, the company admitted to **"aiding and abetting wire fraud" as well as money laundering** and paid a $586 million fine in the United States.[93] In 2015, the Central Bank of Ireland fined and reprimanded the company for failures to prevent "money laundering and terrorist financial transactions."[94]

The Underworld Economy

Western Union is supposed to be tracking and potentially reporting (upon subpoena at the very least) suspicious transactions that could potentially be money laundering, criminal, and/or terrorist transactions. Cryptocurrency offers relief to money launderers, criminals, hitmen, and terrorists by providing an anonymous online financial transaction alternative.

Credit cards, debit cards, ACH, and wire transfers leave a money trail, which can be used for a variety of reasons including reversing fraud (fraud protection) and as evidence for criminal investigations. Western Union and other alternatives also leave some trails. Though, these are less reliable money trails than the trails that exist within the banking system. Bitcoin has superior privacy. It can support global anonymous economic enterprises with transactions that can be nearly untraceable.

---

[93] Reuters. "Western Union Will Pay $586 Million For Aiding Criminals Using Its Service." *Fortune* .Jan 20, 2017. http://fortune.com/2017/01/19/western-union-fraud-money-laundering/

[94] Bodkin, Peter. "Western Union has been leaving the door open for money laundering." *The Journal*. May 19, 2015. http://www.thejournal.ie/western-union-money-laundering-2112147-May2015/

CHAPTER 13
1996

A significant amount of dialogue took place on the Cypherpunks mailing list in 1996 (and later) regarding the viability and mechanics of Assassination Politics (**AP**). Debates ensued regarding the moral and ethical aspects of AP as well.[95]

Debating AP

Initially, Tim May was a bit dismissive of AP, indicating that he thought it was "a watered-down and poorly-thought-out version of what I wrote about in 1988."[96] Yet, AP remained a hot topic discussed on the Cypherpunks mailing list. Jim Bell had clearly struck a chord with some other like-minded individuals on the list and a nerve with others who were uncomfortable with the implications of promoting crowdfunded murder as a means to achieve anarchy.[97]

In a 2016 interview, Bell indicated that "the concept of an assassination market was not mine... There was a guy named Tim May, a controversial person that oddly enough worked for Intel about the same time that I did.... I added a critical set of features, the idea of combining donations. But moreover, I added the concept of not merely of hiring one person but putting out what amounts to a general call. Anyone who wants to collect this... can do it anonymously. And there's a lot more effectiveness in that. And therefore it was a great step forward, and I became one of the important people that had contributed to the Cypherpunks list."[98] AP would continue to be debated on the Cypherpunks mailing list for years.

---

[95] Cypherpunks Email Archive (1996)
[96] Ibid
[97] Ibid
[98] *TheAnarchast*. "World Exclusive: Assassination Politics." (10:30 - 12:30)

Controversies in Advancing Anarchy

At one point in the discussions, May took exception to one comment from Bell, saying "Whoahh! Hold on there, Jimbo! You're crossing the line. You're coming perilously close to calling for the killing of a federal judge. My recollection is that a couple of folks have been arrested and charged for calling for the killing of judges." The debate about AP both pro and con raged on.[99]

Smart Contracts - Extropy Magazine

Shortly after "Assassination Politics" was published by Jim Bell, the article "Smart Contracts: Building Blocks for Digital Markets" by **Nick Szabo** was published in *Extropy Magazine*.[100] This publication focused on advances in technology that might someday allow people to live forever. One possibility pursued by Extropians is The Singularity when human consciousness is uploaded into computer systems.

In addition to potentially providing some rules for human consciousness uploaded into computers, smart contracts could be useful to help realize AP. There are a number of details, which Bell's AP did not fully describe, including how an assassin can be sure that they are paid upon completion of the "hit." These issues might best be resolved by the use of smart contracts on a blockchain.

Cypherpunk Politics & AP

Szabo's article mentions that "The 'cypherpunks' have explored the political impact of some of the new protocol building blocks."[101] The Cypherpunks had worked out a great number of details required to realize crypto-anarchy by this time, including the concept of AP.

Szabo's article listed Tim May's *The Cyphernomicon,* Vernor Vinge's *True Names*, two David Chaum articles, the DigiCash website, and several

---

[99] Ibid
[100] Szabo, Nick. "Smart Contracts: Building Blocks for Digital Markets." *Extropy Magazine*. 1996. http://www.fon.hum.uva.nl/rob/Courses/InformationInSpeech/CDROM/Literature/LOTwinterschool2006/szabo.best.vwh.net/smart_contracts_2.html
[101] Ibid

CHAPTER 13
1996

other references.[102] As discussed in Chapter 6, Szabo was inspired to create smart contracts (computer code on the blockchain) to help realize May's vision of "Galt's Gulch in cyberspace." Smart contracts help make crypto-anarchy practical.

Purchasing an assassination is an (illegal) business transaction. Smart contracts can provide a framework to help coordinate legal or illegal business transactions between parties that never need to know the identity of any other party.

---

[102] Ibid

CHAPTER 14
DECRYPTING CRYPTOGRAPHY - THE ART OF HIDING

Cryptocurrency is a fancy word that combines *cryptography* and *currency*. The basic building block of cryptography is the process of *encryption*. By encrypting a message, you convert it into an unreadable state (*apparent* nonsense). The message appears to be destroyed, but it is still there. It's just hidden so that you cannot see it without the key. With the right key, you can decrypt (unhide) the hidden message so that it may be read.

Encrypted = Hidden

The title of this chapter is *Decrypting* Cryptography because the terms cryptography and encryption have been misused even by the smartest people and "experts." Encryption has been so frequently combined in marketing messages with the terms security and protection that people have begun to believe that if something is encrypted, it must be secure and protected. Encrypted means *hidden*, not necessarily *protected*. Encryption means that something is hidden and someone may have a key to unhide it.

What is Hidden? And from Whom?

Secure banking websites use TLS encryption to hide information *in transit* between your web browser and your bank so that the communication is strictly between you and your bank. This information is hidden from prying eyes on the internet. This encryption offers some protection for you and your bank, though no system is perfectly secure. For example, your PC could become infected with malware, which might silently send your information to some anonymous criminal on the internet.

While banks require transmissions to be encrypted to ensure that there is no eavesdropping across the internet, this is not required for Bitcoin.

Transactions are distributed utilizing a *gossip protocol*. Bitcoin was ostensibly designed to *gossip* for resiliency. However, this randomizing distribution protocol additionally encrypts (hides) the source of transactions by randomly choosing nodes to transmit a transaction, which in turn, randomly choose other nodes. In this manner, it is very difficult to trace the source of transactions since nodes should theoretically be unable to detect if they are talking to the originating node or simply some other random node. Gossiping helps maintain anonymity.

Given that we are talking about *crypto*currency, you may be surprised to learn that (unlike the banking example above) there is no encryption in transit for Bitcoin's blockchain transactions. They are generally transmitted in clear text. Additionally, unlike many secure servers, there is no encryption *at rest* of the blockchain data. This means that the blockchain ledger itself is not encrypted. Which is kind of true, it technically isn't encrypted, at least not in the way that most people usually think encryption works.

Hiding From Everybody, Especially Governments

Although there is no computer-encryption that scrambles the information just before writing it to the ledger, Bitcoin's blockchain ledger is still fundamentally and absolutely encrypted (hidden). It is encrypted because it is a ledger about no one.

These anonymous financial transactions are designed to be hidden from everybody, especially governments. From a technical standpoint, no system is perfectly anonymous. There are always some weak points, which may be exploited. However, Bitcoin and Blockchain can create anonymous systems in cyberspace, operating outside of the control of governments and government controls including anti-fraud and anti-money laundering laws.

CHAPTER 15
1997

Jim Bell didn't just write about ideas like Assassination Politics (AP). According to documentation from one of Mr. Bell's various legal matters:

> Words turned to action following the February 1997 seizure of Bell's automobile for unpaid federal taxes.
>
> Bell responded by contaminating the Vancouver, Washington IRS office with a powerful, foul-smelling chemical, forcing a number of government workers to leave the premises. A subsequent search of Bell's living area in the basement of his parents' home produced a variety of dangerous chemicals, including acid, cyanide and a chemical variant of the dangerous nerve agent sarin—all apparently obtained through the use of false Social Security numbers. Bell's computers also contained the names and home addresses of dozens of IRS employees and messages indicating they were intended for "later targeting."[103]

Mr. Bell has had significant interactions with the IRS, ATF, and others. He has vowed on occasion to obtain revenge on "the system that had imprisoned him."[104] In 1997, Bitcoin did not yet exist. With the advent of Bitcoin and other cryptocurrencies, Mr. Bell's vision of AP is now readily realizable. A logical manner in which a contract killing may be coordinated and funded is with a smart contract on a cryptocurrency blockchain.

---

[103] "United States of America, Plaintiff-appellee v. James Dalton Bell, Defendant-appellant, 303 F.3d 1187 (9th Cr. 2002)." *Justia.com*. Argued Aug 6, 2002. Filed Sep 19, 2002. https://law.justia.com/cases/federal/appellate-courts/F3/303/1187/505708/

[104] Ibid

"Wei Dai" and "James A. Donald" on AP

"Wei" and "James", likely pseudonyms, possibly Szabo and May,[105] offered the following assessment of AP in the summer of 1997:

```
From: jamesd@echeque.com
Date: Sun, 15 Jun 1997 02:05:41 +0800
To: Wei Dai <cypherpunks@toad.com>
Subject: Re: FCPUNX:Untraceable Contract Kill-
ings

At 05:39 PM 6/10/97 -0700, Wei Dai wrote:
> I think the novelty of Bell's scheme is that
> it allows assassination payments to be pooled
> from a large number of anonymous payers
> without explicit coordination (i.e., the
> payers do not have to communicate with each
> other to work out a contract, etc.).
> For killing a neighbor it doesn't improve
> upon the simple untraceable contract, but it
> can make a big difference when the target has
> many enemies (Bell gave politicians as an
> example).
>
> Now in light of the fact that when the target
> has many enemies the assassination becomes a
> non-excludable public good, it is almost
> certain that the scheme cannot actually work
> in practice.  All of the potential payers
> would rather free-ride and let others pay,
> so the public good ends up not being
> "produced".

This not correct:  Public goods are underpro-
duced, but they are produced.

Thus Bell's scheme would lead to less than the
economically optimal number of political assas-
sinations, but this is still a great deal more
than zero, and still likely to have substantial
effect on political behavior.
```

---

[105] See Chapter 8

CHAPTER 15
1997

> We have the right to defend ourselves | http://www.jim.com/jamesd/
> and our property, because of the kind |
> of animals that we are. True law | James A. Donald
> derives from this right, not from the |
> arbitrary power of the state. | jamesd@echeque.com[106]

---

[106] Cypherpunks Email Archive (1996)

CHAPTER 16
1998

In 1998, *Wired Magazine* announced that "Architect John Young nominated [James] Bell for a Chrysler design award for creating an "Information Design for Governmental Accountability."[107] While Bell's Assassination Politics (AP) idea received some praise within the crypto-anarchist community, unsurprisingly, he did not win that award. Instead, Bell had to contend with prison time.

Julian Assange

Several years before Julian Assange would create WikiLeaks and long before he altered the course of the 2016 US presidential election, he forwarded the following email to the Cypherpunks mailing list:

```
From: Julian Assange
Date: Thu, 1 Jan 1998 19:08:37 +0800
To: cypherpunks@toad.com
Subject: Jim Bell... lives... on... in... Hollywood!

Anyone noticed this before?

------- Start of forwarded message -------
Date: 1 Jan 1998 09:54:51 -0000
From: proff@suburbia.net
To: proff@suburbia.net
Subject:home.html

    Scoop the Grim Reaper!
```

---

[107] Wired Staff. "Crypto-Convict Won't Recant." *Wired Magazine*. Apr 14, 2000. https://www.wired.com/2000/04/crypto-convict-wont-recant/

```
Who will live?

Who will die?

And who will win the grand prize in Dewey's
Death Pool—an all-expense paid, two-day
Hollywood Death Tour for two. Or one of four
quarterly prizes—a fabulous celebrity death
library.

It's fun, it's easy—and all you have to do to
win is correctly forecast more celebrity
deaths for the calendar year 1998 than any
other entrant.108
```

Assange's forwarded email detailed out numerous terms and conditions for Dewey's Death Pool. Tim May responded to Assange's email indicating that a few people had already pointed out the presence of death pools, such as Dewey's Death Pool in earlier discussions about AP. In his email, May asserted, "The Feds have shown their hand: they want a ban on domestic cryptography."[109]

B-Money

In November 1998, "Wei Dai" announced b-money to the Cypherpunks mailing list in an email where he simultaneously announced an update to PipeNet, a network anonymization scheme that is similar to the TOR anonymizing network service:

```
From: Wei Dai <weidai@eskimo.com>
Date: Fri, 27 Nov 1998 08:07:43 +0800
To: cypherpunks@cyberpass.net
Subject: PipeNet 1.1 and b-money

I've discovered some attacks against the origi-
nal PipeNet design. The new protocol, PipeNet
1.1, should fix the weaknesses. PipeNet 1.1
uses layered sequence numbers and MACs. This
prevents a collusion between a receiver and a
subset of switches from tracing the caller by
modifying or swaping [sic] packets and then
```

---

[108] Cypherpunks Email Archive (1998).
  http://cypherpunks.venona.com/raw/cyp-1998.txt
[109] Ibid

CHAPTER 16
1998

```
watching for garbage.

A description of PipeNet 1.1 is available at
http://www.eskimo.com/~weidai.

Also available there is a description of b-
money, a new protocol for monetary exchange and
contract enforcement for pseudonyms.

Please direct all follow-up discussion of these
protocols to cypherpunks.[110]
```

The b-money proposal describes the objective: "Until now it's not clear, even theoretically, how such a [crypto-anarchist] community could operate. A community is defined by the cooperation of its participants, and efficient cooperation requires a medium of exchange (money) and a way to enforce contracts. Traditionally these services have been provided by the government or government-sponsored institutions and only to legal entities. In this article I describe a protocol by which these services can be provided to and by **untraceable entities**."[111] [*emphasis added*] A significant discussion thread regarding b-money ensued on the Cypherpunks mailing list.

DigiCash Bankruptcy

1998 is also the year that Dr. David Chaum's DigiCash filed for bankruptcy. The company would ultimately be sold for assets in 2002. However, the dream of untraceable electronic payments remained alive, particularly by those (such as the Cypherpunks) who felt that DigiCash's problem was that **it wasn't untraceable and anonymous enough.**

---

[110] Ibid

[111] "Dai, Wei." *b-money*

CHAPTER 17
FOLLOW THE MONEY

Cryptocurrency literally means "hidden money." *Crypto* comes from the Greek word *kruptos*, which means "hidden" such as when William F. Buckley, Jr. demanded that Gore Vidal stop calling him a crypto-Nazi or "he'd sock him in the goddamn face." Technically, Vidal called him *pro-crypto-Nazi*, a supporter of hidden Nazis, which is certainly inflammatory. Vidal later said he meant to use the word *crypto-fascist*. This happened during a heated exchange in a 1968 debate concerning police response to a particularly provocative Vietnam War protest where protesters raised the Viet Cong flag.

What Are You Hiding?

The banking industry is rife with *crypto-ledgers* such as Collateralized Debt Obligation (CDO) investments, which were blamed for fueling the 2008 banking crisis. Only a handful of investors could see through the facade to uncover the massive crypto-risk and the crypto-truth. Criminals and terrorists hide who they are. They are ***crypto*-criminals** and ***crypto*-terrorists** who hide their financial activities on ***crypto*-ledgers** (which may manage transactions using ***crypto*currency**).

Bitcoin's money trail can be so well hidden that criminals or terrorists feel safe enough to perform data hijacking (ransomware attacks). They encrypt your data and then brazenly extort bitcoins, confident that the payment cannot be traced. This is not to say that everybody who deals in bitcoins is a criminal or a terrorist. It's just that if you are a criminal or terrorist, the utility of untraceable money tends to be very appealing.

Hiding in Plain Sight

Al Capone was never convicted for murder or racketeering. He was convicted for tax evasion after the feds were able to get a hold of his financial ledgers. Ledgers, like blockchain ledgers, can be designed to hold as little information as possible. They may be so cryptic that you cannot make sense of them, but in the hands of highly skilled investigators, even the slightest shadow of evidence may be enough to figure things out. Bitcoin's blockchain ledger is completely anonymous; it is a ledger about no one. This is strong encryption (hiding), but Bitcoin goes even further to achieve anonymity.

When something is in your *possession*, that itself is evidence, such as possessing illegal drugs. "Officer, that is not mine, I swear. A friend borrowed my jacket earlier..." Al Capone's ledger is what finally put him in prison. Possessing certain ledgers can be powerful, but it can also get you into quite a bit of trouble. If you are holding the mafia's financial ledgers, it implies that you may be the bookkeeper for the mob and aware of (involved in) all sorts of activities. Blockchain ledgers avoid this problem by making **everybody** responsible for the ledger, so it appears that ***nobody*** is accountable for the ledger.

Even an anonymous ledger, with an anonymous bookkeeper, can possibly be decrypted by tracing the origin of transactions. So, Bitcoin's blockchain uses a randomizing ***gossip* protocol** to make it difficult to trace transactions back to the source node. Bitcoin **mixing services** (also called "tumblers", explicit bitcoin money laundering) provide *additional* randomization (anonymization) for a fee. Bitcoin gambling sites may offer further bitcoin mixing to make the money trail even more hidden. The Blockchain approach is exceptionally creative and thorough at hiding the money trail.

Ransomware *Powered by Bitcoin*

Ransomware, Bitcoin's first "killer app", is malware that can wreak mass havoc on an organization by infecting a single PC. The ransomware software searches for all information to which the PC has access and begins encrypting everything. It may attack immediately, though it has become more common to patiently lie in wait, doing other things such as disabling backup programs before performing the encryption attack. After all of the information has been encrypted, a pop-up message appears extorting a ransom (demanding payment in bitcoins) for the promise of decrypting (unhiding) your data.

Is the encrypted (ransomed) information *protected*? It depends on your perspective. If you are the victim of a ransomware attack, the encryption has effectively destroyed your data, and you absolutely do not feel safe or protected. If you are the ransomware attacker, *you* have some protection

CHAPTER 17
FOLLOW THE MONEY

from the victim accessing their own information, though they may possibly be able to defeat that protection by restoring from backups (if they are available). The most accurate interpretation of the term *protection* in this situation is that of a mafia-style "protection racket." The digital mafia is now "protecting" your data and promises access for payment in bitcoin.

Realizing Crypto-Anarchy

Bitcoin has been extorted in kidnappings as well.[112] These were aspects of crypto-anarchy that were specifically contemplated by Tim May in his 1988 manifesto. Which states:

> The State will of course try to slow or halt the spread of this technology, citing national security concerns, use of the technology by drug dealers and tax evaders, and fears of societal disintegration. Many of these concerns will be valid; crypto anarchy will allow national secrets to be trade [sic] freely and will allow illicit and stolen materials to be traded. An anonymous computerized market will even make possible abhorrent **markets for assassinations and extortion.** [*emphasis added*] Various criminal and foreign elements will be active users of CryptoNet. But this will not halt the spread of crypto anarchy.[113]

Tim May envisioned anonymous computerized markets that make assassinations and extortion possible. The Cypherpunks "played with the ideas and saw what was needed" from their first meeting in 1992.[114] Crypto-anarchy has been developed and perfected over a very long time horizon.

---

[112] Burke, Jason. "South Africa kidnappers make ransom demand in bitcoin." *The Guardian.* May 22, 2018. https://www.theguardian.com/world/2018/may/22/south-africa-kidnappers-ransom-demand-bitcoin
[113] May. *The Crypto Anarchist Manifesto*
[114] See Chapter 4

CHAPTER 18
2001

On September 11, 2001, the World Trade Center towers fell. The Pentagon was attacked. United 92 crashed due to passengers fighting back against the hijackers that were planning to attack either the White House or US Capitol Building. The United States was at war.

Devolution of a Dangerous List

In a 2018 interview Tim May indicated, "...the Cypherpunks list eventually devolved. Essentially after 9/11 a lot of people got cold feet about participating in something that dangerous. And then the arrest of Jim Bell... I'm credited... that I had come up with the idea of assassination markets. I had not. I mention in *Crypto Anarchist Manifesto* that there could be odious markets for assassinations. I mean it was obvious that if you had untraceable cash that it would enable certain types of ransoms or 'hits' on people."[115] Jim Bell's AP innovation introduced crowdfunded assassinations using untraceable digital cash as a means of achieving political change.

Cypherpunk Mailing List Successor

According to the published archives, Perry Metzger established The Cryptography Mailing List in March 2001.[116] Considering how May indicated that "after 9/11 a lot of people got cold feet about participating in something that dangerous," it is possible that The Cryptography Mailing List was actually established *after* 9/11 and the records backdated to make it appear that this list was established sooner. However, the evidence leads

---

[115] Weatherman. "Under the Microscope - Timothy C. May." (29:45-31:00)
[116] Metzger, Perry E. Email to The Cryptography Mailing List. "The Cryptography Mailing List Returns..." Mar 28, 2001.
http://www.metzdowd.com/pipermail/cryptography/2001-March/000000.html

me to believe that the list was established in March 2001 as the archived messages indicate.

Metzger described his motivations as follows, "The list is a successor to the early Cypherpunks mailing list. I got fed up with the noise levels on it a very long time ago. So, I created a new moderated mailing list that would hopefully be lower noise," said Metzger. He explains, "Moderated implies that when postings go to the list, someone has to manually approve them so that things can't get as out of hand when discussions get heated."[117]

When asked about his early impressions of Bitcoin, Metzger said, "I actually was extremely skeptical about it at the time. The proposal had a number of obvious flaws, all of which are still there, but there was apparently a sufficient hunger for what it could do, and its good points were good enough that it managed to take off."[118]

Bitcoin was announced to the Cryptography Mailing List by the pseudonymous "Satoshi Nakamoto." It was routine for members of the list to use pseudonyms. Metzger indicated, "There were a lot of people who posted to the mailing list under pseudonyms."[119]

Parallel Mailing Lists

The creation of the Cryptography Mailing List created parallel distribution groups since the official Cypherpunk mailing list remained active as well. There are records of postings to both groups and cross-postings between them.[120] Messages to these lists have been published and preserved, but the information published to The Cryptography Mailing List has been explicitly moderated per Metzger. The Cypherpunks list was not moderated, though the email archives of either one of these lists may not be complete.

---

[117] Brockwell, Naomi. "The Mailing List where Bitcoin Began, with Perry Metzger." Video Interview. Sep 9, 2018. https://youtu.be/l0WXFhk3dnU (1:40 - 2:10)

[118] Ibid (2:40 - 3:05)

[119] Ibid (5:55 - 6:00)

[120] Hettinga, R.A. In this example, Hettinga is forwarding an email to The Cryptography Mailing List that Eric Hughes originally sent to the Cypherpunks mailing list. "Eric Hughes sings…" Sep 12, 2001. http://www.metzdowd.com/pipermail/cryptography/2001-September/000715.html

CHAPTER 18
2001

9/11 Email

Metzger posted the following to the Cryptography Mailing List shortly after the attack:

```
From: Perry E. Metzger <perry@piermont.com>
Date: Wed Sep 12 19:11:23 EDT 2001
Subject:    The tragedy in NYC
```

[I sent this originally yesterday, but the, er, problems our mail server in downtown New York suffered for a while caused some delay. Another copy was published on Dave Farber's interesting people. Several people wrote me afterwards vilifying me. Ah well.

The list is now running on a new machine in Virginia, which should be safe even as more buildings collapse and burn. --Perry]

In the wake of the tragedy in NYC today, I was asked by someone if [I] didn't now agree that crypto was a munition. At the time, I thought that a friend of mine was likely dead. (I've since learned he escaped in time.)

My answer then, when I thought I'd lost a friend, was the same as my answer now and the answer I've always had.

Cryptography must remain freely available to all.

In coming months, politicians will flail about looking for freedoms to eliminate to "curb the terrorist threat". They will see an opportunity to grandstand and enhance their careers, an opportunity to show they are "tough on terrorists".

We must remember throughout that you cannot preserve freedom by eliminating it. The problem is not a lack of laws banning things.

I know the pressure on everyone in Washington will be to "do something". Speaking as a New Yorker who dearly loves this city, who has felt deep shock throughout most of the day, watching the smoke still rising from the fires to the south of me, listening to the ambulances

THE BLOCKCHAIN CODE

and police cars continuing to wail about me, let me say this:

I do not want more laws passed in the name of defending my home.

I do not want more freedoms eliminated to "preserve freedom".

I do not want to trade my freedom for safety. Franklin has said far more eloquently than me why that is worthless.

If you must do something, send out more investigators to find those responsible for this and bring them to justice. Pass no new laws. Take away no freedoms. Do not destroy the reason I live here to give me "safety". I'd rather die in a terrorist attack.

--
Perry E. Metzger   perry at piermont.com
--
"Ask not what your country can force other people to do for you..."[121]

Post 9/11

The passage of the Patriot Act and the general expansion of government surveillance had broad support within the United States at that time due to the attacks. Cypherpunks disagreed with this response. The Crypto-Anarchy vision would be challenged and was perhaps more encrypted (hidden) at this time, but the dream remained alive.

---

[121] Metzger, Perry E. Email from Metzger to The Cryptography Mailing List. "The tragedy in NYC". Sep 12, 2001.
http://www.metzdowd.com/pipermail/cryptography/2001-September/000710.html

CHAPTER 19
CATCH ME IF YOU CAN

Before ransomware, the goal of malware was almost entirely to **remain undetected**, silently collecting passwords, credit card information and other data without you realizing it even happened. While this is undoubtedly still the goal of much malware, Bitcoin changed the game, enabling ransomware because it facilitates **untraceable payments**. More accurately stated, bitcoin payments are nearly impossible to trace *when the ransomware perpetrator is careful and an expert in hiding their tracks*.

Speculative Investor & Casual Criminal Beware

Cryptographer *experts* are highly skilled in the proper use of the cryptographic techniques required to remain hidden, and they may remain anonymous. Conversely, the "less than expert" may be terribly exposed. The bitcoin transactions of a casual bitcoin investor or of those incorrectly assuming they are an expert, may potentially be traced through **side-channel analysis,** which can be performed by the truly skilled experts. This means that by merely investing in bitcoin, you are potentially inviting attack. Ironically, this includes weaker, less skilled ransomware criminals who can be potentially identified through the blockchain and certain side channels.

Side-Channel Analysis

A side-channel is a way of seeing information that you are not supposed to be able to see. It is using a stethoscope to crack into a safe by listening to the clicks. Side-channel weaknesses have been the subject of a substantial amount of research by information technology security experts and hackers for a long time.

At the beginning of 2018, CPU flaws were announced that allowed computer programs to access information that was supposed to be hidden within the inner workings of computer processors. These bugs, popularly known as Spectre and Meltdown, could be exploited by malware to measure things that were happening within CPUs, kind of like the clicks of tumblers inside the lock of a safe. These "clicks" (CPU instruction completion timing) allowed the leaking of sensitive information out of the CPU, permitting covert data theft to on a massive scale.

Two Examples of Side-Channel Analysis

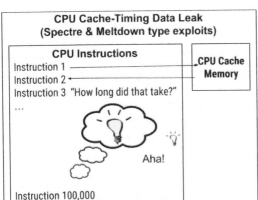 

The story of Spectre and Meltdown flaws that allowed data leaks through side-channel analysis was inaccurately reported in the media. This inaccurate reporting has substantial consequences. We will examine what actually happened in the appendix to *The Blockchain Code*.

Protection Racket

Ransomware forcibly created some reluctant early Bitcoin "customers" who ponied up to pay this "protection racket" to get their hidden data back. Additionally, the bold nature of these attacks helped generate some early press coverage of Bitcoin. The damage inflicted by ransomware can be devastating, and most perpetrators of this crime are never tracked down and brought to justice.

The more information you have at your disposal, the greater the likelihood you may be able to identify a side-channel that could be used to reveal otherwise hidden data. During the writing of this book, I noticed a very interesting opportunity to use side-channel analysis to potentially identify ransomware perpetrators. I reached out to an FBI agent with whom I had previously presented a continuing legal education class to discuss the matter with him.

CHAPTER 19
CATCH ME IF YOU CAN

News had just come out regarding an SEC investigation of **Longfin**, a blockchain technology company that had managed to get itself listed on the NASDAQ stock exchange a couple of months earlier. Part of the apparent business model of Longfin was to perform *cryptocurrency arbitrage*. This process involves buying and selling cryptocurrencies either directly or using option orders. A common use of currency arbitrage is for hedging, a process that seeks to provide exchange price predictability/stability.

Linking Ledgers

Bitcoin is designed to facilitate untraceable transactions, but it is not *perfectly* untraceable. It is untraceable enough for criminals to boldly extort payment, but there are limits. There are potential cracks in that untraceability.

If the New York-based company Longfin was even remotely doing what they say they are doing, this would put the company in a position to potentially break through the anonymity of many cryptocurrency actors, including ransomware perpetrators.

Longfin should theoretically have ledgers that record interactions:

- between multiple cryptocurrencies AND
- between itself and banks AND
- NASDAQ stock trading records

If you wanted to bring ransomware criminals to justice, there might be no better starting point than with the ledgers that should exist at Longfin. I pointed this out to my FBI colleague. I also speculated that some of these ledgers might be accessible due to the SEC investigation into the company.

It would be expected that there are cryptocurrency exchanges that desire as little information about customers as possible. Many Bitcoin users are extremely protective of their privacy. Money transmission laws and transmitter licenses in the United States likely have a certain impact on larger, official cryptocurrency exchanges where there should be some additional ledgers available as well.

Let's assume that there are many cryptocurrency exchanges available around the world (these would be underground/illegal exchanges in the United States) that intentionally retain as little customer information as possible to maximize customer privacy. Longfin should have interfaces between banking institutions and the NASDAQ stock exchange. Records with banking institutions and the NASDAQ are not permitted to be entirely anonymous. Additionally, transaction dates and amounts for cryptocurrency transactions would be publicly recorded on the respective blockchain for the particular cryptocurrency. Dates and amounts may possibly be correlated with banking and/or stock exchange records, which must have at least some personally identifiable information.

While the premise of Bitcoin is that it is supposed to be untraceable, it is a system made by human hands and is therefore imperfect. There is always the potential for some side-channel footprints. We can start with unsolved FBI ransomware case files that should list bitcoins addresses used for ransom demands.

If the ransomware perpetrator is skilled and careful, it can be almost impossible to trace the money. But not all criminals are so careful. For example, a criminal might reuse a bitcoin address that they used to extort ransomware payment for an unrelated business transaction with Longfin. If Longfin ledgers were then available to law enforcement due to an SEC investigation, this might potentially identify the source of a ransomware attack. Additionally, it is common to transfer bitcoins from one of your addresses to another. Therefore, there is a reasonable chance that bitcoin addresses that are only one or two transactions removed from the address may be the same party.

Start with One Ransomware Criminal

Let's get very specific. Here is an image of a pop-up screen that apparently extorted ransom:

CHAPTER 19
CATCH ME IF YOU CAN

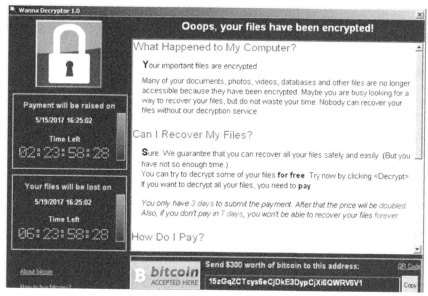

Based on the title, "Wanna Decryptor 1.0", this appears to be a variant of the WannaCry ransomware. On this screen, the perpetrators are demanding $300 worth of bitcoin to the address 15zGqZCcys6eCjDkE3DypCjXi6QWRV6V1. It's difficult to tell for sure solely from the blockchain ledger information, but it appears *this* address may belong to a "less than expert" ransomware criminal(s).

You can review the transactions involving that address by various means. The simplest would be to use the blockchain.com or blockexplorer.com websites. By examining the results at https://www.blockchain.com/btc/address/15zGqZCTcys6eCjDkE3DypCjXi6QWRV6V1, we see that this address received six payments in an amount that would be consistent with a ransom paid within the first three days. Additionally, there is one payment that would be consistent with a payment paid after three days, but before the 7-day deadline. Assuming these are ransoms (which might possibly be confirmed by the FBI or other sources), they would add up to a couple thousand dollars at the then exchange rate.

Additionally, six other apparently *non-ransom* transactions, totaling about 170 bitcoins (equivalent to around $200K at the exchange rate at the time) were processed through the same bitcoin address around the same time. To maximize anonymity, you are not supposed to reuse bitcoin addresses. This ransomware perpetrator did not appear to pay attention to these types of details and needlessly provided additional information. We might theoretically be able to track *this* perpetrator down using the Longfin ledgers as a side-channel.

Blockchain Dominoes

Once you track down one or two of the criminals, links between the others actually get somewhat easier to connect. This is because once you have identified one criminal, this information itself can provide you with more side channels that help you uncover still more hidden information, and so on. Bitcoin is largely untraceable, but not necessarily for criminals who are sloppy. If and when privacy is defeated, the potential exists for a domino effect that could identify multiple bad actors.

Criminal Minds

It is also very interesting that an anonymous party who appears to already have a substantial stockpile of bitcoins would bother to extort a relatively small amount of additional bitcoins. Perhaps the criminals are not necessarily after the bitcoins themselves. Extortion of bitcoins creates new "customers" that buy into the system (albeit under duress), provides hard money liquidity that helps existing bitcoin holders cash out, and provides notoriety (potentially press coverage depending on the target) and validation that bitcoins are valuable.

CHAPTER 20
2003

Cypherpunk Nick Szabo, former DigiCash employee and inventor of the smart contract, began his studies at George Washington Law School around 2003. Szabo's discussions with Tim May inspired him to realize the cryptoanarchy dream. This is a world in which smart contracts would be an essential component. One would expect that this formal legal education was helpful in the implementation of smart contracts.

Tim May's Wikipedia Page Created

On September 29, 2003, the article on Wikipedia describing Timothy C. May, founder of the cryptoanarchy movement, was created. There have been numerous edits to this article over time, which is common with Wikipedia. A persistent error has existed on that page which is still present as this book goes to print. It indicates that he retired from Intel in 2003, which is incorrect. May actually retired from Intel in 1986 at age 34.[122] [123]

Wikipedia - Later (2008) Edits

A "View history" link is accessible at the top of every Wikipedia page to review edits to that page over time. An interesting series of edits to May's page occurred five years later, in July 2008, just three months before the email that would announce Bitcoin to the world.

Per the Wikipedia edit history, on July 26, 2008, an anonymous person with a listed name of 69.86.167.231 added the following material:

---

[122] May. *Thirty Years of Crypto Anarchy*. (4:15-4:40)
[123] Levy, Steven. "Crypto Rebels." *Wired Magazine*. 2/1/93. https://www.wired.com/1993/02/crypto-rebels/

Recent years, and apparent bigotry

Today, Tim May is probably best known for his prolific posts to Usenet and related forums, where he has participated since the early days of the medium. While he has written many information-rich articles on subjects technical and mundane, in recent years his most memorable posts have been those where he espouses more controversial opinions that are frequently held to be racist.

A few exerpts follow.

On the topic of Klan robes, Jews, and the US political situation:

> This is no longer a nation where the First Amendment applies...this is Zionist-Occupied America, with the negroes and Mexicans as the cannon fodder for the Jew generals. [3]

On poverty in Africa:

> What is needed is for the world to stop intervening in Africa and just let the negro/cannibal primitives burn off. Africa needs to lose its negro population. Then, ten years later, after the rot has faded, whites and Asians can move in.

> Fact is, about 2.4 billion on the planet today have no economic hope of survival. Interfering with their departure just means even more have to die out later. Best thing to do is to let the dirts go back to being dirt. [4] [124]

There was one additional quote in this section, but I have not been able to confirm that May is the author, so I have not included it here. The "Recent years, and apparent bigotry" section was immediately removed about one hour later by the Wikipedia user *Skomorokh* with the comments, "appreciate the development, but negative material in the biographies of living people need to be referenced to very reliable sources, which Google isn't." Technically, the sources provided are three discussion threads on Usenet newsgroups. The references included in the Wikipedia article merely happened to link to Usenet by using Google Groups, which is one of several ways to access these public discussion forums.

---

[124] Wikipedia revision of Timothy C. May Wikipedia page from July 26, 2008 20:28. https://en.wikipedia.org/w/index.php?title=Timothy_C._May&oldid=228064270

CHAPTER 20
2003

The first discussion in the old version of the Wikipedia article is from alt.machines.cnc. This link no longer works because this newsgroup is apparently now on a list of "banned content." However, those words of May's appears to have also been posted to a discussion on rec.crafts.metalworking. Here is that full quote:

```
Date: 5/27/08
From: Tim May
Subject: How to REALLY cut US taxes

In article
<ntjp34lu5iks410pcrha53tt4tb55cl3ig@4ax.com>,
Aratzio
<a6ah...@sneakemail.com> wrote:

>
> Bigots that understand they are scum are not
> a problem. Wear your sheet in public, be
> loud, be proud.

The Jews have passed laws banning the wearing
of such garb in public. Many arrests in recent
years for wearing Klan robes, displaying Con-
federate flags, even portraying nooses in truck
decals.

This is no longer a nation where the First
Amendment applies...this is Zionist-Occupied
America, with the negroes and Mexicans as the
cannon fodder for the Jew generals.

Rumors of war, and war.

--Tim May
```
[125]

The second discussion thread referenced, "CostCo – As Inflation Rises, Food Hoarding Begins", is from misc.survivalism. Here is that full quote:

```
Date:    4/23/08
From:    Tim May
```

---

[125] May, Tim. "How to Really cut US taxes." Posting by May to the Usenet newsgroup rec.crafts.metalworking. 5/27/08. https://groups.google.com/forum/#!topic/rec.crafts.metalworking/vR8GNF8NCmk%5B1-25%5D

Subject: CostCo - As Inflation Rises, Food Hoarding Begins

Millions in Africa and other Turd World hellholes are unable to buy food at the (often subsidized) prices they once were (barely) able to.

So?

Is this surprising, that newly wealthy Chinese who build products for the Wal-Marts of American consumers are able to outbid the unproductive, scrape the dirt, farmers of Sudan and Zimbabwe and Chad and Niger and Congo and 30 other pestholes of black Africa?

What is needed is for the world to stop intervening in Africa and just let the negro/cannibal primitives burn off. Africa needs to lose its negro population. Then, ten years later, after the rot has faded, whites and Asians can move in.

Fact is, about 2.4 billion on the planet today have no economic hope of survival. Interfering with their departure just means even more have to die out later. Best thing to do is to let the dirts go back to being dirt.

There are no gods, there is no "sacred." People breed like algae blooms. Right now, a few billion have "bloomed" as fertilizer from the West and Developed World was dumped in the breeding pool.

Algae blooms always die out.

--Tim May[126]

Therefore, the first two quotes in the "Recent years, and apparent bigotry" update to May's Wikipedia page appear to be authentic. Regarding the third quote attributed to May, I was unable to confirm if the words were May's or the words of someone else in the discussion thread. Since I could neither confirm nor deny that the third quote was accurate, I did not

---

[126] May, Tim. "CostCo – As Inflation Rises, Food Hoarding Begins." Posting by May to the Usenet group misc.survivalism. 4/23/08. https://groups.google.com/forum/#!topic/misc.survivalism/9K-X5Nd-pEY

include it here. However, I have included an additional *different* quote from May to bolster the argument that the Wikipedia entry is accurate. According to May, "The key to survival lies in being willing to kill marauding black people (negroes), Mexicans, and Jack-Booted Thugs. Americans can survive if they are willing to kill the 60 million who are basically communists, Papists, and Third Worlders."[127]

About fifteen hours after the "Recent years, and apparent bigotry" section was removed by Skomorokh, this section was once again added to May's Wikipedia page. This time the information was posted not by an anonymous author, but by Perry Metzger.[128] [129]

Metzger is also the creator of the Cryptography Mailing List where "Satoshi" announced Bitcoin. When republishing the "bigotry" section, he commented, "The quotes are accurate. If you email Tim May, he'll almost certainly confirm them to you. He isn't ashamed of his opinions and does not hide them." Fifteen minutes after Metzger reposted this information, Skomorokh removed them a second time (and they remain removed). When deleting the "bigotry" section, this time Skomorokh included the comments "staying super-paranoid about libel while we discuss the issue…" This entire interaction is visible at **https://en.wikipedia.org/w/index.php?title=Timothy_C._May&action=history**.

It is impossible to know all of the reasons why Tim May personally sought to create cryptoanarchy. We are all unique and multiple factors often influence our decisions. However, nations are created and defined by laws that include acceptable ways to interact with fellow citizens. Alexander Hamilton once wrote, "If men were angels, no government would be necessary." It would appear that at least part of May's motivations were based upon frustrations of having to co-exist with all of his fellow Americans according to the current rules of American society.

Wikipedia - Even Later (2013) Szabo Edits

Nick Szabo's Wikipedia page was created on December 8, 2013 and indicated that Szabo was a former law professor at George Washington University (**this is incorrect** and has since been updated, he was a law *student*

---

[127] Ibid

[128] Wikipedia page history - Timothy C. May. https://en.wikipedia.org/w/index.php?title=Timothy_C._May&action=history

[129] Wikipedia user page history for *Pmetzger*. https://en.wikipedia.org/w/index.php?title=User:Pmetzger&oldid=95577412

at the school). This initial entry also noted, "It has been suggested that he is Satoshi Nakamoto."[130]

The second part is accurate. Numerous articles have been written suggesting that Szabo is "Satoshi Nakamoto."[131]

---

[130] Initial Wikipedia Page Entry - Nick Szabo. https://en.wikipedia.org/w/index.php?title=Nick_Szabo&oldid=585068073

[131] Roberts, Jeff John. "Is there any doubt this man created Bitcoin?" *Fortune Magazine*. Oct 31, 2018. http://fortune.com/2018/10/31/satoshi-identity/

CHAPTER 21
PEER-TO-PEER (P2P)

According to emails from "Satoshi Nakamoto", the anonymous software developer(s) that created Bitcoin, the development of Bitcoin began sometime in 2007. The project appears to have *actually* begun by 2006. Additionally, the ideas and concepts behind Bitcoin began decades before that. David Chaum's concepts published in the early 80s were also essential. The other concept was peer-to-peer, which has a history going back to the beginning of the internet.

Responsibility and Accountability

When the internet was first created, things were much less structured than they are today. Each computer might serve information to other computers, which might provide other information back to the original computer or to other computers. This is called a *Peer-to-Peer (P2P)* approach. Over time, most internet applications introduced dedicated *servers*. Today, your computer, phone, or tablet generally acts as a *client* requesting information from a *server*. This is called a *client-server* approach. In the 90s, Napster tried using a P2P approach to facilitate sharing of copyrighted music. Napster claimed that they were not violating copyright laws because the music files were never stored on Napster's servers. Courts disagreed, shutting Napster down because it had a central server component (a central music database - a ledger of sorts).

Several replacement services emerged that were more fully peer-to-peer using a distributed database. Notable examples are **Gnutella** and **BitTorrent**, which facilitate (largely illegal) sharing of music and movies. While copyright holders might wish to have their copyrighted content removed from these more fully peer-to-peer services, it is difficult to hold anyone accountable when, like Bitcoin, there is no official company and no specific servers that are "in charge."

Freedom Fighter

From an email posted by Bitcoin's anonymous creator to the Cryptography Mailing List (a.k.a. "The Cypherpunks mailing list") in 2008:

```
From: Satoshi Nakamoto <satoshi@vistomail.com>
Date: Thu Nov 6 15:15:40 EST 2008
Subject: Bitcoin P2P e-cash paper


>[Lengthy exposition of vulnerability of a
> systm [sic] to use-of-force monopolies
> ellided [sic].]
>
>You will not find a solution to political
>problems in cryptography.

Yes, but we can win a major battle in the arms
race and gain a new territory of freedom for
several years.

Governments are good at cutting off the heads
of a centrally controlled networks like Nap-
ster, but pure P2P networks like Gnutella and
Tor seem to be holding their own.

Satoshi[132]
```

This email from "Satoshi" appears to be a reply to an anonymously sent direct message. Responding publicly on a mailing list to which the sender was presumably a member would be the only way to respond to such a message. As an aside, various speculations and theories about the identity of "Satoshi" have been posted. Some of these speculations are based upon timestamps of email messages. People need to realize that all Cypherpunks mailing list and Cryptography Mailing List messages would have been routed through *anonymizing mail servers*. You cannot trust the accuracy of the email timestamps to deliver a high degree of precision as email metadata was likely altered in the anonymizing "mixing process."

---

[132] "Nakamoto, Satoshi". Email reply from "Satoshi" most likely in response to an anonymously sent email. "Bitcoin P2P e-cash paper." Nov 6, 2008. http://www.metzdowd.com/pipermail/cryptography/2008-November/014823.html

CHAPTER 21
PEER-TO-PEER (P2P)

Bitcoin was built (**mostly**) Pure P2P

It is extremely difficult to build a 100 percent peer-to-peer application. Distribution of the compiled programs and source code of Bitcoin was centralized. New nodes also needed a way to find other nodes to join the network. The initial solution to this problem was through one of the initial computer-mediated social networks, Internet Relay Chat (IRC). About two months before "Satoshi" announced Bitcoin, "**James A. Donald**" published an article where he provided a list of skills that were required to create the system. The last item in the list is "computer mediated social networks,"[133] which makes sense.

This component is *technically client/server, not peer-to-peer*, but it was the final glue (the final design compromise) that made the Bitcoin network work. IRC allowed all the computers running Bitcoin software to find each other (using the #bitcoin channel on chat.freenode.net).

Today, Bitcoin Core software accomplishes the initial connection process not by IRC, but rather by including a *centralized database* of systems bundled with the source code and already-compiled application. There are also a handful of systems hard-coded into the Bitcoin Core code providing a fallback plan for getting new nodes on the network. The hard-coded address list is a kind of backup centralized database built into the computer code. Lastly, there is also a centralized place where the source code and compiled applications are distributed called GitHub.

Might these centralized components allow governments to shut down Bitcoin in a similar fashion to how they shut down Napster? Possibly. If the nations of the world decided to shut down Bitcoin, these centralized points are certainly avenues they might pursue. Although, there are other weak points in the system that might be exploited as well. While the situation is a bit different with Bitcoin than it was with Napster, there are still some similarities in these technical areas.

---

[133] "Donald, James A.". 2008. *The Cypherpunk Program*. https://jim.com/security/cypherpunk_program.html

CHAPTER 22
THE WAYBACK MACHINE

A tool we will use in the next chapter, as well as several other chapters, is The Wayback Machine (a.k.a. The Internet Archive). This website captures snapshots of web pages throughout the internet from various points in time. This archive is helpful to see how the stories told by various web pages change and evolve throughout their history. The address to access the Wayback Machine is archive.org/web.

To use the Wayback Machine, you provide a web address and click the "Browse History" button. There is a calendar as well as forward and backward arrows that allow you to "browse through time" to see the full history of that web page. When exploring our jungle of *intentional* obscurity, the Wayback Machine can help shine a light on the truth. There will be times in this book where we will refer to the Wayback Machine to determine when web pages were published and when certain changes to these web pages occurred.

One thing to note: the list of web pages is not "the entire internet", though it is a lot of the internet. According to the site's FAQ, some sites may be excluded because automated crawlers were unaware of their existence at the time of the crawl. A website owner might also place a file on their site directing search engines not to index their site. Additionally, some sites may be private and require a password, so those sites would not be archived by the Wayback Machine or listed in search engines. Lastly, site owners can submit a request to have their sites excluded from the archive.

TrueCrypt

One notable omission is historical archives of the once popular encryption tool, truecrypt.org. Reports are that Paul Le Roux, the developer of TrueCrypt, was arrested by the US Drug Enforcement Agency and that he cooperated with law enforcement to help get at hidden drug cartel information.[134] All I know for sure is that if you look for truecrypt.org on the Wayback Machine, it says "Sorry. This URL has been excluded from the Wayback Machine."

Backdoors

As an aside, governments have attempted to control the use of cryptography by the private sector. One method was a "backdoor" inserted by the NSA into the Elliptic Curve Deterministic Random Number Generator used by some cryptography tools. Random numbers are central to cryptography. If a random number is, in fact, not so random, encryption may be easily broken. The extent to which this backdoor was actively being used was made public by Edward Snowden in 2013. There is a possibility that Le Roux created a hidden backdoor in *his* encryption code. There have been online discussions questioning this possibility, though the issues with TrueCrypt were likely unintentional bugs, not an intentional backdoor.[135] [136] [137]

The Blockchain philosophy is that centralized control must be avoided wherever possible. There is no centralized code review or change management of the random number generator used by wallets. Everyone is free to use whatever software or service they choose. This is important because the manner in which a deterministic device (a computer) creates a non-deterministic, random number is crucial to the effectiveness of cryptography.

---

[134] Feuer, Alan. "In Spellbinding Testimony, Crime Lord Details Mayhem and Murders." *The New York Times*. Apr 5, 2018. https://www.nytimes.com/2018/04/05/nyregion/crime-lord-le-roux-details-mayhem-and-murders.html

[135] Martin, Alexander J. "Wait what? TrueCrypt 'decrypted' by the FBI to nail doc-stealing sysadmin." *The Register*. Aug 4, 2015. https://www.theregister.co.uk/2015/08/04/truecrypt_decrypted_by_fbi/

[136] Cox, Joseph. "Encryption Program TrueCrypt Has a Critical Vulnerability." *Motherboard*. Sep 30, 2015. https://motherboard.vice.com/en_us/article/3dkxky/encryption-program-truecrypt-has-a-critical-vulnerability

[137] "Was TrueCrypt really broken, or is it a cover for NSA and a VeraCrypt download with an NSA backdoor?" Quora Discussion. https://www.quora.com/Was-TrueCrypt-really-broken-or-is-it-a-cover-for-NSA-and-a-VeraCrypt-download-with-an-NSA-backdoor

CHAPTER 22
THE WAYBACK MACHINE

Anyone using cryptocurrency implicitly places a tremendous amount of trust in the software or services they use. This is especially true of any wallet software, wallet website, or any cryptocurrency organization that manages your cryptocurrency wallet on your behalf. A wallet backdoor is one of several reasons why you may not actually own the cryptocurrency that you think you own. We will explain wallets in detail in Chapter 25.

CHAPTER 23
DECEMBER 2005
BLOCKCHAIN IS BORN

At the end of 2005, **Nick Szabo** published an article on his blog titled "**Bit gold**" [*capitalization is correct*] that requires "minimal dependence on trusted third parties."[138] This name was possibly in homage to Midas Mulligan from *Atlas Shrugged*. This character established a bank, in Galt's Gulch, that dealt exclusively in gold and silver. The specifications outlined by Szabo detail the technical framework for *Bitcoin*. These details include the concept of distributed timestamping, the use of Hal Finney's reusable proof of work, and having the last created amount of currency create the computational problem that must be solved to create the next amount of currency. It is not important to the story that you understand any of these terms, but cryptocurrency programmers should appreciate this.

Additionally, Szabo's specifications indicate that control over bit gold does not depend on sole possession of the bits, but rather a "lead position in the unforgeable chain of title (chain of digital signatures)." This is the birth of Blockchain.

The process describes how to avoid "double spending", a term used in the Bitcoin white paper as well as in the hypertext-linked words in Szabo's article, distributed property title registry that links to Szabo's article *Secure Property Titles with Owner Authority*. To have any semblance of data integrity, one cannot simply repeatedly spend their bit gold, so transactions are timestamped. The distributed property link in Szabo's Bit gold article no longer works (Szabo has moved and updated this article), but the original is still available on the Wayback Machine. The idea is that "proof of ownership" means that you *know a number* that is a solution to a hard math

---

[138] Szabo, Nick. 2005. "Bit gold". *Unenumerated* (Szabo's Blog). Dec 29. http://unenumerated.blogspot.com/2005/12/bit-gold.html (Note: the listed publication date is 2008, but this is incorrect. The date of 2005 has been confirmed by *The Wayback Machine* as will be demonstrated on the following page)

problem and therefore have a key that you can use to create the correct *digital signature*.[139]

March 2006 (3 Months Later) - Bitcoin is Named

The first snapshot captured by Wayback Machine of Szabo's *Bit gold* article is from March 29, 2006. The address to see this snapshot is:

https://web.archive.org/web/20060329122942/http:/unenumerated.blogspot.com/2005/12/bit-gold.html

This historical record shows what this webpage looked like on March 29, 2006. This snapshot of the web page is quite remarkable.

To see what makes this snapshot so surprising, you will need to scroll down to the very first entry in the "LINKS TO THIS POST" section. It is just past "POST A COMMENT." You can locate this near the bottom of the page. It reads:

POST A COMMENT

LINKS TO THIS POST:

Bitcoin

Интересный проект по созданию цифровой валюты без центрального "банка" или сервера. Все P2P, все распределено. Причем в систему встроена автоматическая защита от инфляции: в природе может существовать 21 миллион монеток и ни копейкой

...

posted by Федеральная Служба Опасности @ 10:27 PM

> Per Google Translate, this comment says:
>
> ```
> An interesting project to create a digital
> currency without a central "bank" or server.
> All P2P, everything is distributed. And in
> the system is built-in automatic protection
> against inflation: in nature there can be 21
> million coins and not a penny...
> ```

---

[139] Szabo, Nick. 1998. "Secure Property Titles with Owner Authority."

CHAPTER 23
DECEMBER 2005 BLOCKCHAIN IS BORN

This Russian post from *2006* appears to be the **first historical reference to the name Bitcoin**!

It is also noteworthy that Bitcoin is supposed to have a limit of 21 million coins. This limit has been embedded into the computer code from the outset and is unlikely to change in future releases of the mainstream Bitcoin code (though it has changed in some hard forks of Bitcoin and is different in other cryptocurrencies – we will explain what hard and soft forks are in Chapter 33).

This Russian comment seems to imply that the Bitcoin development project was underway by March 2006 and that at least one Russian Cypherpunk was involved in the project at that time. It also seems that the 21 million coin limit had been determined by then.

This 2006 comment posted to Szabo's *Bit gold* article substantially undercuts the entire "Satoshi Nakamoto" story. This Bitcoin "link to this post" comment was active for about six years. Per the Wayback Machine, it disappeared in early 2012. Some extraordinary steps were taken to *hide this comment*. However, it is visible on the Wayback Machine using the provided link.

It is particularly noteworthy that in October 2009, the publication date of Szabo's article was post-dated by three years from 2005 to 2008, but the URL (web address) was unchanged. It is still *http://unenumerated.blogspot.com/2005/12/bit-gold.html*. It seems that if **Nick Szabo** wanted to make it appear that he had published the *Bit gold* article in 2008 instead of 2005, he would have changed the URL as well from 2005 to 2008. However, that does not appear to be what Szabo was trying to accomplish. This update seems to have been an attempt at *misdirection* to focus attention on that timestamp change, instead of the 2006 Bitcoin comment. Perhaps it was also an attempt to create the appearance that the dates on BlogSpot were somehow unreliable.

December 2006 - B-Money Republished

B-money is the first reference listed in the Bitcoin white paper. The author, "Wei Dai", is likely a pseudonym (possibly an alias for Nick Szabo). This article was *originally* published at *www.eskimo.com/~weidai/bmoney.txt* in 1998. In December 2006, the Wayback Machine captured the first republication of the *b-money* article at *www.weidai.com/bmoney.txt*, the address that would be referenced in the Bitcoin white paper.

The *b-money* article is primarily focused on implementation details of **Nick Szabo's** *smart contracts*. We will look at smart contracts in detail in Chapter 36. Bitcoin had support for smart contracts even in the initially released software.

"Wei"/Szabo/"Satoshi" Honored

"Wei" has since been additionally honored through the naming of the smallest unit of measure in the cryptocurrency Ethereum. This mirrors the honor given to "Satoshi", as a *satoshi* is the smallest unit of measure in Bitcoin. A bitcoin is 100 million satoshis, and an ether is one quintillion *weis*. A *szabo* is one billion weis, and a *finney* is one thousand szabos. Unlike "Satoshi Nakamoto", "James A. Donald", and possibly "Wei Dai", **Nick Szabo** is *not* a pseudonym, this is a true name. **Hal Finney and Timothy C. May** are also true names, though Finney and May died in August 2014 and December 2018, respectively.

Computer-Mediated Social Networking

As the Bitcoin application was closer to being launched, solving the challenging problem of coordinating the various nodes running Bitcoin (tricky to accomplish in a "pure P2P" application) needed to be designed. The approach proposed by *b-money* was a client/server "Usenet-style broadcast channel."[140] This is a computer bulletin-board type of communication protocol. As discussed in Chapter 21, in August 2008, shortly before Bitcoin was officially announced, "James A. Donald" updated this technical detail. He indicated that *computer-mediated social networking* would provide the initial centralized coordination. When Bitcoin launched, nodes found other nodes via the client/server application, Internet Relay Chat (IRC).[141]

---

[140] "Dai." *b-money*
[141] "Donald, James A." 2008. *The Cypherpunk Program.* https://jim.com/security/cypherpunk_program.html

CHAPTER 23
DECEMBER 2005 BLOCKCHAIN IS BORN

August 19, 2008 - Strike at the State from the Jungle of Complexity

"James A. Donald" has a website, jim.com, filled with information about his political views[142] as well as detailed information about CryptoKong (his digital signature application) that uses elliptic-curve encryption. This is the same type of digital signature used by Bitcoin. Per the Wayback Machine, approximately <u>two months before "Satoshi" sent his first email announcing Bitcoin</u>, "James" posted the following apparent **declaration of war** to his website on the page http://jim.com/security/cypherpunk_program.html. The first date that his web page has an archive record in the Wayback Machine is **August 19, 2008**. This webpage begins:

> The Cypherpunk Program
>
> Timothy C. May summarized the plan as
>
> Crypto Anarchy: encryption, digital money, anonymous networks, digital pseudonyms, zero knowledge, reputations, information markets, black markets, collapse of government.
>
> **Which is *intentionally* obscure. The plan is to strike at the state from the jungle of complexity, to strike at the state from beyond the state's intellectual and temporal horizons.** [*emphasis added*] The evil minions of the state will not be coming after cypherpunks, because they will not understand what cypherpunks are doing, and because when things start going bad for them the [*sic*] will not be able to link cause and effect.[143]

When "James" talks about "The Cypherpunk Program", he is talking about far more than just the Bitcoin Computer Program. This is a Crypto (hidden) Anarchy Program, which is built upon *intentional obscurity*. To quote Cypherpunk Eric Hughes (from a YouTube video where he proudly

---

[142] James Liberty file collection index, https://jim.com/, see jim.com/rights.html
[143] "Donald, James A." *The Cypherpunk Program*

113

promotes Anarchy and misdirection), "off is on, bad is good, plain text is ciphertext."[144]

Even this message from "James" appears to be intentionally obscure. Although *The Cypherpunk Program* contains a rather direct message that "the plan is to strike at the state from the jungle of complexity," confusing statements were included in this declaration. One such statement is that "the cypherpunk movement collapsed." It clearly had not and was only a couple of months away from launching Bitcoin. The reasons listed for the supposed "collapse" was due to four problems, the last of which is "violently unpopular criminal misuse of net centered money."[145] It is quite possible that "James" who referred to "Timothy C. May" in the third person, was in fact, May, himself. There is significant evidence that suggests that "James" was an alias for May.[146] Additionally, the style of the message (and typo) is consistent with *The Crypto Anarchist Manifesto* and *The Cyphernomicon*.

Halloween, Friday - October 31, 2008

On Halloween 2008, "Satoshi Nakamoto" sent an email titled "Bitcoin P2P e-cash paper" to The Cryptography Mailing List.[147] The paper referenced in the email was formatted to read like an academic paper where it ended with a list of references.

The first listed reference is *b-money*, as discussed above. The *Bit gold* article authored by Nick Szabo in 2005 was curiously *not* one of the eight listed references. This is despite it being effectively the published specification of Bitcoin and apparently being the "kick-off announcement" of the Bitcoin development project, per the March 2006 Russian comments.

---

[144] "Hackers on Planet Earth: Cryptography and Privacy." Video Presentation. Channel2600. 1994. https://youtu.be/v5kayD5IQQU (1:10-1:30, 26:55-27:10, 48:18-50:10)

[145] "Donald, James A.". *The Cypherpunk Program*.

[146] See Chapter 8

[147] "Nakamoto, Satoshi." Email from "Satoshi" to The Cryptography Mailing List. "Bitcoin P2P e-cash paper." Oct 31, 2008). http://www.metzdowd.com/pipermail/cryptography/2008-October/014810.html

CHAPTER 23
DECEMBER 2005 BLOCKCHAIN IS BORN

Sunday - November 2, 2008

The first response to "Satoshi's" email came from "James A. Donald", which begins:

```
From: "James A. Donald"
<jamesd@echeque.com>

Date: Sun Nov 2 18:46:23 EST 2008

Subject: Bitcoin P2P e-cash paper


Satoshi Nakamoto wrote:
> I've been working on a new electronic
> cash system that's fully peer-to-peer,
> with no trusted third party.
>
> The paper is available at:
> http://www.bitcoin.org/bitcoin.pdf

We very, very much need such a system,
but the way I understand your proposal,
it does not seem to scale to the required
size....[148]
```

The email thread between "Satoshi" and "James" helped sell the community on the idea. In his reply, "James" raised the scalability question while simultaneously pitching a basis for a monetary value of Bitcoin. "Satoshi" immediately provided an extremely reassuring reply to the scalability concern, indicating that Bitcoin could achieve Visa-level transaction volume with "about $18 worth of bandwidth at current prices."[149]

Among the Bitcoin faithful working to advance the cause of this cryptocurrency, scalability has been reported as the basis of ongoing technical concerns. At the time of Bitcoin's announcement, "James" and "Satoshi" ensured that the scalability question had been immediately asked and answered before anybody else could.

---

[148] "Donald, James A." Email reply to "Satoshi" Bitcoin announcement email. "Bitcoin P2P e-cash paper." Nov 2, 2008.
http://www.metzdowd.com/pipermail/cryptography/2008-November/014814.html
[149] Ibid

CHAPTER 24
A "TRUSTLESS" SYSTEM

An email from a January 2009 discussion thread begins:

```
From: Satoshi Nakamoto <satoshi@vistomail.com>
Date: Fri Jan 16, 2009 18:35:32
Subject: Re: [bitcoin-list] Bitcoin v0.1 re-
leased

> Dustin D. Trammell wrote:
> > Satoshi Nakamoto wrote:
> > You know, I think there were a lot more
> > people interested in the 90's, but after
> > more than a decade of failed Trusted Third
> > Party based systems (Digicash, etc), they
> > see it as a lost cause. I hope they can
> > make the distinction that this is the
> > first time I know of that we're trying a
> > non-trust-based system.
>
> Yea, that was the primary feature that caught
> my eye. The real trick will be to get people
> to actually value the BitCoins so that they
> become currency.[150]
```

"Satoshi" hopes "they can make the distinction that this is the first time I know of that we're trying a **non-trust-based** system." Dustin D. Trammell agrees, saying **non-trust is <u>the</u> "primary feature."**

Trustless

This is a big deal because **<u>trust</u> is the foundation of all human relationships *and* computer security**. A truly trustless system would work something like, "first, hand over all of your money to former Nasdaq Chairman-

---

[150] "Nakamoto, Satoshi." Email from "Satoshi" to Bitcoin Project Email List on SourceForge. "Re: [bitcoin-list] Bitcoin v0.1 released." Jan 16, 2009. https://sourceforge.net/p/bitcoin/mailman/message/21356305/

turned-Ponzi-scheme-fraudster Bernie Madoff...." *Nobody* would voluntarily use a system that they do not trust. The term **trustless** is a vine of misdirection in the jungle of complexity surrounding Bitcoin and Blockchain. <u>Words matter</u>. *Especially* here in the jungle. Our jungle is a jungle of words.

In Code We Trust

DigiCash was a company, like Visa, that attempted to work with banks. With Bitcoin, *unlike* DigiCash (or Visa), there are no central authorities. The design requires no companies like traditional banks and also hides from government laws and regulators. The premise is that anyone can download and run the Bitcoin software to become their own bank and participate in an anonymous economic community. **Trust in the software itself is required.**

It's theoretically possible that anyone could download the source code of what is now known as Bitcoin Core, read it, understand it (ideally updating and fixing some of the problems), and build a specialized environment that would allow one to compile it into an executable program. As a practical matter, almost everyone that will download the software will do so as a pre-compiled program, which should theoretically (though not necessarily) run the same software as the source code. Downloading and running software implicitly assumes trusting the software.

While running your own software is possibly the only somewhat secure way to transact bitcoins, I am not specifically advising it. I downloaded the Bitcoin Core software on an old PC on a completely isolated network. Beyond all of the Bitcoin-related connections, which could be doing who knows what to your PC, all software installations carry risk. Consider the source of this software and proceed at your own risk.

Development & Debugging

Hal Finney and "Satoshi" appear to have worked on the Bitcoin code prior to the release. There were two "Satoshi" accounts and one "Hal" account for the project in the original source code repository on sourceforge.net (per Wayback Machine capture from January 5, 2009):

CHAPTER 24
A "TRUSTLESS" SYSTEM

Developer	Username	Role/Position	Email	Skills	
Hal Finney	hal		hal at users.sourceforge.net	Private	
Satoshi Nakamoto	nakamoto2		nakamoto2 at users.sourceforge.net	Private	
Satoshi Nakamoto	s_nakamoto	Project Manager	s_nakamoto at users.sourceforge.net	Private	[151]

On January 8, 2009, "Satoshi" sent an email titled "Bitcoin v0.1 released" to The Cryptography Mailing List. This email officially launched the software. Hal Finney was the first to reply to this message, congratulating "Satoshi" on this first alpha release of the software, that per the above Wayback Machine capture, Hal had been working on with "Satoshi":

```
From: Hal Finney < hal@finney.org>
Date: Sat Jan 10 21:22:01 EST 2009
Subject: Bitcoin v0.1 released

Satoshi Nakamoto writes:
> Announcing the first release of
> Bitcoin, a new electronic cash
> system that uses a peer-to-peer network
> to prevent double-spending. It's
> completely decentralized with no server > or
central authority.
>
> See bitcoin.org for screenshots.
>
> Download link:
> http://downloads.source-
forge.net/bitcoin/bitcoin-0.1.0.rar

Congratulations to Satoshi on this first alpha
release.  I am looking forward to trying it
out.[152]
```

---

[151] The address to see the Wayback Machine snapshot is https://web.archive.org/web/20090105145118/http://sourceforge.net:80/project/memberlist.php?group_id=244765

[152] Finney, Hal. Email from Finney replying to email from "Satoshi." "Bitcoin v0.1 released." Jan 10, 2009. http://www.metzdowd.com/pipermail/cryptography/2009-January/015004.html

On January 11, "Satoshi" released the first bug fixes, which were focused on problems in the client/server portion of the code. "Satoshi" indicated that he could not really test the IRC portion of the code prior to going live. This is the computer-mediated social networking connection discussed earlier that initially allowed nodes to find each other:

```
Date: Sun Jan 11 22:32:18
From: Satoshi Nakamoto <satoshi@vistomail.com>
Subject: [bitcoin-list] Bitcoin v0.1.2 now
available

Bitcoin v0.1.2 is now available for download.

See http://www.bitcoin.org for the download
link.

All the problems I've been finding are in the
code that automatically finds and connects to
other nodes, since I wasn't able to test it in
the wild until now.  There are many more ways
for connections to get screwed up on the real
Internet.

Bugs fixed:
- Fixed various problems that were making it
hard for new nodes to see other nodes to con-
nect to.
- If you're behind a firewall, it could only
receive one connection, and the second connec-
tion would constantly disconnect and reconnect.

These problems are kind of screwing up the net-
work and will get
worse as more users arrive, so please make sure
to upgrade.

Satoshi Nakamoto
```
[153]

Development and bug fixes are ongoing to this day. One of the more serious bug fixes was in response to an overflow error in August 2010. A

---

[153] "Nakamoto, Satoshi". Email from "Satoshi" to the Bitcoin project distribution list on SourceForge. "[bitcoin-list] Bitcoin v0.1.2 now available." Jan 11, 2009. https://sourceforge.net/p/bitcoin/mailman/bitcoin-list/thread/CHILKAT-MID-bb997183-6436-3f0e-d4f9-2eae6f7e5128%40server123/#msg21303153

CHAPTER 24
A "TRUSTLESS" SYSTEM

single transaction managed to manufacture **184 billion bitcoins**. This problem was corrected, and the blockchain was effectively "rolled back to a past state" so it was as if the transaction never happened.[154]

Who Is In Charge?

Another particularly interesting incident happened in 2013 with the 0.8 release of the code. The 0.8 release included a migration from a database called Berkeley DB to a different database called LevelDB (apparently, to help reduce the time it takes to initially synchronize the blockchain). Version 0.7 had a bug that caused it to reject a block that version 0.8 of the software accepted. This caused a split in the Bitcoin blockchain (an unplanned hard fork) where miners were actively building two separate blockchains. The larger pools, representing the majority of the computing power (known in the Bitcoin world as "hashpower"), were running the newer software. The more "hashpower" your pool has, the more likely it will create the next block and extend the blockchain.[155]

According to the "rules of the game", the longest blockchain is supposed to win. Instead, the core developers and the handful of large mining pools decided to downgrade and temporarily stop mining to allow the shorter blockchain "catch up." This was understandable, but also a curious decision. Bitcoin is supposed to be untrustworthy if a few people collude to represent more than 51% of the hashpower.[156]

In the Bitcoin white paper, "Satoshi" argues that Bitcoin can be trustworthy as long as no single party or collusion of parties controls "51% or more of the hashpower." This is a fundamental concept of the Bitcoin system, as detailed in the Bitcoin white paper.[157] Most recently, the distribution of Bitcoin hashpower appears to have established effectively one **single "trusted party" in charge of the Bitcoin blockchain**. This is the Chinese company **Bitmain**. As Ethereum creator Vitalik Buterin said in July

---

[154] Bruno. "The Curious Case of 184 Billion Bitcoin." *Bitfalls*. Jan 14, 2018. https://bitfalls.com/2018/01/14/curious-case-184-billion-bitcoin/

[155] Buterin, Vitalik. "Bitcoin Network Shaken by Blockchain Fork." *Bitcoin Magazine*. Mar 12, 2013. https://bitcoinmagazine.com/articles/bitcoin-network-shaken-by-blockchain-fork-1363144448/

[156] Ibid

[157] "Nakamoto." "Bitcoin: A Peer-to-Peer Electronic Cash System."

2018, "Bitmain and affiliated pools now have ~53% of all bitcoin hashpower. Isn't this a really big problem?"[158]

Validating Transactions

It is also very interesting that performance of the synchronization of the blockchain remains a significant opportunity to improve the code. I downloaded and ran a Bitcoin full node on an old PC using the Bitcoin Core application. A *full node* does everything that a Bitcoin *miner* does (it validates transactions and gossips), except it does not try to guess the next magic number to win bitcoins and extend the blockchain.

I ran the pre-compiled, ready-to-run program on an old PC that I had isolated on an entirely separate network. When you run the program for the first time, it appears that the Bitcoin blockchain is downloaded as expected. This contains the entire history of *every* Bitcoin transaction *that has ever happened* in the world since the beginning of Bitcoin. A verification process occurs which is supposed to validate *all* the Bitcoin transactions that have ever happened in the entire world since the beginning of Bitcoin.

This initial, one-time, validation of every Bitcoin transaction that has ever happened took several days, during which the limiting factor was *disk drive performance*. While this was not entirely unexpected because of all of the lookups (which translate to a bunch of random disk reads), it really should not be the case on a more well-tuned application. Bitcoin Core has performance problems in this area that are fixable. I would expect that the code running on Bitmain mining systems (the largest manufacturer of Bitcoin mining systems as well as the largest operator of Bitcoin mining pools) has likely been written to be more efficient. Since the primary objective is to win bitcoins, they may possibly not even bother to spend time revalidating past transactions. There is no enforceable requirement that mining systems expend any resources validating historical transactions; they need only concern themselves with a relatively small collection of new transactions. We will look at how "mining" works in Chapter 27.

---

[158] Borman, David. "Vitalik Buterin comes up with seven difficult questions for the cryptoverse." *Chepicap*. July 13, 2018. https://www.chepicap.com/en/news/2124/vitalik-buterin-comes-up-with-seven-difficult-questions-for-the-cryptoverse.html

CHAPTER 24
A "TRUSTLESS" SYSTEM

Number Guessing

Even with the inefficient code, an old PC, with an old slow hard drive (not a speedy modern SSD) was able to perform the validation of every Bitcoin transaction that has ever occurred in the entire world within a few days. After the initial blockchain validation was complete, the resources required to validate new transactions was minuscule. There is a myth that a giant network of powerful computers exists to validate Bitcoin transactions or to somehow make Bitcoin "more secure." This is completely untrue.

"Miners" are machines that spend virtually all of their computing power searching for (guessing) the next magic number, nothing more. A difficulty factor determines how hard it should be to guess the next magic nonsense number (called a nonce). The concept of proof-of-work is that the system regularly updates the difficulty factor (up or down) to ensure that the "miners" have enough "busy work" to keep them busy for about 10 minutes.

Recent Bug Fixes

New versions of the Bitcoin Core code continue to be released, including significant bug fix releases. From the release notes to Bitcoin Core, version 0.15.1 (an update released late 2017):

- <dumpwallet> no longer allows overwriting files. This is a security measure as well as it prevents dangerous user mistakes.
- <backupwallet> will now fail when attempting to backup to source file, rather than destroying the wallet[159]

Wallets are the place where each Bitcoin user is supposed to be the only person in the world that knows the magic numbers (keys) that unlock bitcoin addresses. If wallets are overwritten or destroyed without adequate backup, you lose all your bitcoins. If anybody else, other than you, ever sees any of these magic numbers, you also may lose all your bitcoins.

---

[159] "Low-level RPC changes." Bitcoin Core 0.15.1 Release Notes. https://bitcoincore.org/en/releases/0.15.1/

Trust

Bitcoin is designed to realize Crypto-Anarchy (hidden anarchy), which has been in development for more than 30 years. Governments around the world have some real problems (some more than others), and the crypto-anarchists seek a new way. But is a global online hiding place of anonymous and untraceable business really the solution?

In addition, beyond the consequences for society, one must take some serious leaps of faith to trust Bitcoin as an investment. The exchange rates of cryptocurrencies have clearly been manipulated.[160] Moreover, trade volumes of cryptocurrencies have been grossly misrepresented which overstate liquidity.[161] Prices for cryptocurrencies may collapse overnight, or they may continue to skyrocket to new highs. I have no crystal ball on the short-term direction of cryptocurrency exchange prices, though the level of manipulation appears to be extreme.

From a fundamental technical perspective, there are numerous challenges with cryptocurrencies that threaten any speculative cryptocurrency investment. Beyond the potential for a liquidity crisis and price collapse to nearly zero, the underlying ownership mechanism of Bitcoin is extremely problematic. Any speculative investor may find out that they do not even own the cryptocurrency that they think they own. We will explore some of the reasons why in the next chapter.

---

[160] Vigna & Osipovich. "Bots Are Manipulating Price of Bitcoin in 'Wild West of Crypto'." *The Wall Street Journal*. Oct 2, 2018. https://www.wsj.com/articles/the-bots-manipulating-bitcoins-price-1538481600

[161] Coppola, Frances. "Cryptocurrency Trader Says The Market is Manipulated." *Forbes Magazine*. June 1, 2018. https://www.forbes.com/sites/frances-coppola/2018/06/01/cryptocurrency-trader-says-the-market-is-manipulated/#b49ccb725cde

CHAPTER 25
WALLETS

WARNING: This is not a "how to" chapter on cryptocurrency wallets. We now discuss the theory and engineering trade-offs inherent in this anonymous system. While previous lessons in our story help prepare for this chapter, this is indeed a jungle of complexity. If you do not understand everything in this chapter, do not fear. All readers will likely be able to at least get the gist of what is being said in this chapter, and the remainder of this book is much simpler.

This book was written to provide useful information to non-technical readers and blockchain developer experts alike. <u>For a shorter and less technical read, you may skip this chapter.</u> You can always return to it if you later want to gain a deeper understanding of cryptocurrencies and wallets.

Normal bank accounts or investment accounts are registered to *an entity*. The entity could be a person, a trust, LLC, or another sort of company. The intrinsic value of Bitcoin, cryptocurrencies in general, and Blockchain is anonymity through mathematics. In Bitcoin, there is no "entity registration." For simplicity, this chapter will solely refer to Bitcoin, though the basic concepts should apply to all cryptocurrencies. Wallets authorize spending bitcoins, which means sending bitcoins from one bitcoin address to another.

Hashing

To understand wallets, it is helpful to understand how cryptographic hashing works. Hashing functions take a variable length input, intentionally scrambles the information in a way that is reproducible when supplied with the same input, and produces a fixed length output. It is also designed to be essentially non-reversible if all you have is the output. It is considered to be a *one-way* function. Cryptographic hashing is useful to create **digital signatures** that can be used to prove to others that you that you know

THE BLOCKCHAIN CODE

something which theoretically only you should know. This digital signature can provide this proof to others while keeping precisely what it is that you know private. This is something called a *zero-knowledge proof*.

What's In Your Wallet?

A (hopefully truly random) number generator provides a number between 1 and 2^{256} (an astronomically large number). The size of this number is important because the entire hope is that you cannot have a computer guess every possible number and see which guess is correct.

This random number (key) is then *hashed* to produce a bitcoin address. The amount of time that it takes computers to perform this hash function is important as well, because the easier it is for a computer to perform the hash, the easier it would be for a computer to guess every possible number and determine which guess is correct. Wallets are a collection of **bitcoin address and key** *pairs* that describe where your bitcoins may be stored (bitcoin address) and the key that is required to access each storage location. The overall wallet creation process can be described as follows:

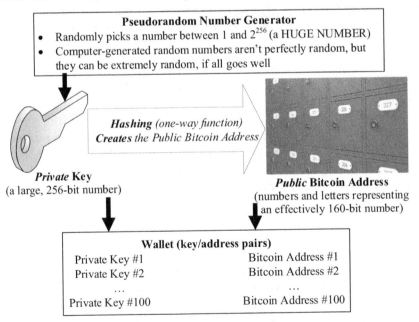

Technically, a bitcoin address is merely the solution to a math problem that anybody could solve. However, the one-way nature of hashing means that, as long as the private key is truly random, and other implementation

126

CHAPTER 25
WALLETS

pitfalls are avoided, it should be extremely difficult for anyone to start with the bitcoin address and figure out what private key was used to create it. Wallets are a collection of *pairs* of private keys and the bitcoin addresses that work together, and they work together purely because of a mathematical relationship between the two numbers.

So, even though the bitcoin address is just a solution to a math problem that, theoretically, anyone *could* figure out, there are just too many possible math problems (defined by each possible key) for anybody to easily figure all of them out.

Key Space

A key space is a measure in cryptography of just how many guesses you would have to make to figure out a key by pure guessing. The key space size defines how hard the guessing game can be for an adversary if everything goes right with your cryptographic security. Cryptanalysis (code breaking) generally seeks to reduce the actual size of the key space to help figure out a key.

It is noteworthy that the hashing performed on private keys starts out with a 256-bit key, but when the process is completed, it results in a 160-bit number that is the significant part of the bitcoin address.[162] The total possible number of bitcoin addresses is 2^{160}. This means that there are about 10,000 trillion trillion trillion trillion trillion trillion trillion trillion trillion trillion trillion trillion possible bitcoin addresses. While this is a huge number, it is a trillion trillion trillion trillion trillion trillion trillion trillion times smaller than 2^{256}. This is an interesting fact when considering the Large Bitcoin Collider (LBC), discussed later in this chapter.

Coins Owned by Math, Not People

The entire authorization mechanism of Bitcoin is based upon the fact that there are such a vast number of possible keys. Any of these possible keys are the potential inputs to the hashing function that generate bitcoin addresses. It is very difficult from a computational standpoint and a data storage standpoint for anyone to know *all* of the possible math problems. If

---

[162] A bitcoin address is actually slightly larger than 160-bits because of some additional information (a description of if this address is on the main, test or other networks, plus a checksum) that is also encoded into the address. However, none of this additional information affects the key space.

you did, you would be able to spend bitcoins at every possible bitcoin address. This creative design avoids the need to have any sort of registration process that could be tied back to a person or entity. Coins are truly "owned by math" in the most literal possible sense.

There are no usernames, no passwords, nothing personally identifiable in Bitcoin. If you happen to know the private key that creates a particular bitcoin address, perhaps through some sort of wallet leak or even sheer guessing, the bitcoins are "yours." Additionally, if you know what random numbers might be used by wallet software to pick the keys used to create these hashes (addresses), figuring out a valid key can be simple[163] and again bitcoins may be "yours."

Authorization

Unlike traditional banking systems, Bitcoin does not technically incorporate the concept of *authentication*. It would be more accurate to describe Bitcoin's approach as *authorization*. This may be a bit semantical, but authentication is generally understood to be a means of authenticating that you are who you purport to be. Since Bitcoin is anonymous, there are no person records against which someone might be authenticated.

Multi-factor authentication is commonplace in modern security. When you access your bank account for the first time from a particular device, you will almost certainly be prompted for some additional form of authentication. This is most commonly implemented as a text message to your mobile phone. There are better, more secure secondary factors, which have become commonplace, such as apps on phones, and physical USB dongles. Voiceprint identification has also become commonly used as an additional factor with financial institutions, often as a third-level of verification.

Banks require multi-factor authentication because passwords (something you *know*) are generally insufficient security. Other types of authentication are something you *have* (like a mobile phone) or something you *are* (biometrics). Banks require at least two-factor authentication because the stakes are high and they need to positively determine your identity. This level of authentication is impossible to achieve in cryptocurrencies like Bitcoin.

---

[163] See discussion on backdoors in Chapter 22

CHAPTER 25
WALLETS

Single Factor

While some wallet solutions purport to offer two-factor authentication, the underlying Bitcoin system is designed around the concept of one-factor authentication. The coins are "owned by math" and math alone. If you know the correct math problem associated with a bitcoin address, even by *extremely* lucky guessing, you are authorized to spend bitcoins at that address. Any two-factor authentication claims are misleading. **There is no way to implement true two-factor authentication for cryptocurrency wallets.**

This is true even for multi-signature (multisig) wallets; these are bitcoin addresses that start with 3. Multisig wallets provide a mechanism to require multiple keys to authorize, but this is still something you *know*. It requires that you know something that is more complex than a single key, but it is not something you *have* or something you *are*.

There are implementations of multi-signature wallets that can *simulate* two-factor by storing one of the keys on a mobile phone, for example, but this is not true two-factor. If someone learns the keys via some sort of wallet leak, they know the keys. Cryptocoin access authorization is inherently **single-factor** authentication (something you *know*).

Without a Trace

If the contents of your wallet are leaked, and your bitcoins are spent, it may be nearly impossible to determine who it was that spent your bitcoins or how they got a key. Bank systems are built around the concept of identities and logging. When you log in to your bank website, your identity is confirmed, and a history of transactions is maintained. When bank employees access information or perform transactions, this is logged. Unlike Bitcoin, banks will always have records of who the payee is for all payments. Bank fraud may occur, but there will be almost certainly always be an audit trail.

THE BLOCKCHAIN CODE

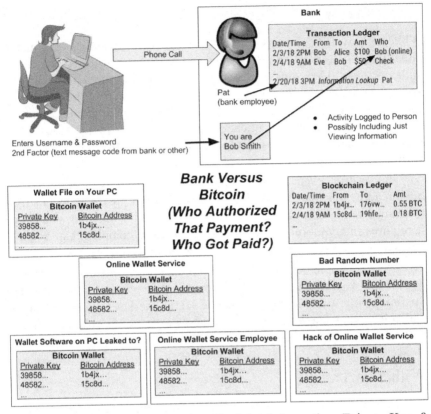

Wallets are files that contain **all** of the information (Private Key & associated Bitcoin Address) that are required to authorize a payment. The question from the diagram above is "which wallet authorized the payment?" The answer is "any one of these wallets, and you have no reliable way to tell which wallet was used or who it was that was paid." Transactions are anonymous. The "from" and the "to" addresses are random strings of numbers and letters. It does not matter how you acquire wallet information, if you have the information, you can authorize transactions and you yourself can remain anonymous.

In general, if bank fraud results in unauthorized transactions, banks have the responsibility to make things right. You are trusting your bank and bank employees not to snoop and invade your privacy concerning transaction history. Regarding fraudulent payments, there are laws, regulators, and robust processes standing behind this process. If your wallet information is compromised and bitcoins are stolen, there will be a transaction record on the blockchain that records money moving from a bitcoin

CHAPTER 25
WALLETS

address that you thought was "yours." You will be able to identify the bitcoin address that received the bitcoins, but it is merely a random-looking string of numbers and letters. Bitcoin addresses are designed to be untraceable.

This why the Mt. Gox "hack" story strains credulity. Mt. Gox was a cryptocurrency exchange that was shut down in February 2014. The story is that Mt. Gox was hacked. This is certainly possible. What seems unlikely is any claims of 100% certainty that this was not an inside job. How do you prove that someone did not perform an anonymous, untraceable act? What is also problematic is what happens with exchanges during times of Bitcoin liquidity crises. We will look at what happened with Mt. Gox in more detail in Chapter 35.

Others may obtain keys via many mechanisms such as data theft or leaks, bugs, or *address collision* (accidental or forced). As a reminder, an address collision is when more than one person creates a key/address pair that has the same value for the address. This can happen by a wallet generator picking the same key or by a *hash collision* (when more than one key hashes to the same address).

Bitcoin was designed to live outside of governments and all laws. Transactions are designed to be untraceable. Once someone spends coins, they are spent. Reliable avenues for hacking or other fraud investigation in Bitcoin are limited. This is why fraud protection is effectively impossible in Bitcoin. When things go wrong, it may be nearly impossible to get the straight story on what happened, and there is no undo.

Hash Collisions

For any given hash, while it is highly *improbable* that any given input will generate the same hash as another input, theoretically *many possible inputs* will generate the same hash result. This is much more likely (expected) when the expected inputs are larger than the hash output, as is the case with the hashing process to take 256-bit Bitcoin unshared (private) keys to create a 160-bit hash used for the significant portion of the bitcoin address. Every such input that produces the same hash is what is known as a *hash collision*.

With 2^{256} possible inputs (private keys) being hashed into 160 bits (2^{160} possible bitcoin addresses), we might expect about 2^{96} possible hash collisions for every possible bitcoin address. This means that for every bitcoin address in your wallet, your key is not the *only* key that will work to authorize spending those bitcoins. There should be about a trillion trillion

trillion trillion trillion trillion trillion trillion *different* keys that will produce the correct hash value (digital signature) required to spend bitcoins.

Large Bitcoin Collider

There is a project called the Large Bitcoin Collider (LBC), created by Ryan Castellucci, that pools together computers to generate Bitcoin address collisions. With every successful collision, the pool grabs all of the bitcoins at that address. However, the intent of the project (as publicly described) is simply to prove that they can do it. The pool has apparently been returning all bitcoins that they have "collected" to someone that can reasonably prove that they were the original owner. How does that work? As we have discussed, there is no such thing as an official "owner" of any bitcoins!

The answer is interesting and instructive. The LBC targets the vast 160-bit bitcoin address space, not the tremendously larger 256-bit key space of the private key. There are, theoretically, about a trillion trillion trillion trillion trillion trillion trillion trillion *different* keys that should work for any given bitcoin address (see above). So, when address collisions happen via the mechanism of the LBC, these collisions are far more likely (statistically "guaranteed") to be *hash* collisions. According to the LBC website, if someone can prove that they have a *different* valid private key to the bitcoin address than the one the pool found (a **hash collision**, not a key collision), they will apparently assume that this person is the "true owner" of the bitcoins. The pool's stated policy is to return the bitcoins to the "true owner."[164]

Code Cracking Hardware

The Large Bitcoin Collider is an interesting project, but it is a computationally expensive approach and should not yet have anywhere near the kind of hashpower (running specially designed hardware called Application Specific Integrated Circuit or ASIC) that organizations like Bitmain and other mining pools are running.

It is noteworthy that the mining and intentional colliding design requirements are similar. Dual use specialized ASIC hardware could be designed (or possibly has already been designed). In theory, systems could

---

[164] "Part IV: Theory". *Large Bitcoin Collider Manual*. https://lbc.cryptoguru.org/man/theory

CHAPTER 25
WALLETS

actually be designed to be triple use. Many secure protocols, such as TLS (secure website encryption) are dependent on SHA-256. While I am unaware of such deployments, the potential combination of resources motivated to perform cryptanalysis to potentially find general weaknesses in SHA-256, and code-cracking horsepower could potentially pose a general security threat to global computer security.

Worst Wallets

There is no such thing as a perfect hashing algorithm. There is also no perfectly random computer-generated number. In addition, numerous possible implementation details may create flaws in the wallet creation process. As a result, we may be able to use more sophisticated cryptanalysis to reduce the key space required to crack Bitcoin wallets. In the YouTube presentation, *Stealing Bitcoin with Math*, Castellucci and Valsorda demonstrate the ease in which particularly bad wallets called *brain wallets* can be cracked. Cracking brain wallets uses a different approach than the LBC above.[165]

Brain wallets take user input (a password), instead of a random number, and turn that into a Bitcoin private key and associated bitcoin address. These bitcoin addresses are vulnerable to dictionary attacks. For short-enough passwords, every possible bitcoin address has been pre-calculated (a rainbow table, in cryptographer-speak), so that these bitcoin addresses can be instantly cracked if they ever appear in the Bitcoin blockchain.

In the *Stealing Bitcoin with Math* presentation, Valsorda additionally discusses how the brain wallet generator had an option to generate a "random" password. This "random" option relied on a function called *math.random*, which is not a cryptographically secure random number generator. Since the numbers it would generate are not very random, figuring out the key for bitcoin addresses that it created was easy. Brain wallets are the poster child for the worst of the worst wallets.

Castellucci and Valsorda are excellent presenters. During a particularly humorous portion of the presentation, they intentionally place a small amount of bitcoin into an address created with a brain wallet. The presenters and audience laugh as they watch the money being taken, very rapidly, presumably by some unknown bot. This bot would be a computer program

---

[165] Castellucci, Ryan and Valsorda, Filippo. "Stealing Bitcoin with Math." Video Presentation. July 23, 2016. https://youtu.be/f2s3_UG9IPU

looking for easy-to-crack bitcoin addresses appearing on the Bitcoin blockchain.

Bad Wallets

Going beyond expected brain wallet-style wallets, Castellucci and Valsorda were able to generate collisions in several other ways. Castellucci indicated that in February 2016, he performed a simple scan of private keys from 1-150 billion and was able to generate 149 collisions. The process was from literally trying 1, 2, 3... etc. for the keys, attacking the 256-bit key space of the private key. Castellucci was able to generate collisions mechanisms that were indicative of other wallet coding problems. Every software ever created is susceptible to bugs, Bitcoin wallet software is no exception. With Bitcoin wallets, the risks are high, and the ability to audit and track down what went wrong can be exceedingly difficult.

More Efficient Pure Guessing

Later in that year, Castellucci launched the more refined approach of the LBC discussed above where he is attacking the 160-bit bitcoin address space rather than the substantially larger key space of the private key.

What Can Go Wrong

An awful lot has to go right for anybody to ensure that they are the only person with the magic numbers in their wallet. Even astronomically bad luck can randomly give another wallet access to your bitcoins. This is extremely unlikely, though, so let's look at all the other things that must go right for your wallet to be reliable.

First, you are trusting that the code that generates the wallet is reasonably bug-free. Even Bitcoin Core released some significant bug fixes related to wallets in late 2017. Nobody is perfect, and software is made by human hands. There is no way to be 100% sure that any wallet generator does not have a wallet generation problem or a wallet leak problem.

Second, you are trusting the platform upon which the software resides. The platform would be your PC if you are running Bitcoin Core. PCs can be infected with malware, hard drives may crash, or myriad other potential problems.

CHAPTER 25
WALLETS

Third, if you are trusting a third party, such as an online service, or a cryptocurrency exchange to be a caretaker for your wallet, you are violating every tenet of reasonable cryptocurrency security. The concept put forth in the Bitcoin white paper is that you are not supposed to trust third parties. You have no reasonable idea what is going on with your wallet whatsoever. All of the above items are still valid concerns, but now you add to the mix risks of a rogue employee or rogue organization compromising your secret numbers.

If Anything Goes Wrong

If any of the above problems occur, you can lose all your bitcoins. If your bitcoins are stolen, you can expect no reasonable way to know who took the bitcoins. Unlike traditional banking systems, Bitcoin is designed around the concept of anonymity. It is built around a ledger, maintained by everyone, which means no one is accountable. The transaction records are about no one.

Great Privacy & Great Opportunity for Fraud

In the hands of *experts*, a high degree of privacy may be accomplished. This extreme privacy makes this technology ideal for use by criminals and terrorists. For speculative investors, beyond the price manipulation, there are many ways in which wallets can be compromised. This means that although you believe you own cryptocurrency, you may find out that you actually own nothing. When you discover that you own nothing, you have virtually no recourse.

Cryptocurrencies create a system where both money laundering and fraud can be accomplished more efficiently and at a larger scale than with any other technology in history.

CHAPTER 26
2013

In June 2013, Edward Snowden, a former CIA employee and former contractor for the NSA released thousands of classified documents.

Snowden Surveillance Revelations

The revelations detailed a massive surveillance apparatus, including the controversial XKeyscore. This tool could collect a massive amount of information. In the words of Snowden, "I, sitting at my desk [could] wiretap anyone, from you or your accountant, to a federal judge or even the president, if I had a personal email." U.S. government officials have denied the accuracy of this specific claim of Snowden's.[166]

Snowden's accusations and released documents painted a picture of a US government collecting information with little restraint under the auspices of the then still active, Patriot Act. On the other hand, Snowden's massive disclosure of documents displayed a lack of restraint on his part concerning U.S. national security concerns.

Snowden indicated, "I carefully evaluated every single document I disclosed to ensure that each was legitimately in the public interest. There are all sorts of documents that would have made a big impact that I didn't turn over."[167] However, Snowden released thousands of documents to journalists.

An improper redaction of one of those documents published resulted in the exposure of intelligence activity against al-Qaeda in Mosul (a group

---

[166] Greenwald, Glenn. "XKeyscore: NSA tool collects 'nearly everything a user does on the internet'." *The Guardian.* July 31, 2013. https://www.theguardian.com/world/2013/jul/31/nsa-top-secret-program-online-data

[167] Greenwald, McAskill, and Poitras. "Edward Snowden: the whistleblower behind the NSA surveillance revelations." *The Guardian.* Jun 11, 2013. https://www.theguardian.com/world/2013/jun/09/edward-snowden-nsa-whistleblower-surveillance

that became part of what we now know as ISIS). Therefore, Snowden's actions compromised some activities the U.S. government was performing to combat Al Qaeda/ISIS.[168]

Natural tension and trade-offs exist between security and privacy. Following the 9/11 attacks, the government was given more or less free reign to collect any information via the Patriot Act. The Snowden revelations are likely the reason why the Patriot Act was not extended and renewed in 2015.

Al-Qaeda Cypherpunks

In July 2013, the **al-qaeda.net node of the Cypherpunks** anonymizing remailer experienced technical difficulties. The problem was ultimately corrected, and Riad S. Wahby let everybody know that service had been restored:

```
Date: Sat, 20 Jul 2013 03:06:13 -0400
From: "Riad S. Wahby" <rsw@jfet.org>
To: cypherpunks@al-qaeda.net
Subject: back on the airwaves


All,

Welcome back to the Cypherpunks mailing list.
You've received a subscription notice and are
receiving this message now because you were a
member of the cypherpunks@al-qaeda.net or cy-
pherpunks@jfet.org mailing list before it went
offline several (?) weeks ago.
```
[169]

While some Cypherpunks might wish to distance themselves from Al Qaeda, the Cypherpunks/Anonymous seek anarchy. No one is in charge, so we have this Cypherpunk affiliation with Al Qaeda. Anonymous, untraceable digital cash, Bitcoin and cryptocurrencies, are a particularly useful tool for terrorists and criminals alike.

---

[168] Oliver, John. "Government Surveillance: Last Week Tonight with John Oliver (HBO)." Oliver Interviews Snowden Video. *Last Week Tonight*. Apr 5, 2015. https://youtu.be/XEVlyP4_11M (17:30 - 33:00)

[169] Whaby, Riad S. Email from Whaby to cypherpunks@al-qaeda.net. "back on the *airwaves*." July 20, 2013. https://cryptome.org/2013/07/cpunks-half-down.htm

PART II.

DECRYPTING BLOCKCHAIN

CHAPTER 27
"MINING" DECRYPTED

The term "mining" is very misleading. So is the term "bit*coin*." Pictures of gold coins are pure marketing. Cryptocurrencies are numbers managed by computer programs and have nothing whatsoever to do with gold or precious metals.

Multiple Ledgers Cannot Always Agree

In Chapter 3, we described Blockchain as a group of people recording what they believe happened on their own separate piece of paper. While computerized accounting should be more accurate than manual paper ledgers, separate digital ledgers will disagree for many reasons. These reasons may be honest (code differences between "miners", bugs, propagation delay). This may also be due to attacks, such as the Bitcoin transaction malleability attack, a man-in-the-middle attack where nodes could alter transactions during the gossiping process.

Pick a Ledger

In Blockchain, there is no authoritative custodian of the ledger. Instead, "honest" nodes and "miners" keep their own, personal copy of the blockchain ledger containing every Bitcoin transaction that their ledger indicates has ever happened in the entire world, forever. Because there is no approval process to become a member of this economic society, "attacker miners and nodes" are expected to selfishly undermine the system.

Tag, you're It!

Since there is supposed to be no authoritative custodian of the ledger, one "miner" (honest or attacker) must be "elected" to extend the blockchain and define "the truth." Without this process, there would be no way to

THE BLOCKCHAIN CODE

resolve conflicting transactions and make sense of the ledger. For Blockchain systems built on "proof-of-work", like Bitcoin, miners effectively vote for themselves with *hashpower*. Miners need to find a nonsense number (nonce) that when hashed with information from the previous block has a minimum number of leading zeros (we will explain hashing and leading zeros later on in this chapter). Hashpower is a measure of how many nonsense number (nonce) guesses you can perform per second. The more guesses, the more likely you will guess the next number that will work. When you win the guessing game by guessing a number that will work, you also win free bitcoins.

In the example below, Bob, Alice, and Mary are running three Bitcoin miners. There is some disagreement about what the next transactions are, which can happen. So, to make sense of the ledger, one of the nodes is effectively chosen to write the next block. For the next block, it will be Alice's block. She got lucky (found a good next nonce), and as a reward not only does she get to define The Truth, she gets fifty brand new bitcoins. The sender (from) is empty, since the new coins have been fabricated out of nothingness.

Bob's Miner

From	To	Amount
Bob	Alice	.1 BTC
Alice	Eve	.2 BTC
Eve	Bob	1.1 BTC

Alice's Miner

From	To	Amount
Bob	Alice	.1 BTC
Alice	Eve	.2 BTC
Bob	Mary	2.2 BTC

Mary's Miner

From	To	Amount
Bob	Alice	.1 BTC
Alice	Eve	.2 BTC
Mary	Max	3.3 BTC

I found a good next nonce!!!
Hey everybody, use my block!

The Truth
(Alice's truth becomes the official truth)

From	To	Amount
	Alice	50 BTC
Bob	Alice	.1 BTC
Alice	Eve	.2 BTC
Bob	Mary	2.2 BTC

The above example is simple and only has three miners. We are also assuming that Alice is playing by the rules and her block is good (all the transactions in the block have valid signatures). We are also assuming that Bob and Mary are playing by the rules. In a situation when there are many miners, there is a higher chance that more than one miner might find a good next nonce at the same time. When that happens, there will be a race to see whose truth will be the next truth and who will win those next new bitcoins.

CHAPTER 27
"MINING" DECRYPTED

Bitmain

From a practical standpoint, for your Bitcoin transactions to be approved, the Chinese company **Bitmain** must approve of the transaction.[170] The vast majority of Bitcoin blocks are "mined" in China. Most of these blocks are "mined" by the Chinese company Bitmain that operates the BTC.com and AntPool Bitcoin mining pools (and are affiliated with ViaBTC, possibly others).

It is difficult to report the hashpower of Bitmain with 100% accuracy, but by mid-2018 Bitmain appeared to conservatively control over 40% of the total hashpower, probably over 50%. Ethereum founder Vitalik Buterin estimated Bitmain's hashpower at 53% in July 2018.[171] This is well beyond the level required to assume unilateral control over the Bitcoin blockchain. In addition to this, Bitmain is a popular manufacturer of Bitcoin mining hardware used by other mining pools. It is difficult to confirm the accuracy of mining pool hash rate estimate reports, but it seems safe to say that as this book goes to print, Bitcoin Mining = Bitmain.

"Decentralized" Mythos

The popular notion is that when a single party controls more than 50% of the hashpower, that party effectively controls the Bitcoin blockchain. However, a 2013 Cornell University research paper, "Majority is not Enough: Bitcoin Mining is Vulnerable" by Emin Sirer and Ittay Eyal, demonstrates "the current reality where a group of any size can compromise the system." This paper demonstrates how 25% of the mining power of the network is sufficient to misdirect other mining pools' efforts into building on what will ultimately become useless blockchains. With at least

---

[170] If Bitmain does not like your transaction, it should consider any blocks published that contain your transaction to be invalid and refuse to build future blocks upon any such block. There are constant disagreements about which blocks are valid on the tip of the Bitcoin blockchain that are resolved over time. Bitmain's ability to build blocks far faster than anybody else should effectively allow the company to have the final say in rejecting any given transaction.

[171] Ritter, Bauer, and Melnikoff. "The Buterin Questions, #1 Bitmain and Affiliated Pools Now have Approximately 53% of all Bitcoin Hashpower. Isn't this a Really Big Problem?" *Medium*. July 17, 2018. https://medium.com/penta-network/the-buterin-questions-1-bitmain-and-affiliated-pools-now-have-approximately-53-of-all-bitcoin-fb65576393df

25% of the hashpower, the largest pool can effectively assume unilateral control of Bitcoin's blockchain ledger.[172]

Bitmain's dominant position makes it a centralized authority that threatens to destroy Bitcoin's perceived data integrity. Bitmain's controlling position also threatens to destroy the "decentralized" marketing message that is designed to appeal to not only anarchists, criminals, and terrorists, but also everybody who is frustrated by governments (aren't we all?).

Proof-of-Stake (PoS) systems are also centralizing. In PoS, the individuals that have the most of a given cryptocurrency are effectively in charge of authoring new blocks, and they receive the bulk of the rewards. If Bitcoin or hard forks of Bitcoin were to adopt a proof-of-stake approach, presumably that would put the original Cypherpunk creators in an even greater position of power over that cryptocurrency. For Ethereum or hard forks of Ethereum, it would presumably put Vitalik Buterin and others from Ethereum's ICO in this position. Curiously, there are elements of PoS mentioned in the *b-money* paper. It appears that PoS may have been considered, though ultimately rejected, for Bitcoin during the development process.

"Mining" = Lottery Gambler

There are two modes for running Bitcoin Core, "miner" and "full node." Both modes gossip to distribute transactions throughout the network. Both modes review transactions to ensure that they are valid. "Miners" perform one additional function. "Miners" are extremely busy trying to guess the next nonsense number (nonce) that lets them extend the blockchain and win the lottery of free bitcoins. "Miners" are lottery gamblers, but "miner" sounds much more impressive.

Getting lucky more frequently is what hashpower is all about. A minuscule amount of processing power is required to validate and communicate the next group of transactions. This validation and the gossiping process is successfully running on an old PC of mine. This old, slow PC is literally doing the same amount of validation and gossiping work that even the largest of mining pools, like Bitmain's pools, are doing. My old PC just isn't trying to guess a nonsense number that will win bitcoins.

---

[172] Eyal, Ittay and Sirer, Emin Gün. 2013. "Majority is not Enough: Bitcoin Mining is Vulnerable". https://www.cs.cornell.edu/~ie53/publications/btcProcFC.pdf

CHAPTER 27
"MINING" DECRYPTED

More Hashpower = More Lottery Tickets

You may have heard of bitcoin "miner" machines that consume large amounts of power. These systems do exist, though reports on the nature of the systems, aggregate electricity use, and predominant geographic location, have been distorted in "news" reports. They are not using all that electricity for any sort of encryption or transaction validation. This is a common misconception, a vine of misinformation in the jungle of complexity. This electricity is used for astronomically energy-inefficient nonsense number (nonce) guessing.

Nonsense Number Guessing

Electricity consumed by Bitcoin nonsense number guessing translates to natural resource consumption and greenhouse gas emission. Yet, for some cryptocurrency enthusiasts, this grossly wasteful system design seems to lead to a perverse justification of the importance of Bitcoin, based upon how much energy can be consumed by this nonsense number guessing.

Atmospheric Carbon

Shortly after "Satoshi" announced Bitcoin, Cypherpunk co-founder John Gilmore lamented, "The last thing we need is to deploy a system to burn all available cycles, consuming electricity and generating carbon dioxide all over the internet... Can't we just convert actual money in a bank account into bitbux -- cheaply and without a carbon tax? Please?"[173] It has been estimated that more than 500,000 times the amount of electricity is being consumed per Bitcoin transaction than per Visa transaction![174]

Gross Power Inefficiency

Bitcoin nodes and "miners" do perform some actual meaningful work. They listen for new transactions to record in their copy of the ledger, validate, and transmit transactions to other nodes. It is just that this work takes almost zero processing power to accomplish with the current volume of

---

[173] Gilmore, John. Email from Gilmore to the Cryptography Mailing List. "Proof of Work -> atmospheric carbon." Jan 25, 2009.
http://www.metzdowd.com/pipermail/cryptography/2009-January/015042.html
[174] "Bitcoin Energy Consumption Index." *Digiconomist*. http://bitcoinenergyconsumption.com

transactions. Even with the current grossly inefficient code running on my full node, my old, slow spare PC can process the entire world's volume of Bitcoin transactions without a problem. My old PC has a record of every Bitcoin transaction that has apparently happened in the entire world since the beginning of Bitcoin, it validates all incoming transactions, just like all the other full nodes and mining systems. This work consumes less than 2% of an old, slow PC's resources. Hashpower is all about *decrypting* the next nonsense number to win bitcoins and define "the truth."

Code Breaking

Bitcoin "miners" are not encryption machines. If anything, the computing power of these systems is focused on code breaking, or decrypting. The idea behind Bitcoin's "proof-of-work" system is that there has to be a reasonable way to perform the "tag you're it" process of electing one miner to extend the blockchain ledger. A time interval of "about 10 minutes" was chosen to "elect" one node to resolve conflicts between ledgers by publishing the next list of "official" transactions and extending the blockchain.

As a new block is appended to the blockchain, this creates a new hash. A new nonsense number (nonce) must then be found that will produce a new random hash that will work to extend the blockchain. This nonsense number is strictly that. It is a nonsense number. This nonsense number will not be used solve mysteries of the universe or even doing anything to make Bitcoin "more secure" or anything like that. It is merely **a guessing game** where each miner spends almost all of their processing time trying to guess the next nonsense number.

Guessing the nonsense number requires repeatedly performing hash functions with new guesses until you finally guess a nonsense number (nonce) that creates a hash with a certain number of leading zeros that will successfully link the new block with the block before it in the chain.

There is nothing magical about having leading zeros in the hash. When a hash is performed, the output should appear completely random, so there is a fifty percent chance that a hash will have a single leading zero. There is a twenty-five percent chance that a hash will have two leading zeros, and so on. It is fifty percent less likely that a hash will have three leading zeros than two, etc. The **difficulty factor** *automatically* **increases up and down**, making the guessing game harder or easier. The goal is to keep the average interval between blocks to be about 10 minutes.

CHAPTER 27
"MINING" DECRYPTED

"About Every 10 Minutes"

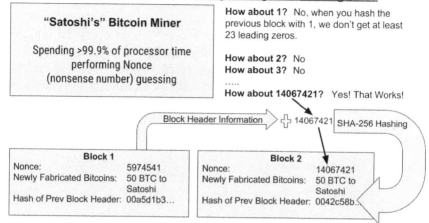

- Satoshi just "got lucky" and guessed the next nonce that worked. He creates the next block in the blockchain and just won **50 newly created bitcoins**!
- Bitcoin mining machines spend a negligible amount of time processing transactions, they spend virtually all of their processor time guessing nonsense numbers to try to win newly created bitcoins.
- New blocks are supposed to be created (and new bitcoins won) about every 10 minutes. If numbers are guessed too quickly, the difficulty *automatically increases* to 24 leading zeros. If the guessing is taking too long, the difficulty *decreases* to 22 leading zeros.

The targeted timeframe of "about 10 minutes" makes a lot of sense. If it was set to be shorter than that, you would frequently have many miners guessing the next nonsense number around the same time, and a great deal of "races" would happen to see which block propagated more quickly. If the target was longer than this, it would take longer than the "about an hour" for reasonable confirmation.[175]

---

[175] Several other cryptocurrencies, such as Ethereum, have shorter target intervals between blocks, to accomplish faster transaction speed, at the cost of increased "block creation race" chaos at the tip of the blockchain. Blocks must be "buried" behind a certain number of blocks before one may have some degree of confidence in a report of a transaction completion being reliable. With Bitcoin, consensus appears to be that after six blocks (about an hour), transactions may assumed to be reasonably confirmed. There does not seem to be the same degree of consensus about Ethereum. Some popular guesses appear to be 12 blocks (3 minutes), 250 blocks (1 hour), and 500 blocks (2 hours).

THE BLOCKCHAIN CODE

When a miner guesses a nonsense number that works, they extend the blockchain, defining "the truth." However, the most important reward that miners receive are **the bitcoins that they win** when they get to extend the blockchain.

To keep the spacing between the blocks "about every 10 minutes apart", the difficulty factor automatically adjusts how many leading zeros are required in the block linking hash every 2016 blocks (about every two weeks). The Blockchain system would run just as well (and arguably be more secure) with far less hashpower. The hashpower code-breaking arms race is about improving odds of winning bitcoins and being the authority that writes the blockchain.

CHAPTER 28
TRADITIONAL & SOCIAL MEDIA

> I want the truth!
> You can't handle the truth!
> —Lt. Kaffee (Tom Cruise) and Col. Jessup
> (Jack Nicholson), <u>A Few Good Men</u>

Information is everywhere, yet the truth often eludes us. First, we tend to believe **what we *want* to believe**. As the late comedian George Carlin once said, "The reason I talk to myself is because I'm the only one whose answers I accept." Carlin's witty comments frequently cut to the core reality of the human condition. He is missed, but his words of truth live on.

Traditional Media

Even the best traditional media reporters are mere mortals and struggle to overcome personal perceptions and biases. When it comes to reporting on financial or investment matters, such as when the stock market goes up and down, many reports are on shaky ground. What passes for financial news reports is often just *speculation*, though they may appear to speak with authority. "The S&P rallied on today's unemployment report," "the Dow declined on earnings reports", etc. The logic on the reporting is often sound, but there are certain assumptions and "guessing" that may be reported essentially as fact when the reality is not so cut and dried.

When it comes to cryptocurrency (literally *hidden money*), news reports are often wildly speculative "news by rumor." Cryptocurrency fund manager Tom Lee has been covered in financial news media quoting price/"mining cost" ratios as if it was something meaningful, like a P/E ratio.[176] Mining costs? Initially, blocks were created by "Satoshi's" computer(s) alone. A single computer <u>remains</u> sufficient to create new blocks!

Blocks should be created about every 10 minutes, regardless if there is a single PC performing the bitcoin "mining" or if it is a huge network of specialized bitcoin "miners." Half of all of the bitcoins that will ever be mined were mined in the first four years. Based on message board posts, it appears that around mid-2010, when about 20% of the bitcoins ever to be mined had already been mined, there were perhaps three PCs mining bitcoin. This is based on a reference to someone mining thousands of coins per day. Per the bitcoin lottery schedule, about 7,200 coins were mined per day at that time.

During the early years, the "mining" was performed by a small group using Windows PCs, using the CPU. Eventually, a few more PCs started "mining", and a clever person realized that they could win more bitcoins by using their video card to "mine." Eventually, a hardware "arms race" ensued to increase the chance to win more bitcoins. Nothing has fundamentally changed from when only a handful of PCs were mining. There are simply more people using more hardware guessing nonsense numbers.

The "mining" **difficulty factor** automatically adjusts <u>every 2,016 blocks</u> (about every two weeks) to try to create about <u>one block every 10 minutes</u>. If blocks end up being created faster than that, per the Bitcoin computer code, the difficulty factor **automatically *increases***. If blocks are created more slowly, the difficulty factor **automatically *decreases***. Speculations in the media regarding cryptocurrency exhibit a fundamental lack of understanding of the basic mechanics of how Bitcoin actually works.

History Repeats Itself

Buffet has predicted "a bad ending" for cryptocurrencies.[177] His partner, Charlie Munger, has called it "stupid and immoral" and "rat poison squared," a viewpoint echoed by Buffett himself.[178] Yet, several "experts"

---

[176] Belvedere, Matthew J. "Bitcoin bull Tom Lee wants Wall Street to know he didn't cut his year-end forecast." CNBC. July 5, 2018.
https://www.cnbc.com/2018/07/05/fundstrats-tom-lee-cuts-his-year-end-bitcoin-forecast-to-20000.html

[177] "Warren Buffett: Cryptocurrency Will Come to a Bad Ending." Video Interview with Buffett. CNBC. Jan 10, 2018. https://youtu.be/YWMmd7hlwNI

[178] Fearnow, Benjamin. "Warren Buffett, Bill Gates Blast Bitcoin as 'Non-productive Asset', Bad Investment." *Newsweek Magazine*. May 7, 2018.

CHAPTER 28
TRADITIONAL & SOCIAL MEDIA

have dismissed Buffett's concerns.[179] This is the same Warren Buffett whose critics disparaged him during the dot-com bubble only to see Mr. Buffett proven right after the crash! As others like Matthew Frankel of The Motley Fool point out, you may doubt Mr. Buffett at your peril.[180]

Technology Spin & Encrypted Stories

When reporting on technology matters, news reporters must frequently deal with less than reliable sources. It can be very difficult to challenge the information that they are receiving. As a result, they may report what their source wants them to say, not the truth, and certainly not the whole story.

The most outrageous recent example is how Intel was able to spin their Meltdown fiasco. This huge technical problem received substantial news coverage in early 2018, though the story was heavily spun/reported as a Spectre/Meltdown problem, which encrypted (hid) the fact that the *real* story was **Meltdown** alone. To be fair, the story was highly technical and involved two types of *speculative execution* flaws. Meltdown is by far the more serious problem, and this story was not accurately reported in the media, which has far-reaching ramifications. We will discuss Meltdown in detail in the appendix to the *Blockchain Code*.

Unfriended on Facebook

Many beliefs (true or false) develop, spread, and are reinforced by social media's "news by rumor" distribution mechanics. Additionally, social media's friend/unfriend mechanism encourages *islands of ideology*. Over time, there is a tendency to *friend* people whose posts validate your beliefs and **unfriend** those whose posts do not. Posts from people whose posts you liked, re-tweeted, or commented on in the past are likely to be featured prominently in your feed. Content may be boosted by paid advertisements with signals of extra validity provided by notification that a friend of yours *likes* the promoted content.

---

https://www.newsweek.com/bitcoin-bill-gates-warren-buffett-cryptocurrency-berkshire-hathaway-investment-912850

[179] Mourdoukoutas, Panos. "Warren Buffett Is Wrong About Bitcoin." *Forbes Magazine*. May 7, 2018. https://www.forbes.com/sites/panosmourdoukoutas/2018/05/07/warren-buffett-is-wrong-about-bitcoin/#390b816379c8

[180] Frankel, Matthew. "Think Warren Buffett Is Wrong About Bitcoin? Read This." *The Motley Fool*. Jun 28, 2018. https://www.fool.com/investing/2018/06/28/think-warren-buffett-is-wrong-about-bitcoin-read-t.aspx

Reality Distortion Field

Social media is generally a wonderful thing. In many ways, it has brought humanity closer together than ever. However, with respect to the truth, it presents a picture of the world that looks more like <u>how you *want* to see it</u> than <u>how it *truly* is</u>. As George Carlin pointed out, this is already our built-in human bias! Through the use of social media, this personal reality distortion field around each of our lives grows ever stronger. When it comes to ideology, social media is a powerful tool to energize and rally the troops and to shape public opinion.

Hello, My Name is...

Social media has weak identity controls allowing you to indicate that you work for virtually any organization without verification. Pyramid scams can spread on social media where people encourage friends and family to buy into a system with promises of a great financial result. To continue to make money, you need to convince even more friends and family to buy into the system as well. Such pyramid schemes are designed to profit those who create the system. The last to buy in are the biggest losers when the system ultimately collapses.

Dangerous Times

During 2018 congressional hearings, Mark Zuckerberg stated that Facebook is in "an arms race" with Russia. He indicated that his company was constantly battling "people in Russia whose job is to try to exploit our system."[181]

This problem goes far beyond just Facebook, though social media has serious challenges managing the truth. Additionally, the messages are not just Russian propaganda. Numerous parties seek to have their message, with their spin, communicated to the world. This includes Blockchain and cryptocurrency promoters seeking money from investors, anarchists seeking to destroy all governments, and politicians and political forces seeking your vote.

---

[181] Picchi, Aimee. "Facebook hearings: 6 surprises from Mark Zuckerberg." *CBS MoneyWatch*. Apr 11, 2018. https://www.cbsnews.com/news/facebook-hearings-6-surprises-from-mark-zuckerberg/

CHAPTER 28
TRADITIONAL & SOCIAL MEDIA

We must be diligent and seriously validate information. Your wealth, safety, and even the democracies of the world like the United States are at risk.

CHAPTER 29
GREAT STORIES

Code breaking horsepower (or "hashpower") is useful to someone looking to crack certain codes. Much more important than this are *cryptanalysis* (code breaking) techniques, which find ways to vastly reduce the problem and the amount of cryptographic brute force power required. For the past 100 years, machine-based cryptography and cryptanalysis (code breaking) have played important roles in virtually every military conflict.

Cracking the Code

The groundbreaking work performed in Poland and by the UK's Bletchley Park (featured with some artistic license in the movie *The Imitation Game*) has been credited with shortening World War II. **Every code can be and will eventually be cracked by someone with enough determination to crack the code**. The fact that the Lorenz and Enigma ciphers had been cracked was an *extremely* carefully protected secret. This was critical so that the Nazis did not get suspicious and change their codes. **When very important codes get cracked, these become the most closely guarded secrets of all**.

Hiding the Fact that You Are Hiding

This brings us to what is often the most challenging, but sometimes most important cryptography skill of all: hiding the fact that you are hiding. Consider the Zimmermann Telegram sent by Arthur Zimmermann:

Decrypting War Plans

The story goes that the British had severed Germany's transatlantic cable facilitating Germany's communications with North America. In the interest of peace, the United States agreed to receive and forward Germany's encrypted messages to Mexico and Canada with the understanding that these messages would be used for "peaceful purposes."

According to historians, British cryptanalysis experts were covertly monitoring all transatlantic messages. It was no secret that these messages could contain important information. No effort was made to hide the fact that they were hiding messages. Look at the telegram. It is clearly a secret message. It screams, "Please decrypt me. I'm an important hidden message!" Which, according to the history books, is exactly what the British cryptanalysis experts did![182]

The *decrypted* German message contained the following proposal:

> We make Mexico a proposal of alliance on the following basis: **make war together,** make peace together, generous financial support and an understanding on our part that **Mexico is to reconquer**

---

[182] Bellamy, Jay. "The Zimmermann Telegram." *Prologue Magazine* (Winter 2016, Vol. 48, no. 4). https://www.archives.gov/publications/prologue/2016/winter/zimmermann-telegram

CHAPTER 29
GREAT STORIES

```
the lost territory in Texas, New Mexico, and Ar-
izona.
```
 [183] [*emphasis added*]

Invent a Great Story

Clearly, hiding the fact that you are hiding is an *extremely* valuable skill for any master cryptographer! The story goes that, at first, the British were uncertain about what to do with this information. They could not simply show the decrypted message to the Americans without revealing that they were secretly monitoring all transatlantic messages. So they invented a story, a James Bond-style story that the message was intercepted by one of their agents in Mexico! The mysterious operative was not Ian Fleming's famous 007, but was known only as mysterious "Mr. H."[184] At the time, the British were quite possibly the best codebreakers in the world and the best at hiding the fact that they were codebreakers in the first place!

Hiding the fact that you are hiding means making up a story and getting others to believe it, just like the British did. The British were able to hide the fact that they were expert code breakers. They also maintained an extreme level of secrecy after they had cracked key codes such as the Lorenz Cipher and Enigma Cipher. The Germans had no idea that the British had cracked the code, which allowed British cryptanalysts to alter the tide of World War II. The full scope of their code breaking work remained hidden for 30 years until it was declassified.[185]

Poof

At the reveal of the central secret of the 1995 movie *The Usual Suspects*, the narrator tells us "The greatest trick the Devil ever pulled was convincing the world he didn't exist." This is a reference to a line in the French poem, "The Generous Gambler" by Charles Baudelaire. **The Blockchain Story is a really great story**. It will revolutionize everything!

---

[183] Ibid

[184] Ibid

[185] Hamill, Jasper. "UK spooks STILL won't release Bletchley Park secrets 70 years on." *The Register*. Feb 6, 2014. https://www.theregister.co.uk/2014/02/06/mi5_still_holds_bletchley_park_secrets/

The Devil is in The Details

As with Bitcoin, the primary intrinsic value of Blockchain is anonymity. To understand (decrypt) any system, consider **who** created the system, for **what** purpose, and **how** it works. Echoing the central question of *The Usual Suspects:* "Who is Kayser Söze?"

And who is "Satoshi Nakamoto?"

CHAPTER 30
BLOCKCHAIN - HIGHER EDUCATION & BUSINESS

Here is the original version of the C++ code that created bitcoins:

```
int64 nSubsidy = 50 * COIN;

// Subsidy is cut in half every 4 years
nSubsidy >>= (nBestHeight / 210000);
```

This is two lines of computer code (three, if you count the comment line). Who knew that it would be so easy to mint enough money to potentially eliminate every government on earth? The term "subsidy" is used because the idea is that "the system" initially *subsidized* "miners" by creating **50 new bitcoins about every 10 minutes** (24 hours per day, 365 days per year). The subsidy is cut in half every 210000 blocks (about every 4 years).

You May Have Already Won...

Through the initial Bitcoin subsidy lottery, which ended in November 2012, 10.5 million bitcoins in winnings were anonymously distributed to the anarchist Cypherpunk community and other early adopters. This represents a staggering $210 BILLION based on bitcoin price at the peak of the market in early 2018, or roughly twice the estimated wealth of Jeff Bezos, the wealthiest man on earth. Combining this with the second lottery, which ended in 2016, increases total anonymous subsidy winnings to 15.75 million bitcoins ($315 BILLION)**,** or more than the wealth of Jeff Bezos, Bill Gates, and Warren Buffett combined!

To Claim Your Prize

Now before we resign ourselves to the inevitable takeover of the world and prepare for the new world order, it's hardly a done deal. Remember the dot-com millionaires? They had lots of theoretical wealth, in the form of stock or stock options that were ultimately worthless. Investors threw money at Bernie Madoff because his hedge fund was producing "unbelievable returns." And who could forget Enron?

Playing the Game

The cryptoanarchy game is not over. John McAfee, the founder of McAfee, Inc., the political activist, the former murder suspect, and generally colorful character, has promised to eat a certain part of his anatomy on national television if Bitcoin does not hit $1M/bitcoin by the end of 2020.[186]

John McAfee
@officialmcafee

When I predicted Bitcoin at $500,000 by the end of 2020, it used a model that predicted $5,000 at the end of 2017. BTC has accelerated much faster than my model assumptions. I now predict Bircoin at $1 million by the end of 2020. I will still eat my dick if wrong.

This should coincide with his run for President of the United States as a candidate for the Libertarian Party or possibly his own party.[187] Talk about campaign promises! While Warren Buffett has been clear in his condemnation and indicated that he "would short Bitcoin if he could,"[188] he would not provide timeframes or prices. Let's not speculate, that got Intel (the company that bought out McAfee) into trouble. Let's stick to the facts.

---

[186] McAfee, John. Tweet from McAfee. Nov 29, 2017. https://twitter.com/officialmcafee/status/935900326007328768?lang=en

[187] Marinova, Polina. "John McAfee Says He Will Run for President in 2020." *Fortune Magazine*. June 4, 2018. http://fortune.com/2018/06/04/john-mcafee-president-2020/

[188] Microsoft founder Bill Gates has also indicated he would short Bitcoin as well if there was an easy way to do it.

CHAPTER 30
BLOCKCHAIN - HIGHER EDUCATION & BUSINESS

Bitcoins for Sale

For the first several years, bitcoins were mined and collected at a rate of 50 coins about every 10 minutes and relatively little else was done with them. By November 2012, the first lottery was completed after distributing 10.5 million bitcoins to a very small collection of individuals within the Cypherpunk community and other early adopters.

Early on, prices were listed on some exchanges that purported to list a value, but with extremely small trading volumes, these initially posted prices might be analogous to a lemonade stand type of sign saying "bitcoin for sale, 1000 coins for a dollar" or "bitcoins for sale $5000/bitcoin." The bitcoin exchange rate is communication from an exchange of what they say the price is. Unless there is substantial transaction volume, exchange prices are somewhat arbitrary and not terribly meaningful. Let's say you have one person who might buy into your price for, say 100 bitcoins, and you have 5 million bitcoins. The value of the 100 bitcoins is the price you get in the trade. The value of the remaining 4,999,990 bitcoins is effectively zero until another buyer comes along.

There appears to be a substantially higher volume of bitcoin transactions today than there was when bitcoin first started with the lemonade stand days. However, the volume of transactions is still dramatically lower than what is generally being reported by exchanges. Simply reviewing transactions on the Bitcoin blockchain shows a clear pattern of automated shuffling of coins.

However, even if this were to somehow stop, the trade volumes are *reported by the exchanges*, which have substantial conflict of interest concerns. The exchanges, as cryptocurrency businesses, stand to benefit by higher prices and perceived higher transaction volumes. Additionally, the *owners* of these exchanges likely have significant cryptocurrency holdings as well, so there are personal financial interests. It is very difficult to accurately measure true transaction volume because we must consider the source of this information. We will look at exchanges in detail in Chapter 35.

Buying Allegiance

Especially in the time when we were clearly in the lemonade stand days, where the price of bitcoin was at its most arbitrary point, there was extremely little true liquidity. There was no way to sell a significant amount of bitcoins for any meaningful amount of money. There were far too few buyers. What could you possibly do with all of this newly minted money? Initially, they were given away to buy interest.

Bitcoin giveaways made a lot of sense. An exchange (which is theoretically anyone who purports to assign a value and perhaps might theoretically consider trading) could list an arbitrarily high price - "free bitcoins (a $100 value)" to give people a reason to load the software. Once they loaded the software, they were entering into a regular lottery with a promise of possibly occasionally winning even more free bitcoins. The initial Bitcoin **Faucet** on July 3, 2010, started out offering five free bitcoins to anybody who would install the software:

Wayback Machine archive, July 03, 2010 snapshot of
http://freebitcoins.appspot.com/

This faucet ran for a couple of years, though the number of bitcoins given away was reduced **one month later** (per the August 5, 2010 capture) with the following message:

```
Hey! I thought you were giving away FIVE!
When I started the Faucet, Bitcoins were worth
about a half a US penny each, so five were
worth about 2.5 US cents. Since then, Bitcoins
have gone up in value more than ten times. The
rules are now: 0.50 bitcoins per visitor when
the Faucet has more than 500 BTC in it, and
0.05 when it is starting to run dry.
```

CHAPTER 30
BLOCKCHAIN - HIGHER EDUCATION & BUSINESS

They could have said the price increased 100-fold or 1000-fold if they wanted to, but a 10-fold increase in one month perhaps sounded more sustainable and believable. More targeted bitcoin faucets (also known within the cryptocurrency community as **airdrops**) were used over time, and college students were the primary target. In 2014, **all 4,500 undergraduates** at the Massachusetts Institute of Technology (MIT) were *given* $100 worth of bitcoins (nearly half a million dollars total bitcoin value at the then exchange-provided price) to buy college students interest and validation.[189]

The cryptocurrency exchange Coinbase performed an additional bitcoin giveaway that same year. Coinbase gave free bitcoins to more than 20,000 additional students representing universities throughout the United States.[190] Per a Coinbase blog article, the largest number of these bitcoins appear to have been received by students located at Stanford, University of Illinois, University of Texas, UC Berkeley, Purdue University, Drexel University, University of New Mexico, UCLA, Rutgers, University of Michigan, UC Davis, UC San Diego, the Rochester Institute of Technology, and NYU. The original Coinbase blog articles have since been deleted, but this information has been archived on the Wayback Machine.[191]

Blockchain U

Through the help of cryptocurrency (hidden money), stories in campus newspapers and other publications mentioning Bitcoin began to appear. Bitcoin and Blockchain interest groups were established on campuses, ultimately leading to presentations and even college courses on the topics. In January 2018, the cryptocurrency Dash (which has a DAO where parties can vote with cryptocurrency on efforts to be funded), donated $350K to Arizona State University. This purchased undergraduate and graduate research fellowships to encourage students to publish papers, thereby elevating and validating Blockchain technology. This $350K even bought the

---

[189] Hern, Alex. "MIT students to get $100 worth of bitcoin from Wall Street donor." *The Guardian*. Apr 30, 2014. https://www.theguardian.com/technology/2014/apr/29/mit-student-bitcoin-wall-street-donor

[190] Hajdarbegovic, Nermin. "Over 20,000 Students Receive Bitcoin in Coinbase Giveaway." *CoinDesk*. May 30, 2014. https://www.coindesk.com/20000-students-receive-bitcoin-coinbase-giveaway/

[191] School list compiled by reviewing Wayback Machine page archives of https://blog.coinbase.com/post/85758038492/10-of-free-bitcoin-for-college-students

creation of an official ASU Blockchain Research Laboratory as well as the creation of a series of online graduate courses on Blockchain.[192]

Overstock

In 2014, the internet retailer overstock.com became the first major retailer to accept bitcoin as payment.[193] 2014 was also when massive amounts of bitcoins were given away to college students, as discussed above.

Overstock has a great deal of experience with performing promotional giveaways involving colleges. The 2011 article by the Wall Street Journal, "Google Penalizes Overstock for Search Tactics", highlighted the company's practices of creating fake websites to link back to its own site. Additionally, Overstock was penalized for encouraging college and university websites to post links to overstock.com in order to receive discounts for students and faculty.[194]

This goes to perception versus reality of noble scientific research. At the time that Overstock was penalized by Google, Google was apparently providing a certain amount of higher weight to .edu domains. In theory, institutes of higher learning might be expected to produce certain content that represents the noblest pursuits of knowledge, research, and advancing human understanding. Overstock apparently leveraged this for their own gain and was called out by Google for doing this. In a very real sense, Overstock was buying a certain amount of undeserved legitimacy with links coming from .edu domains.

Legitimacy for Sale

At MIT, a half a million dollars bought a fair amount of interest and legitimacy for Bitcoin and Blockchain. Slightly less than that purchased substantial legitimacy at Arizona State University. The list of universities

---

[192] Grant, Terry. "Dash, Arizona State University Elevate Blockchain Research, Offer Graduate Course and Scholarships." *ASU Full Circle Magazine.* Jan 18, 2018. https://fullcircle.asu.edu/research/dash-arizona-state-university-elevate-blockchain-research-offer-graduate-course-scholarships/

[193] Wile, Rob. "Someone already bought a $2,700 12-piece patio set on overstock.com using bitcoin." *Business Insider.* Jan 9, 2014. https://www.businessinsider.com/overstockcom-is-now-officially-accepting-bitcoin-2014-1

[194] Efrati, Amir. "Google Penalizes Overstock for Search Tactics." *The Wall Street Journal.* Feb 24, 2011. https://www.wsj.com/articles/SB10001424052748704520504576162753779521700

where a certain amount of legitimacy of Blockchain has been purchased is staggeringly long.

Selling Legitimacy

A great number of consulting organizations appear to be scrambling to sell their expertise in Blockchain and win consulting gigs. In the process, they have been telling quite a story about Blockchain technology and how it will change the world.

CHAPTER 31
THE BLOCKCHAIN TECHNOLOGY STORY

> And like that—poof—he's gone!
> —*The Usual Suspects*

The above quote is the last line of the movie, as the identity of Kayser Söze is revealed. Throughout this book, we have looked at the inventor of what would become known as Blockchain. His name is **Nick Szabo**. It's only the "Satoshi Nakamoto" persona/pseudonym that has disappeared.

A Great Story

The legend of "Satoshi Nakamoto" is a great story. When "Satoshi" was no longer needed, poof—he disappeared. However, the *story* of "Satoshi" lives on and is an entertaining distraction. The story continued to grow and evolve and became no longer just about Bitcoin.

A vast number of other cryptocurrencies appeared with great stories of why they exist. And the story continues to grow... the TECHNOLOGY of Bitcoin became called "Blockchain" and has become a truly magical story of how the world will be transformed. A great story often *encrypts* (hides) the truth.

Technobabble

The romanticized concept of the "magical distributed ledger" that will *eliminate the middleman* connects with people because everyone has experienced frustrations with clunky systems. Everyone feels there has to be a better way. The problem is that Blockchain's great stories are often full of fancy words that explain nothing.

Water is a liquid. Assets can also be described as liquid. So, we have AquaRights.com with the slogan "Water Rights on the Blockchain." This is a rather dubious use case for Blockchain, of course, but many other popular ideas do not fare much better when we dig into the details.

Blockchain's Backstory

Technology always exists for a particular reason. There is always some design objective or goal. Bitcoin is the initial implementation of Blockchain; it is the pilot program of this technology. Tim May, the creator of cryptoanarchy, and Nick Szabo, the creator of Blockchain, describe a common vision for cryptoanarchy. They are creating a global online hiding place, beyond the reach of governments, beyond national borders, and beyond laws.[195]

The references in the Bitcoin white paper give credit for prior work and provide perspective for Bitcoin and Blockchain. "Wei Dai's" *b-money*, the first reference, begins:

> I am fascinated by Tim May's crypto-anarchy. Unlike the communities traditionally associated with the word "anarchy", in a crypto-anarchy the government is not temporarily destroyed but permanently forbidden and permanently unnecessary. It's a community where the threat of violence is impotent because violence is impossible, and violence is impossible because its participants cannot be linked to their true names or physical locations.[196]

"Wei" appears to acknowledge that "anarchy" is traditionally associated with chaos and the disintegration of society, but believes that May's vision of cryptoanarchy will be different. He talks about violence, but when crypto-anarchists talk about violence, there is often an unstated implication that they are talking about *state-sponsored* violence, such as the threat of law enforcement. By creating this hidden corner of cyberspace, the state will be "impotent" as "Wei" describes it. State "violence [law enforcement] is impossible, and violence [law enforcement] is impossible

---

[195] Chapters 2 & 6 of this book describes this with direct quotes from May and Szabo.
[196] "Dai, Wei." *b-money*

CHAPTER 31
THE BLOCKCHAIN TECHNOLOGY STORY

because its participants cannot be linked to their true names or physical locations."[197]

The second paragraph of *b-money* provides additional thoughts about realizing cryptoanarchy:

> Until now it's not clear, even theoretically, how such a community could operate. A community is defined by the cooperation of its participants, and efficient cooperation requires a medium of exchange (money) and a way to enforce contracts. Traditionally these services have been provided by the government or government sponsored institutions and only to legal entities. In this article I describe a protocol by which these services can be provided to and by untraceable entities.[198]

When advocates proclaim the potential of Blockchain, they often speak in grandiose terms. They view it as a *revolutionary* technology, which it is. It was specifically created to *revolt* against the concept of governments. The vision is to create a society that exists where "government is not temporarily destroyed but permanently forbidden and permanently unnecessary."[199]

B-money describes how ensuring the exchange of money and enforcing contracts has traditionally been the role of governments and government-sponsored institutions. Blockchain was created to build "how such a [crypto-anarchist] community could operate." As the final sentence of this second paragraph describes, Blockchain describes how "these services can be provided to and by untraceable entities." The article outlines five objectives that it seeks to accomplish to create this hidden society can function outside of the visibility and interference of governments by establishing protocols for:

1. The creation of money
2. The transfer of money
3. The effecting of contracts
4. The conclusion of contracts
5. The enforcement of contracts[200]

---

[197] "Dai, Wei." *b-money*
[198] Ibid
[199] Ibid
[200] Ibid

The final paragraph of *b-money*, before the appendix, explains:

```
The protocol proposed in this article allows
untraceable pseudonymous entities to cooperate
with each other more efficiently, by providing
them with a medium of exchange and a method of
enforcing contracts. The protocol can probably
be made more efficient and secure, but I hope
this is a step toward making crypto-anarchy a
practical as well as theoretical possibility.[201]
```

Bitcoin and cryptocurrency are first steps towards cryptoanarchy, but truly achieving the huge vision of building a fully functional separate hidden society will require a substantial amount of further development. Building systems that allow "untraceable pseudonymous entities to cooperate with each other" remains the primary use case for Blockchain technology. However, as with any technology, it is possible for creative individuals to adapt it for other purposes.

Public, Permissionless Blockchain

Bitcoin, and most cryptocurrencies, are an example of public, permissionless Blockchain. Some would consider permissionless Blockchain to be the only true or "real" Blockchain, though there are many who would disagree with that assessment.

In public, permissionless Blockchain, the blockchain ledger is theoretically visible to anyone. In practice, applications may be designed to avoid revealing certain details, such as identities. By requiring no permission, or authorization, to participate, every participant may remain anonymous. This type of Blockchain is well suited for cryptocurrencies and crypto-anarchist applications.

Some may seek to make public, permissionless Blockchain somewhat less anarchistic, but they will be facing an uphill battle due to the nature of the technology. Jen Wieczner, in a *Fortune Magazine* article, "How a New Blockchain Aims to Shut Down Assassination Markets", highlights a company that is trying to build a Blockchain governance system. "The biggest criticism of blockchain technology is generally that the decentralization and anonymity—or at least pseudonymity—it affords will also facilitate illegal activity outside the reaches of government, such as illicit

---

[201] Ibid

CHAPTER 31
THE BLOCKCHAIN TECHNOLOGY STORY

marketplaces where you can buy anything from drugs to hitmen," Wieczner said.[202]

The idea put forth in the *Fortune* article is that a system using artificial intelligence could try to detect all of the evil things that can happen in an anonymous, anarchist system powered by Blockchain and shut those transactions down. It is unclear how this artificial intelligence "Blockchain police" would work. As Wieczner indicates, permissionless Blockchain "facilitates illegal activity outside of the reaches of government." How do you build an artificial intelligence "Blockchain government" when the underlying technology is designed to resist such authority in the first place through anonymity and obfuscation?

Permissionless cryptocurrency (which is nearly all cryptocurrency) inherently circumvents Anti-Money Laundering laws and associated Know Your Customer objectives. While no technology is flawlessly anonymous and untraceable, permissionless Blockchain applications can achieve a high degree of anonymity and untraceability. Most cryptocurrencies, and potentially a number of permissionless Blockchain applications are a giant metaphorical middle finger to every Anti-Money Laundering law, every Know Your Customer rule, and effectively every government on earth.

However, just because an application is built with public, permissionless Blockchain, that does not mean it is necessarily designed for illegal purposes. For example, a whistleblower type application, where someone can anonymously report something would be an excellent application for public, permissionless Blockchain. Public, permissionless Blockchain is an imperfect technology, but Bitcoin and other cryptocurrencies have clearly demonstrated a certain degree of viability of this technology.

Decentralized Autonomous Organization (DAO)

Cryptoanarchy may be facilitated by public, permissionless Blockchain applications. Governments may be theoretically "permanently forbidden and permanently unnecessary"[203] and everyone can be anonymous. However, there is still a need to retain a certain amount of order to create a functional anarchist society. A Decentralized Autonomous Organization,

---

[202] Wieczner, Jen. "How a New Blockchain Aims to Shut Down Assassination Markets." *Fortune Magazine*. Oct 23, 2018. http://fortune.com/2018/10/23/dfinity-blockchain-assassination-market/
[203] "Dai, Wei." *b-money*

or DAOs, seeks to provide a possible framework of coordination within a post-government, anarchist world.

Bitcoin itself is generally considered to be a DAO to some extent. Other systems such as Dash and "The DAO" are focused on creating organizations run by smart contracts implemented on a blockchain. A DAO could be used to perform coordinated voting and funding. This may include decisions about how the DAO itself will work or coordinating assassinations (as discussed in Chapter 11).

Permissioned Blockchain

A while after Bitcoin was created, the name Blockchain was coined to describe the way that Bitcoin works. It is a system designed to facilitate untraceable transactions between anonymous parties. This was *the only* reason the technology was created. "Satoshi" created it to be permissionless, since it manages a ledger about no one. There is no concept of "user accounts" or "people" who might be granted or denied permissions. It was designed to be as anonymous and untraceable as possible.

The term *permissionless* came along much later. At a certain point in time, creative developers attempted to limit the inherent extreme anonymity and untracablility inherent in Bitcoin and created a "permissioned" version of the technology. Now that a "permissioned" (watered-down) version of the technology was created, and it still had "Blockchain" in the name, the original technology needed a new name. Blockchain was renamed "Permissionless Blockchain" and the watered-down version of Blockchain was called "Permissioned Blockchain."

Permissionless Blockchain attempts to leave no trail of breadcrumbs to tie activity back to anyone. From a crypto-anarchist point of view, this provides security and protection of anonymous individuals from governments and others. However, this anonymity is generally considered incompatible with the traditional view of real-world security. The traditional foundation of security is **identity**. Bad things, security-wise, tend to happen in the shadows. Streetlights are present in cities for a number of reasons, and a very important one is security. We generally do not walk down poorly lit alleys at night. *Permissioned* Blockchain may be used to put restrictions on the inherent anonymity of Blockchain.

With *permissioned* Blockchain, mechanisms may be built where trusted parties (the thing that Blockchain was originally built to avoid) might verify someone's true name when creating an account, for example. There are a number of options for how one might build such a system. In

CHAPTER 31
THE BLOCKCHAIN TECHNOLOGY STORY

one scenario, identity might be globally known; in others, identity might still largely be withheld except under certain tightly controlled circumstances such as account creation.

Permissioned Blockchain itself is a high-level concept that is open to numerous implementation approaches. However, the general concept is that deliberate steps are taken to mitigate the natural anonymity inherent in the base public, permissionless Blockchain. The Hyperledger project is an example of a permissioned Blockchain.

The merits of permissioned (watered-down) Blockchain are not entirely clear. In the words of an article by *The Economist*, "The advantages of blockchains are often oversold. Because of the overheads involved in shuffling data between all participants, blockchains are less efficient than centralised databases, a problem that gets worse as the number of users rises. When the Bank of Canada tried using blockchains to process domestic payments, which are already quite efficient, it found they offered no benefit. Stripe, a big digital-payments firm, has abandoned its blockchain experiments after three years of trying, describing the technology as 'slow and overhyped'."[204]

That hype not only serves to promote Blockchain technology and encourage Blockchain consulting engagements but also helps boost the perceived value of cryptocurrencies since they are "Powered by Blockchain." There is a little bit of technical reality and a tremendous amount of misinformation and spin.

Blockchain as a Database

Permissionless Proof-of-Work (PoW) systems such as Bitcoin are outrageously inefficient by design. PoW establishes an intentional nonsense-number-guessing "arms race" in the hopes that no single party or collusion of parties will have more than 50 percent of the nonsense-number-guessing power.[205] As the Bitcoin whitepaper puts it, "The system is secure as long as honest nodes collectively control more CPU power than any cooperating group of attacker nodes."[206]

---

[204] "The promise of the blockchain technology." *The Economist*. Sep 1, 2018. https://www.economist.com/technology-quarterly/2018/09/01/the-promise-of-the-blockchain-technology

[205] In Chapter 27, we demonstrated how, contrary to popular belief, the actual threshold is 25 percent, not 50 percent

[206] "Nakamoto, Satoshi". *Bitcoin: A Peer-to-Peer Electronic Cash System*

PoW Blockchain is one of the least efficient database systems of all time. However, the existence of electrical power-hungry systems creates great theatre and misdirection that can be exploited to create an undeserved perception of "power and importance."

Other approaches such as Proof-of-Stake, Proof-of-Authority, and private, permissioned approaches can improve efficiency and processing speed. However, we must keep things in perspective. Blockchain was specifically created to build a hidden corner of cyberspace. The engineering trade-offs required to accomplish this objective are substantial, and it would be hard to call any implementation of Blockchain *efficient*.

Even in the most efficient permissioned Blockchain system, where certain trusted parties can be simply authorized to perform block creation, there are enormously more efficient and performant approaches than Blockchain. Which is why it seems particularly confusing to see the Internet of Things (IoT) suggested as a use case for Blockchain.

Internet of Things (IoT)

There has been a fair amount of talk about The Internet of Things (IoT), yet few people have any idea of how this really works. This is probably because it is a terribly vague name. Everything is a "thing", so how is the Internet of Things not just "the internet?" Perhaps the thinking is that since "things" can be *chained* together, Block*chain* will somehow magically be great for IoT?

Most serious technical discussions about IoT are generally concerned with enabling low-power devices that can run for a very long time on batteries. For example, it is impossible to develop "things" like a sensor that can run for years on a battery if we use Wi-Fi.

Wi-Fi is the common name given to a standard called 802.11. IoT research and development is typically concerned with protocols like Z-Wave or 802.15.4 (Zigbee, Thread) that consume a fraction of the power of typical 802.11 networks. There is a variant of 802.11 (802.11ah) that is designed to be a low-power, long-range alternative that could potentially be in the IoT discussion, although this probably still requires too much power for IoT.

Blockchain may be many things, but it was not designed to be low-power. Permissionless PoW blockchain is possibly the least power-efficient technology ever conceived! Even with permissioned Blockchain,

CHAPTER 31
THE BLOCKCHAIN TECHNOLOGY STORY

there are technologies that are orders of magnitude more efficient. Blockchain seems completely inappropriate for IoT. Yet, there is an article in Computerworld, published June 25, 2018, titled "IoT could be the killer app for blockchain."[207] This is a dubious assessment from what otherwise appears to be a reputable source of information. Several news sources routinely recycle questionable Blockchain use case assessments like this.

Food Safety

According to the World Health Organization, "An estimated 600 million - almost 1 in 10 people in the world - fall ill after eating contaminated food and 420,000 die every year."[208] This report notes how food supply chains cross multiple national borders and calls for collaboration between governments, producers, and consumers.

The problem is global in nature and Blockchain is a technology that was designed to exist as a global system outside of the concept of governments and national borders. There are multiple ways to accomplish food supply chain tracking, and Blockchain may make sense for this application, though it is far from clear that Blockchain is the best approach.

Let's consider a Blockchain project that Walmart and IBM announced. The plan is to require all suppliers of leafy green vegetables for Walmart and Sam's Club to upload tracking information into the IBM Food Trust Solution. This is an application built on Hyperledger (a permissioned Blockchain-based technology) and per a quote from an IBM VP, "it runs on IBM Cloud."[209]

The announced solution will reportedly reduce the amount of time to trace the source of food from 7 days to 2.2 seconds. This sounds impressive, and it would be wonderful if this goal were reached. However, this is being accomplished by creating a digital tracking system that replaces paper. This does not require Blockchain.

---

[207] Mearian, Lucas. "IoT could be the killer app for blockchain." *Computerworld Magazine*. June 25, 2018. https://www.computerworld.com/article/3284024/blockchain/iot-could-be-the-killer-app-for-blockchain.html

[208] "Food Safety Fact Sheet." Oct 31, 2017. World Health Organization. http://www.who.int/news-room/fact-sheets/detail/food-safety

[209] Miller, Ron. "Walmart is betting on the blockchain to improve food safety." *TechCrunch Magazine*. Sep 24, 2018. https://techcrunch.com/2018/09/24/walmart-is-betting-on-the-blockchain-to-improve-food-safety/

Given the fact that "it runs on IBM Cloud," it is unclear why Blockchain makes sense for this application. If there is one central authority managing the database, it is hard to understand why IBM would use Hyperledger instead of a non-Blockchain-based database such as IBM's own DB2 or Oracle, SQL Server, MySQL, or perhaps PostgreSQL. Because it is being hosted all on one cloud infrastructure, virtually any technology *other* than Blockchain should make more sense.

Online food supply chain tracking seems extremely valuable and may save lives. However, Hyperledger appears to increase complexity and potentially introduces unnecessary performance and transparency risks.

Identities

While Blockchain is rooted in a foundation of privacy and anonymity, some Blockchain applications actually seek to use Blockchain to implement a sort of distributed identity system. Because privacy is a philosophical foundation of Blockchain and built into the DNA of Blockchain, these approaches may choose to offer blinded (anonymous) identity verification services.

For example, in situations where you might need to provide some proof, perhaps proof of age to purchase alcohol, or proof of ownership, these applications may theoretically offer options to provide this proof without revealing anything more than this information. Personally identifiable information, such as your name may be omitted where not required. Similar functionality may be implemented with non-Blockchain approaches, but Blockchain begins with privacy as the foundation.

As with every computing system ever created, there is an inherent scope of utility and inherent limitations and risks. The devil is always in the details. It is unclear if Blockchain technology approaches would be a good approach for any particular identity management application. However, it should be abundantly clear that public, permissionless blockchain is extremely well suited to *circumvent* Know Your Customer Laws and **facilitate money laundering.**

Techno-Reality

The technical merits of *permissioned* Blockchain, such as the Hyperledger Project versus alternative approaches, are unclear. Anything designed with

CHAPTER 31
THE BLOCKCHAIN TECHNOLOGY STORY

permissioned Blockchain may likely be implemented with a non-Blockchain approach more simply, cheaper, with higher performance, and higher security. We will examine this further in the next chapter.

Cryptocurrencies prove that there is some technical merit to public, *permissionless* Blockchain to create anonymous systems. The Blockchain Story encourages the development of anonymous systems of questionable value for everyone other than anarchists. Additionally, the Story of Blockchain technology misdirects some focus from what is going on with cryptocurrency and cryptoanarchy while simultaneously affording some degree of hyped validation for the technology beyond its true merit.

CHAPTER 32
WHO CAN YOU TRUST?

Facebook's struggle with information accuracy is emblematic of the fundamental question in modern society of "who can you trust?" Reports on Facebook's efforts appear mixed. One report on September 8, 2018, proclaimed, "Facebook's fight against fake news isn't going so well,"[210] while another report less than a week later indicated, "Researchers say Facebook's anti-fake news efforts might be working."[211]

Going Viral

Social media has helped advance the phenomenon of the "viral story" (or video), though the concept of popularity breeding popularity is nothing new. Virality is an indicator of popularity, not necessarily quality. Often, when a story or video goes viral, it is interesting, and we can understand why it went viral. Occasionally, we are left scratching our heads, wondering how this thing got so many views or likes.

Viral Topics

When a story is told, and people find it interesting, it becomes news. If enough interesting stories are told about a particular topic over time, it becomes a newsworthy, *viral topic*. Publications need to be *topical* and write about the kind of stories that people want to hear.

Cryptocurrencies and Blockchain have been in the news often enough to the point where some media outlets have created recurring programs or

---

[210] Kozlowska, Hanna. Quartz. "Facebook's fight against fake news isn't going so well" (Sep 8, 2018) , https://qz.com/1382740/facebooks-fight-against-fake-news-isnt-going-so-well/

[211] Locklear, Mallory. Engadget. "Researchers say Facebook's anti-fake news efforts might be working" (Sep 9, 14, 2018), https://www.engadget.com/2018/09/14/facebook-fake-news-efforts-working/

columns on the topic. The people that provide the content about controversial topics like cryptocurrency and Blockchain tend to have a significant bias that is favorable to the topic. Otherwise, they would not be someone who is able to continually produce the content. To be fair, many media outlets will seek to provide some contrary viewpoints, though they tend to be individuals who are rotated in and dismissed by "the experts."

Questionable Validation

Regardless of the merits or accuracy of reports, once a topic has gone viral, the very fact that it has gone viral tends to provide a certain amount of inherent validation. *Forbes Magazine* is an example of a publication with cryptocurrency "experts", like Billy Bambrough,[212] on staff. Bambrough is an example of a cryptocurrency and Blockchain "expert" regularly churning out pro-cryptocurrency and pro-Blockchain articles. When a magazine with the clout of *Forbes* publishes these articles, the story is frequently carried by other news organizations.

Wonderful, Empty Definitions

The popular message of Blockchain is that it will "change everything for the better." This story is dominated by wonderful-sounding yet meaningless, empty definitions. This creates the perfect environment for people to fill in the gaps with projections of their hopes and dreams for the world.

Deloitte and the U.S. Government

Brian Lee is the Chief Public Health Informatics Officer for the Centers for Disease Control. Prior to working at the CDC, Mr. Lee was a Senior Manager at Deloitte Consulting where he performed work for the CDC and other government organizations.

    Mr. Lee's presentation "Blockchain 101 for Public Health" asks, "What is a blockchain?" and answers this question with the following five bullet points,[213] which are listed along with my response to each bullet:

---

[212] See *Forbes* Contributor Page for Billy Brambrough, https://www.forbes.com/sites/billybambrough

[213] Lee, Brian. "Blockchain 101 for Public Health." US Centers for Disease Control. https://www.cdc.gov/ophss/chiic/forums/CDC-Blockchain-Overview_-v16_tgs_2_2018-508.pdf

CHAPTER 32
WHO CAN YOU TRUST?

- `A distributed immutable ledger of transactions`

    The term "immutable" overstates the reality of the technology. It is fair to say there are implementations of Blockchain that may achieve a certain level of *resistance* to change over time. However, the devil is in the details.

    It is somewhat troubling to see a similarly overstated assessment in a Blockchain white paper involving US National Intelligence, the FBI, and the US Department of Defense. This paper includes the statement "Blockchain is a cryptographically-secured distributed ledger that records transactions chronologically, permanently, and unalterably." [214]

    Blockchain is inherently a system of "every ledger for themselves." There is no authoritative custodian of the ledger and therefore no authoritative ledger. This inherently requires a system of resolving ledger conflicts between nodes.[215]

- `The underlying technology behind the cryptocurrency known as Bitcoin`

    This is accurate.

- `What TCP/IP (internet protocol) has been for the exchange of information, blockchain can be for the exchange of value`

    This broad statement offers Lee's optimistic opinion. It also appears to be concerned with cryptocurrency. It is unclear how this relates to health care.

- `A set of tools for cryptographic assurance of data integrity, standardized auditing, and formalized contracts for data access`

    All of these claims are inaccurate.

---

[214] US Government (National Intelligence, FBI, DoD, DHS) & Private Sector (SAS, FIS, Sojourn Consulting, Truman National Security Project, and Cisco) "Blockchain and Suitability for Government Applications." 2018 Public-Private Analytic Exchange Program. 2018. https://www.dhs.gov/sites/default/files/publications/2018_AEP_Blockchain_and_Suitability_for_Government_Applications.pdf, p5

[215] See Chapter 27

Blockchain Does NOT Assure Data Integrity: Blockchain is an "every ledger for themselves" technology, which requires a mechanism to resolve data integrity problems (disagreements between nodes regarding the contents of the ledger). Timestamping provides "tag you're it" selection of *one* of the nodes to extend the blockchain. This hardly qualifies as "assurance of data integrity."[216]

Blockchain Does NOT Assure Standardized Auditing: Blockchain is a concept where there is no authoritative ledger. However, after a block becomes "buried" in the blockchain behind a certain number of blocks, the likelihood of older blocks becoming de-facto "official blocks" continually increases. Because every node in the system has a copy of the ledger, the system may have the *appearance* that these ledger copies allow independent audits. There may be *a limited amount of* truth to that. However, you could also make the argument that no node can ever truly be sure of the truth in a Blockchain system. Any given node may possibly be seeing merely what someone wants them to see.[217]

When it comes to creation of Blockchain (permissionless Blockchain), it was specifically designed to facilitate untraceable transactions in a hidden corner of cyberspace. It was designed to be ***un**-*auditable with respect to identity. One may glean certain information from the Blockchain ledger. However, it may require extremely tough forensics work to try to track down certain information if someone is highly skilled, careful, and does not want you to know what they are doing. Moreover, that forensics work may ultimately be unsuccessful. The impetus of creating Blockchain in the first place was to facilitate anonymous and untraceable transactions.[218]

Now, it is possible for someone to build virtually any type of application with almost any technology. One may possibly build auditing tools using Blockchain. However, it is a gross

---

[216] See Chapter 27
[217] See Chapter 17
[218] See Chapter 19

CHAPTER 32
WHO CAN YOU TRUST?

overstatement to say that Blockchain itself assures standardized auditing. Many implementations of Blockchain obfuscate, misdirect, and frustrate attempts to audit.[219]

Blockchain Does NOT Assure Formalized Contracts for Data Access: Blockchain natively has support for the concept of smart contracts. However, the originally created *permissionless* Blockchain has zero access controls around data access. Instead, the concept was that *everybody* keeps a copy of the ledger so that *nobody* can be held accountable for the ledger.[220]

Permissioned Blockchain has bolted on the concept of permissions to the original Blockchain concept. Even *permissioned* Blockchain does not necessarily assure formalized contracts for data access. One may develop virtually any functionality with any technology. There may be certain implementations that attempt to provide this functionality, but Blockchain itself does not.[221]

It is also important to remember that it is far from clear that *permissioned* Blockchain will be a broadly useful technology. The jury is still out on that and there are a great number of skeptics. The paper discussed earlier whose authors include representatives from US Intelligence, the FBI, and the US Department of Defense (DoD) cautions, "View with skepticism claimed 'successful uses' of blockchain, recognizing that for many applications, there's another - and potentially easier - way to accomplish the task."[222]

The above caution comes from a report that otherwise appears to be relatively pro-Blockchain (particularly pro-Blockchain research). However, this government assessment offers far more measured guidance than Mr. Lee does. Blockchain was created to facilitate anonymous and untraceable applications. Therefore, defense and "spy stuff" use of Blockchain

---

[219] See Chapters 2, 4, 5, 7, 8, 9, 10, 11, 12, 13, 14, 16, 17, 19, 21, 24, 25, 27, 31, 33, 34, 35, 36
[220] See Chapter 17
[221] See Chapter 31
[222] "Blockchain and Suitability for Government Applications." 2018 Public-Private Analytic Exchange Program, p35

seems more promising than most other areas of government. It is a technology created to *destroy* governments, so it makes sense that US Intelligence and DoD would want to study it!

- A technology which empowers participating members to exchange items of value through a distributed ledger
    - that each member owns
    - and who's content is always in sync

The statement "always in sync" is incorrect. First, a Blockchain is a data structure managed by imperfect computer programs, made by imperfect human beings, and runs on the planet Earth.

Second, even if the computer programs themselves were somehow magically perfect, this is a distributed ledger system where each node runs independently. There is no 2-phase commit or other traditional database synchronization mechanism. Therefore, the situation is actually the *opposite* of "always in sync."

Unlike traditional database systems, it is almost guaranteed that the ledgers will be **out of sync** to a certain extent. A timestamping mechanism seeks to provide a certain degree of order and synchronization to what otherwise would be pure chaos. Over time, as a blockchain grows, you may have increased confidence in older blocks that reside on what you believe is the longest blockchain. Within a single Blockchain-based application, one may expect several disagreeing copies of the blockchain, each with different transactions, all purporting to speak the truth.[223]

Once again, Mr. Lee brings up exchanging value, which seems focused on cryptocurrency. Why is this a point of focus of a presentation titled "Blockchain 101 for Public Health?"

Blockchain and cryptocurrency propaganda, such as this presentation, advocates and sells the technology, while distorting and exaggerating the reality of it. This presentation appears to mirror the strong pro-Blockchain selling performed by Lee's former employer, Deloitte.

---

[223] We will discuss this in detail in the next chapter

CHAPTER 32
WHO CAN YOU TRUST?

Blockchain Consulting

Consulting organizations have an inherent need to appear knowledgeable about topics like Blockchain in order to demonstrate that they are indeed experts in everything that their clients might need help with. The more material that they present on Blockchain, the more consulting work they stand to gain. Deloitte has created a diagram (below), which has been featured in several magazine articles, including the troubling article that compelled me to write this book in the first place[224]:

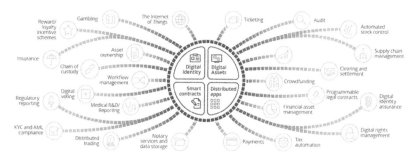

While you may be able to do all of those things with a blockchain, it is not at all clear that you should. Consider the government study that advises, "View with skepticism claimed 'successful uses' of blockchain, recognizing that for many applications, there's another - and potentially easier - way to accomplish the task."[225] This echoes the assessment of *The Economist* that, "The advantages of blockchains are often oversold."[226]

Even more troubling, cryptocurrency and Blockchain excel at facilitating money laundering like no other technology in history. Despite this, the two items featured in the top right corner of the above diagram are KYC - *Know Your Customer* and AML- *Anti-Money Laundering*.

---

[224] See Preface
[225] "Blockchain and Suitability for Government Applications." 2018 Public-Private Analytic Exchange Program, p35
[226] "The promise of the blockchain technology." *The Economist*.

- Know Your Customer: Blockchain facilitates **anonymous transactions** where transactions are possible between two parties that never know the other party![227]
- *Anti*-Money Laundering: Blockchain technology is a creative solution, with enormous engineering trade-offs, specifically designed to facilitate **anonymous and untraceable payments!!!**[228]

While it is possible that AML and KYC applications can be developed using virtually any technology, including Blockchain, this takes the likely core societal objections to the technology, and seems to try to flip it around!

Truly researching and understanding Blockchain is extremely difficult. It becomes even more difficult when questionable information sources are being recycled. Writing comprehensible, meaningful material on this topic is even more challenging than understanding it. We have an extremely problematic situation where numerous parties have effectively become Blockchain salespeople by writing articles and white papers. This material is recycling and selling the great story of Blockchain to the world. Some of this material may appear to be a balanced treatment of the subject, but almost all of it is hopelessly biased.

When organizations feel that they need to understand what the buzz is all about on any topic, they will generally assign this responsibility to someone who appears to know the most about this topic. Who ends up writing these stories or performing this research? The people who are *already involved* with cryptocurrency and/or Blockchain. These are the people who are *already sold* on cryptocurrency and Blockchain. They may have personally invested in cryptocurrency and are hoping that the values of cryptocurrency will rise. Consider the source.

---

[227] See Chapter 5
[228] See Chapters 2, 4, 5, 7, 8, 9, 10, 11, 12, 13, 14, 16, 17, 19, 21, 24, 25, 27, 31, 33, 34, 35, 36

CHAPTER 33
A FORK IN THE ROAD

A fork in Blockchain means a disagreement. The various types of disagreements and the ramifications of these disagreements is, you guessed it, *complicated*. For the purpose of simplicity, this chapter will refer to the Bitcoin blockchain. However, the concepts discussed will generally apply to all cryptocurrencies and to non-cryptocurrency Blockchains as well.

Whose Truth?

With Blockchain, nobody is in charge. Everybody keeps their own personal copy of what they think happened. Bitcoin is designed where one miner should guess the right nonsense, pseudorandom, number (nonce) that allows them to potentially extend the blockchain. It is a random number, and it will take a random amount of time to guess. However, there are so many guessers making so many guesses per second that it averages out to about every 10 minutes.

Truth Race

When a miner guesses the right nonce, they will broadcast "WE WILL USE <u>MY</u> TRUTH, which has *these* particular transactions, including these brand new bitcoins which have been created out of nothingness and deposited into this particular bitcoin address that I choose." More than one miner may guess a nonce that can extend the blockchain around the same time. When this happens, a race throughout the network ensues to see which truth wins. In theory, miners are supposed to accept the first, longest chain that they receive that has is valid and build on that chain.

    I say in theory, because every miner is free to run whatever software they choose. As a result, they may possibly decide to ignore the longest chain they receive in favor of another chain. These are so-called "selfish mining" strategies. For example, Bitmain, the company with the largest pool of hashpower by far, could decide to intentionally hold back releasing the next block, and start guessing the next nonce to extend its blockchain a second time on its blockchain in private. With its dominant hashpower, this would cause others to waste their guesses on blockchains that will ultimately be rejected. This would allow Bitmain to win even more bitcoins.

Because of these races and other blockchain disagreements, this is why Bitcoin transactions are not considered reasonably confirmed until they are buried in the blockchain behind six other blocks (~10 minutes per block = 1 hour). At least that's how it *usually* works.

Unexpected Hard Fork

In Chapter 24, we discussed how a software upgrade that was implemented by several larger mining pools accepted a block that was rejected by a large number of nodes and miners. This resulted in what is called a hard fork of the Bitcoin blockchain. Two parallel blockchains were being built, which was unexpected and a huge problem. In this case, a large number of nodes/miners were building on a different blockchain than the blockchain being produced by the mining pools with the most hashpower. Confusion ensued, which was resolved by the largest mining pools all agreeing to downgrade their software and rewrite the blockchain.

Whose Rules?

Every node may run whatever hardware and software they choose. However, for nodes to cooperate, there are certain rules that they need to play by in terms of the format of blocks that they accept and blocks that they create ("mine"). Sometimes there are differences of opinion on software development path.

One group of software developers might release a different version of the Bitcoin program than the Bitcoin core group, for example. As long as the differences are compatible, this is called a "soft fork."

It is hard to know for sure how often soft forks are taking place in Bitcoin since everybody is free to run whatever software they choose. However, it does not appear that soft forks happen frequently with Bitcoin because, as the above example shows, even a basic software upgrade on a consistent development path can result in an unexpected hard fork of the blockchain. Unexpected hard forks indicate utter chaos, a disintegration of all data integrity.

CHAPTER 34
CRYPTO-COIN COPYING

Since cryptocurrencies are digital and built to realize a crypto-anarchy (hidden anarchy) ideal where nobody is in charge, they are incredibly easy to copy. Why wouldn't you copy them? You literally double your money every time!

Forking Over Your Money

New cryptocurrencies seem to appear every day, looking for new "investors." The vast majority of these crypto-coins are **duplicated bitcoins**. I am not talking about reusing computer code. This is actual "coin copying." You can copy dollars, too, but it's tricky. You need to find the right kind of paper, and there are a few other technical details. Additionally, it's frowned upon by the authorities, so you could go to prison. When you copy bitcoins or another cryptocurrency in this manner, it could not be simpler, and it is called an intentional **hard fork**.

Bitcoin Cash blockchain

... 478557 — 478558 — 478559 — 478560 — 478561 ... 491406 — 491407 — 491408 ...

Bitcoin blockchain 8/1/17 - Bitcoin Cash Hard Fork, **Spend Your bitcoins HERE**, too!

... 478557 — 478558 — 478559 — 478560 — 478561 ... 491406 — 491407 — 491408 ...

Bitcoin Gold blockchain   10/24/17 - Bitcoin Gold Hard Fork   ... and HERE!

... 478557 — 478558 — 478559 — 478560 — 478561 ... 491406 — 491407 — 491408 ...

... and HERE!

Spend your bitcoins *again* on the Bitcoin Cash blockchain and *again* on the Bitcoin Gold blockchain and *again* on the Bitcoin Diamond blockchain and *again* on the Bitcoin Dark blockchain and *again* on the Bitcoin Private blockchain, and so on and so on...

This fork creates a new cryptocurrency where everybody that already owns bitcoins now gets duplicated brand new coins as well. This is helpful to get people to care about your new cryptocurrency. Everybody who already had bitcoins at the time of the fork (split) in the blockchain can spend the same coins twice. They can spend them in the "Bitcoin world", and they can spend them again in the "new coin world."

Hard forks give the creators and early adopters, who own the vast majority of the coins that are being copied, the same stockpile of coins again; they're simply copied and given a new name like "Bitcoin Cash", "Bitcoin Gold" or "Bitcoin Diamond" instead of just "Bitcoin." Primary recipients of the copied bitcoins would be Cypherpunk crypto-anarchists. All existing bitcoin holders have an incentive to say this fork is a good cryptocurrency and solicit new "investors" so that they can cash out.

Duplicating Coins, Duping the Public

Coming up with a good name for the new coin is important because you want new "investors." The only way that new "investors" can buy in is for existing "new coin" holders to cash out. Now, you likely will not get any takers from *knowledgeable* bitcoin holders that realize that they already have a bunch of your "new coin." However, there are many less knowledgeable bitcoin holders, with entirely too many dollars, that have no idea what is going on and may just buy these new coins again!

Additionally, you have a great opportunity to get new investors that have not invested before! Press that copy button. Press it now! Play up the mining costs. Advertise that you mine for these coins with a crypto-diamond drill. They'll love that.

I cannot tell you how many times I have seen the image of a gold coin on news stories about Bitcoin. Whenever the term fork has come up in reporting (which is far less frequent, this is more common in cryptocurrency "news" advocate websites), there is a picture of a gold coin with a fork dining utensil positioned like you can use the fork to eat the coin. The message is not coin splitting or copying chaos and investor exploitation. The message is "Bitcoin is gold, here comes a fork... eat it up. Yummy!"

Blockchain & ICO Distractions

The level of misinformation and misdirection surrounding cryptocurrencies is mind-blowing but understandable. There are so many plot lines, who could possibly keep up? ICOs (Initial Coin Offerings) sound like IPOs, and they are kind of like that, but different. People can kind of wrap their head around an IPO and see how people can be scammed. ICOs may

CHAPTER 34
CRYPTO-COIN COPYING

be scams, but ICOs themselves are distracting from what is happening with all of the hard forks. The Blockchain story itself seeks to validate cryptocurrencies and distracts from what is going on with cryptocurrencies. Confused? That appears to be the plan.

The "21 Million Limit" Story

There are certain elements of the Bitcoin story that have been repeated many times by the Bitcoin storytellers. One of the most popular story points is that Bitcoin has a "21 million limit" of bitcoins. It seems very important to the storytellers, which is understandable. The Bitcoin blockchain has been hard forked (copied and renamed) multiple times.

The "21 million" limit helps shift the focus away from what is really going on with hard forks. Bitcoin hard forks give Cypherpunks an endless supply of crypto-coins that they can sell to whoever will buy. ICOs have gotten more attention than hard forks, which works out great to distract from the coin copying of bitcoin and ether. Are all cryptocurrencies Ponzi schemes?

While cryptocurrencies certainly have all of the characteristics of a Ponzi scheme, and may very well suffer a Ponzi scheme ending, they are far more sophisticated than anything created by Charles Ponzi or Bernie Madoff. Might cryptocurrencies go to zero or nearly zero overnight? Even Vitalik Buterin, the creator of Ethereum cryptocurrency, has tweeted in February 2018, "Reminder: cryptocurrencies are still a new and hyper-volatile asset class, and could drop to near-zero at any time."[229]

Exchanges are the financial heart of cryptocurrencies. They are the source of liquidity. When someone is buying, someone else MUST be selling (cashing out). That is the only way that the transaction can occur. We will review how liquidity crises work (how Ponzi schemes often end) and how this can make your cryptocurrency worthless overnight in the next chapter (Exchanges).

---

[229] Buterin, Vitalik. Tweet from Buterin. Feb 17, 2018. https://twitter.com/vitalikbuterin/status/964838207215955969?lang=en

CHAPTER 35
EXCHANGES

> "Why, sometimes I've believed as many as six impossible things before breakfast."
> —The White Queen, *Through the Looking Glass*

The primary consideration of those who invest in cryptocurrencies is the **exchange rate** with traditional currencies such as dollars, euros, or yen. The cryptocurrency market is substantially different from every other market, particularly the stock market and the credit markets. While there are significant differences, the most similar market to the cryptocurrency market would probably be the foreign currency exchange (Forex) market.

Foreign Currency Exchange (Forex)

The Forex market is the largest market in the world in terms of volume. Like cryptocurrency exchanges, Forex is decentralized with relatively little regulation. When you travel overseas and purchase something on your credit card in a different currency, you are engaging in this market.

In the early 90s, I was the primary systems administrator of a system, designed by Swiss Bank, that performed foreign currency exchange arbitrage (hedging) analysis for the Treasury Department of Motorola. The company had bank accounts with sizable foreign currency assets. Forex hedging was used by the company to help minimize the impact of volatility in foreign currency asset valuation. We needed to have our earnings reports represent true financial results and not be skewed by fluctuations in exchange rates. These above examples are routine uses for Forex. As with every market, there are also speculators.

Forex Manipulation

All exchanges can be manipulated, and the Forex market is no exception. In June 2013, *Bloomberg* reported on collusion in the Forex market that resulted in significant manipulation of foreign currency exchange rates.[230] Investigations resulted in five banks pleading guilty to currency manipulation and fines of $5.7 billion in 2015.[231] By October 8, 2018, the number had ballooned to 16 banks and $14 billion in fines.[232]

On August 2, 2018, thirteen executives and employees of the Maxim Trader Group in Singapore were convicted of running a **Forex Ponzi scheme** to defraud investors.[233] Numerous Forex scams and Ponzi schemes have been in the news over the years.

Cryptocurrency Exchange Manipulation

As high as the risks are for manipulation and fraud in the Forex market, this risk pales in comparison to the fraud and manipulation risks in cryptocurrency exchanges. To begin with, there are enormous conflicts of interest in virtually all cryptocurrency exchanges. The **exchanges publish the price**, and the owners and operators of cryptocurrency exchanges will almost certainly benefit from an increase in price. The owners of the exchanges may personally have substantial cryptocurrency holdings. In the case of the Cypherpunks and other early adopters, they were the recipients of the initial, very generous lotteries. Additionally, every time the Bitcoin blockchain is **hard forked and copied**, these same individuals receive additional **copies** of the coins.[234]

---

[230] Vaughan, Finch and Choudhry. "Traders Said to Rig Currency Rates to Profit Off Clients." *Bloomberg.* June 11, 2013. https://www.bloomberg.com/news/articles/2013-06-11/traders-said-to-rig-currency-rates-to-profit-off-clients

[231] Reuters. "Five Banks To Plead Guilty to Global Currency Manipulation." *NBC News.* May 19, 2015. https://www.nbcnews.com/business/markets/five-banks-plead-guilty-global-currency-manipulation-n361921

[232] Nguyen and McLaughlin. "Currency 'Cartel' Traders on Trial for Chats That Cost Billions." *Bloomberg.* Oct 8, 2018. https://www.bloomberg.com/news/articles/2018-10-09/currency-cartel-traders-on-trial-for-chats-that-cost-billions

[233] Pan, Jason. "Thirteen found guilty over massive Ponzi scheme." *Taipei Times.* Aug 3, 2018. http://www.taipeitimes.com/News/taiwan/archives/2018/08/03/2003697901

[234] See Chapter 34 for a description of hard forks

CHAPTER 35
EXCHANGES

There are *several* exchanges, *each* reporting numbers. The transaction prices reported by each cryptocurrency exchange provides communication to *the entire world* regarding what someone was purportedly willing to pay for bitcoin or another cryptocurrency. Reports of higher prices on a sustained basis from even *one* exchange will fraudulently communicate higher prices throughout *all* of the exchanges. **If even *one* exchange fudges the numbers, the entire system ends up with inflated, fudged numbers**. There is no inherent reason to trust any given cryptocurrency exchange. It is even harder to expect that all exchanges will act in a trustworthy manner, especially with such potentially enormous **conflicts of interest**.

Wash Sale Manipulation

Even if we assume that *all* cryptocurrency exchanges throughout the globe magically overcome conflict of interest temptations, *and* are always completely honest in reporting the exchange rate, *and* always work 100% correctly, **the price of cryptocurrency can *still* be manipulated by even a single party**. Even in a scenario where all exchanges are assumed to be perfectly honest in reporting, one party can be both the buyer and the seller and drive up the price. This would be accomplished by a single party creating a ladder of limit orders to sell a cryptocurrency at a series of above market asking prices while simultaneously placing orders to buy the same cryptocurrency at market price. This is a *wash sale*, where a single party can theoretically drive the price to any level desired within constraints involving other sell orders in the system and transaction fees.

For anyone who holds a substantial amount of cryptocurrency (such as those in the initial Bitcoin subsidy lottery), the rewards of driving the price higher should outweigh virtually all other concerns. For anyone who owns a substantial amount of anonymous cryptocurrency and operates an exchange, the cost to do this is effectively zero. There is significant evidence that wash sales and basic fraudulent transaction reporting by exchanges are the primary (only?) reason why the price of bitcoin has risen from under a penny per bitcoin to thousands of dollars per bitcoin. Let's look at the story of Mt. Gox, including the time when the price of bitcoin briefly returned to nearly zero. In the final collapse of Mt. Gox, many investors who thought they owned bitcoins found out that they did not really own them at all.

Mt. Gox

Mt. Gox was a bitcoin exchange based in Tokyo, Japan, operating from 2010 until it suddenly shut down in February 2014. By all accounts, Mt. Gox was the largest bitcoin exchange in the world at the time of its bankruptcy filing and sudden closure. It has been estimated that Mt. Gox was then responsible for 70% of all bitcoin exchange transactions worldwide.[235]

The former CEO of Mt. Gox, Mark Karpelès, has spent a substantial amount of time in court defending himself following Mt. Gox's collapse. During his trial in Tokyo, Mr. Karpelès admitted to operating a computer program known as "Willy bot", to manipulate the price of bitcoin.[236]

As indicated above, exchanges can manipulate prices by reporting whatever transactions they wish to indicate, regardless if they are real or not. To make things look more legitimate, they can perform automated wash sales to increase the price with laddered orders. If you consider the paper *Price Manipulation in the Bitcoin Ecosystem* by Gandal, Hamrick, Moore, and Oberman, alongside the testimony of Karpelès, it seems apparent that Mt. Gox did BOTH of these things![237]

Make-Believe Bitcoin Price and Volume

The Gandal, Hamrick, et al. paper indicates "Willy bot" performed automated transactions designed to artificially increase the prices, but at least these were actual transactions of bitcoins. The description of the "Markus bot" computer program describes an even simpler, more straightforward approach. According to the paper, "Markus did not actually pay for the bitcoins he acquired; rather, his account was fraudulently credited with claimed bitcoins that almost certainly were not backed by real coins."[238]

---

[235] Vigna, Paul. "5 Things About Mt. Gox's Crisis." *The Wall Street Journal.* Feb 25, 2014. https://blogs.wsj.com/briefly/2014/02/25/5-things-about-mt-goxs-crisis/

[236] Suberg, William. "Mt. Gox Trial Update: Karpeles Admits 'Willy Bot' Existence." *Cointelegraph.* Jul 11, 2017. https://cointelegraph.com/news/mt-gox-trial-update-karpeles-admits-willy-bot-existence

[237] Gandal, Hamrick, et. al. 2017. "Price Manipulation the Bitcoin Ecosystem." *Workshop on the Economics of Information Security.* May 16. https://weis2017.econinfosec.org/wp-content/uploads/sites/3/2017/05/WEIS_2017_paper_21.pdf

[238] Ibid

CHAPTER 35
EXCHANGES

Put more simply, the Gandal, Hamrick et al. paper indicates that "Markus bot" was pure fictional reporting by Mt. Gox of transactions that never actually occurred. These fictional trades were used to fraudulently communicate to the world, "here are transactions that just occurred and they show that the price of bitcoin just went up."

"Willy bot" (automated transactions to manipulate the price by Mt. Gox) and "Markus bot" (fraudulent trade reporting by Mt. Gox) were responsible for pushing up the price of bitcoin from $150 to $1000 over a two month period.[239] "Willy" and "Markus" not only succeeded in artificially inflating the price of bitcoin, but also the reported *volume* of transactions. The higher reported volume of transactions helped make the increase in bitcoin price seem more believable and helped create the false perception of increased interest in and liquidity of bitcoin.

There have been **no meaningful changes** to the controls of the bitcoin marketplace after Mt. Gox's demise to prevent other bots from taking "Willy's" place. It is unclear precisely how much of the price of bitcoin is the result of other bots or simple, "Markus-style", fictitious transaction reporting by one or more of the exchanges.

Cryptocurrency (literally "hidden money") was explicitly designed to exist outside of the reach of governments. It seems unlikely that governments or any entity would be able to implement meaningful controls to avoid rampant exchange rate manipulation short of the outright banning of cryptocurrency exchanges.

Liquidity

"Willy Bot"-style laddered order, wash sale price fixing is possible as long as there is a reasonably *limited* number of sell orders. Cryptocurrencies and cryptocurrency exchanges are fairly "dark markets" where it can be nearly impossible to tell what is actually going on. This is what allows "Markus Bot"-style fraudulent order reporting to occur. These dark markets can become illiquid markets (where the price can go to nearly zero, and you cannot cash out) if a sufficient number of sell orders are placed at the same time at market price. This is called a ***liquidity crisis***.

Per a Mt. Gox 2011 press release, "Clarification of Mt. Gox Compromised Accounts and Major Bitcoin Sell-off," the price of bitcoin dropped

---

[239] Ibid

on the Mt. Gox exchange from $17.50 to $0.01 within the span of 30 minutes. Mt. Gox reported that this was the result of hacking.[240]

However, it is noteworthy that a collapse of the price of Bitcoin to zero or nearly zero is also precisely what would occur during a basic liquidity crisis. This is when a sufficient volume of at-market-price sell orders dramatically reduces the price. If Mt. Gox could simply not deliver enough cash in dollars or other traditional currency to meet the demand, this is the same behavior we would expect. These dollars would be primarily provided by corresponding buy orders, possibly secondarily from the exchange itself, should the operators of an exchange decide to support the price of bitcoin by temporarily buying back bitcoins during heavier sell volume periods.

The Story

Whenever a liquidity crisis occurs, an exchange has a choice. They can be honest and drive the price of bitcoin down (possibly to nearly zero), which would eliminate the cryptocurrency exchange owner's personal cryptocurrency wealth. Alternatively, they ironically have a far better choice to proclaim, "We've been hacked! Or sorry, you've been hacked!" Not only does this provide a far better answer than "bitcoin just went to zero," it provides convenient excuses for why others who thought they owned bitcoins will never be able to cash out.

While several cryptocurrency exchanges have impressive looking websites and project an image of security, the fundamental situation remains unchanged versus Mt. Gox with respect to both fraud risks and simple illiquidity risk. A sufficient volume of bitcoin sales to dollars or other currency can drive any given exchange or even the entire cryptocurrency system into a state of illiquidity, and this can happen overnight.

The Great Story of Mt. Gox

Mt. Gox closed for good in February 2014. The closure was accompanied by additional stories of hacking to explain why many of their customers

---

[240] Mt. Gox. "Clarification of Mt. Gox Compromised Accounts and Major Bitcoin Sell-Off". Company Press Release. June 2011. Wayback Machine Archive captured Sep 19, 2001. https://web.archive.org/web/20110919162635/https://mtgox.com/press_release_20110630.html

CHAPTER 35
EXCHANGES

had lost all of their bitcoin deposits. I have reviewed some very engaging reports explaining how these hacks have apparently occurred, and it may very likely have been an outside hacker that finally destroyed Mt. Gox as has been claimed.[241] However, I have also seen no evidence that definitively *proves* that bitcoins were lost due to outsider hacking and not an insider job. Since bitcoins are never registered to a person, they truly are owned only "by math"[242], it is extremely difficult to prove how someone got access to a key to access bitcoins. It is also extremely difficult to definitively prove who that someone is if they don't want you to know.

Exchange Crypto-Risks

Let's set aside if, as a society, we want to be living the cryptoanarchy dream by embracing cryptocurrency. There are inherent risks that are unique to working with cryptocurrency exchanges, most notably the very nature of cryptocurrency ("hidden money") ownership. For purposes of simplicity in this section, we may refer to Bitcoin, though these statements apply to cryptocurrencies more broadly than just Bitcoin.

Nobody truly owns bitcoins. There is no official registration. There is no official record of ownership. They are "owned by math." The basis of bitcoin ownership is that you know a magic number (key) associated with a particular address. Once someone else knows that key, they can spend the bitcoins at the associated address, and you cannot get them back unless they voluntarily send them back to you. Once someone else has your special digits (key), there is no reliable way to determine how they figured it out. The system is specifically designed to hide the money trail.[243]

Several exchanges (and possibly their insurers, if any) have a great story about "hot" wallets and "cold" wallets. Coinbase, a major cryptocurrency exchange explains, "98% of customer funds are stored offline. Offline storage provides an important security measure against theft or loss. We distribute bitcoin geographically in safe deposit boxes and vaults around the world." Coinbase further explains:

---

[241] McMillan, Robert. "The Inside Story of Mt. Gox, Bitcoin's $460 Million Disaster." *Wired Magazine*. Mar 3, 2014. https://www.wired.com/2014/03/bitcoin-exchange/
[242] See Chapter 25
[243] Ibid

1. Sensitive data that would normally reside on our servers is disconnected entirely from the internet.
2. Data is then split with redundancy, AES-256 encrypted, and copied to FIPS-140 USB drives and paper backups.
3. Drives and paper backups are distributed geographically in safe deposit boxes and vaults around the world.

The Coinbase security information page then indicates that 2-step verification is required on all accounts.[244]

This sounds great, and there is likely a limited amount of merit to these procedures. However, the fact remains that if you know the magic number (or multiple magic numbers in the case of multi-signature wallets) and you know the associated cryptocurrency address, you can spend any bitcoins stored at that address. This can happen multiple ways. There may be a technical problem or leak in the wallet generation code or perhaps an operational error. Even an extremely lucky guess has the potential to generate a key that can allow someone to spend bitcoins at that address.[245]

Are bitcoins stored at addresses managed by "cold wallets" vulnerable to theft? Absolutely! It has been reported that Mt. Gox had bitcoins stolen from its "cold wallets" as well as its "hot wallets."[246] So, "cold storage" of the wallets did not appear to help out Mt. Gox.

The concept of a "cold wallet" is a limited control. Software errors and hacking may occur while the wallets must be "hot" in order to function. Cryptocurrency may then be stolen later, while the wallets are in "cold storage." At all times, insider theft of wallet information remains a significant risk and this risk exists for "hot" or supposedly "cold" wallets. A rogue employee may compromise "hot" or "cold" wallet information, leave the company, leave the country, and then pilfer the cryptocurrency from wallets that are supposedly in "cold storage." Bitcoin was designed around the concept of trusting NO third parties. Relying on third parties to manage cryptocurrency wallets is a dangerous proposition.

---

[244] Per Coinbase website, see https://www.coinbase.com/security

[245] See Chapter 25

[246] Norry, Andrew. "The history of the Mt. Gox Hack: Bitcoin's Biggest Heist." *Blockonomi*. July 2, 2018. https://blockonomi.com/mt-gox-hack/

CHAPTER 35
EXCHANGES

The primary consideration with "hot" and "cold" wallets may be how insurers can limit their liability. The Coinbase website describes how "hot" and "cold" wallets relate to their insurance:

> Digital Currency Balances
> Coinbase secures customer digital currency through a combination of secure, online servers and offline ("cold") storage. Coinbase maintains 98% or more of customer digital currency in cold storage, with the remainder in secure online servers as necessary to serve the liquidity needs of our customers.
>
> Coinbase maintains commercial criminal insurance in an aggregate amount that is greater than the value of digital currency we maintain in online storage. Our insurance policy is made available through a combination of third-party insurance underwriters and Coinbase, who is a co-insurer under the policy.
>
> The policy insures against theft of digital currency that results from a security breach or hack, employee theft, or fraudulent transfer.
>
> Our policy does not cover any losses resulting from unauthorized access to your personal Coinbase or Coinbase Pro account(s). It is your responsibility to use a strong password and maintain control of all login credentials you use to access Coinbase and Coinbase Pro. Digital currency is not legal tender and is not backed by the government. Digital currency, such as Bitcoin, Litecoin, and Ethereum, is not subject to Federal Deposit Insurance Corporation ("FDIC") or Securities Investor Protection Corporation protections.[247]

Coinbase has limited insurance (with Coinbase itself as a co-insurer) of effectively only 2% of their cryptocurrency assets, specifically the "hot wallets." Cryptocurrency ("hidden money") is unlike most other online investment accounts where there is generally a clear audit trail when funds move between various accounts. Ultimately, if fraud occurs at a bank or

---

[247] Per Coinbase website, see https://support.coinbase.com/customer/portal/articles/1662379-how-is-coinbase-insured-

major investment institution, there will almost certainly be a money trail. The entire premise of cryptocurrency is that it is supposed to be untraceable.

Liquidity Limits

There is no reason to assume that any given exchange is financially stable. Additionally, a repeat of the 2011 bitcoin price drop to $0.01 can absolutely reoccur at any time. If this happens again, there is no guarantee that the price will recover.

If a severe liquidity crisis occurs, this time across the now multiple exchanges, will the story be "we've been hacked" and will it be believable? Or will it be the end of the line for cryptocurrency? If the price drops precipitously or if trading is halted, what will the story be and should you believe it?

CHAPTER 36
SMART CONTRACTS

> The first thing we do, let's kill all the lawyers.
> —*Dick "the Butcher"*
> *from Henry VI by William Shakespeare*

A smart contract is "code on the blockchain." Smart contracts provide a way to guarantee execution of an agreement between **anonymous parties** via Blockchain. Once all parties agree to a smart contract, execution of the agreement is to occur with zero recourse beyond what happens by computer code. Since no parties should know the identities of any of the other parties, normal societal laws, and legal recourse should be impossible by design.

Kill the Middleman

The concept of eliminating the middleman is something with which everybody should be familiar. This is also something that is generally viewed favorably unless you are the middleman being eliminated. Nobody wants to suffer through systems that are more complicated and/or expensive than necessary. The internet has already eliminated many middlemen, but more remain that we would like to eliminate.

Governments in the Middle

The primary middleman that smart contracts eliminate is *government*. Additional middlemen may also be eliminated depending upon the details of the smart contract. By creating anonymous systems that exist outside of governments and laws, an environment can be created where "what happens, happens" and legal recourse is essentially impossible. In theory, smart contracts could create systems that support completely unrestricted and untraceable commerce where parties can transact without judgment by governments or others.

The first reference from the famous Bitcoin white paper, *b-money*, was focused on the potential of *smart contracts* to make the dream of **crypto-anarchy practical and achievable**. The paper summarized the potential as follows:

> ```
> The protocol proposed in this article allows un-
> traceable pseudonymous entities to cooperate with
> each other more efficiently, by providing them
> with a medium of exchange and a method of enforc-
> ing contracts. The protocol can probably be made
> more efficient and secure, but I hope this is a
> step toward making crypto-anarchy a practical as
> well as theoretical possibility.[248]
> ```

Anonymity

Blockchain creates systems where everybody can be *anonymous*. No matter how iron-clad a computerized *smart contract* (or any kind of contract) is, if one or both of the parties knows the name of another party in the real world, lawsuits or other action (legal or otherwise) is still possible. Smart contracts provide a means of coordination in an anonymous, anarchist society where lawyers and courts do not exist. The smart contract establishes rules, order, and coordination between **two (or more)** *anonymous* **parties**.

Longfin

One company that appeared to have embraced these concepts is the Blockchain-focused company Longfin. This company was briefly listed on the NASDAQ stock exchange. Within a few months, the SEC initiated action, and the company was delisted from the NASDAQ.[249] By late 2018, the company began the process of being dissolved entirely.

Longfin Chairman and CEO, Venkat S Meenavalli explicitly stated that it is his goal to perform **Shadow Banking** on the homepage of his website, www.longfincorp.com:

---

[248] "Dai, Wei." *b-money*
[249] Beaty, Grant. "9 Reasons Why Nasdaq Should Delist LongFin Immediately." *Seeking Alpha*. Apr 17, 2018. https://seekingalpha.com/article/4163537-9-reasons-nasdaq-delist-longfin-immediately

CHAPTER 36
SMART CONTRACTS

> Reimagining the world of Alternative Finance (Shadow Banking), $72 trillion industry powered by Artificial Intelligence, Machine Learning and Blockchain enabled Smart Contracts.
>
> — Venkat S Meenavalli
> *Chairman & CEO*

The firm's website listed three business divisions to reimagine shadow banking[250] (potential misuses of shadow banking have been added in parentheses):

- Importer/Exporter Financing (potentially black market transaction financing)
- Electronic Market Making (potentially anonymous, automated manipulation of the stock market and/or other markets)
- Blockchain powered Smart Contract Solutions (which may potentially be used by criminals and terrorists and may potentially be used to support the other two listed activities)

According to their pre-IPO *1A* filing with the SEC, Longfin had **three EMPLOYEES** and the plan, post-IPO, was to merge with a 20 employee Singapore company called *The Stampede*.[251] Longfin is/was a blockchain company with the slogan "calculating the incalculable":

This slogan seems appropriate given that the market capitalization of the start-up ballooned to $7B at one point.[252] It is unclear how much of this lofty valuation was due to the electronic market making or possibly strong demand for such boldly proclaimed solutions to support the world of underworld financial operations.

---

[250] From the company website, https://www.longfincorp.com archives of which may be viewed on the Wayback Machine (web.archive.org).

[251] SEC Form 1A, Longfin, Corp. - Submitted May 8, 2017, https://www.sec.gov/Archives/edgar/data/1699683/000169968317000007/Longfin1_A.pdf

[252] Richter, Wolf. "LongFin is under investigation — but investors aren't giving up yet." Business Insider. Apr 3, 2018. https://www.businessinsider.com/longfin-is-under-investigation-but-investors-arent-giving-up-yet-2018-4

For perspective, consider Beijing-based bicycle sharing company, ofo, which according to Wikipedia, in 2017 was valued at 2 billion dollars and was operating in 250 cities and 20 countries with over 62.7 million monthly active users.[253] Longfin's SEC filings indicate roughly 20 employees, yet their stock was trading with a valuation more than three times a company with 62.7 million customers! As an aside, ofo's CEO is Dai Wei (not to be confused with "Wei Dai").

Longfin has/had a Smart Contracts business called Ziddu. When Bitcoin was originally released in 2009, the Ziddu website looked like this:

Additionally, the company's tagline at that time was "Upload - Share - Earn":

Earn
Get paid every time others download your videos or photos or documents .   [254]

Ziddu later pivoted into Smart Contracts and became the Smart Contract division of Longfin. The new slogans for Ziddu became "The Only Marketplace for Decentralized Smart Contracts" and:

"If it is not in Blockchain, then it is not a Smart Contract"   [255]

To the casual observer, this last slogan might appear to be a just tagline.

---

[253] Wikipedia Page for ofo, https://en.wikipedia.org/wiki/Ofo_(company)
[254] Ziddu Wayback Machine Archive from Mar 03, 2009. https://web.archive.org/web/20090303165818/http://www.ziddu.com:80/
[255] Ziddu Web Page. https://www.ziddu.com (it is unclear if the site will remain after Longfin is dissolved, if the site is unavailable, see the Wayback Machine at web.archive.org for this website)

CHAPTER 36
SMART CONTRACTS

Although this is quite disturbing, it turns out that in my home state of Arizona, we actually have a legal definition officially codifying, recognizing and elevating Blockchain technology and establishing it as the legal foundation of a "Smart Contract." In Arizona, the Longfin slogan is not a slogan. In Arizona, if it is not in Blockchain, it appears that it is legally not a Smart Contract.[256]

Arizona Blockchain Law

In 2017, a law was passed which established Arizona Revised Statutes (A.R.S.) § 44-7061 with the following definitions:

1. **"Blockchain technology"** means distributed ledger technology that uses a distributed, decentralized, shared and replicated ledger, which may be public or private, permissioned or permissionless, or driven by tokenized crypto economics or tokenless. **The data on the ledger is protected with cryptography, is immutable and auditable and provides an uncensored truth.** [*emphasis added*]
2. **"Smart contract"** means an event-driven program, with state, that runs on a distributed, decentralized, shared and replicated ledger and that can take custody over and instruct transfer of assets on that ledger.[257]

The terms distributed, decentralized, shared and replicated ledger are questionable and misleading, but beyond that, we have legislative assurances that the data on the ledger is "protected with cryptography." As we have discussed in Chapter 14, this is a meaningless phrase unless we can describe from whom the data is hidden, who has the key, and how this is protective. The legislative assurances of immutability and auditability are rather curious. Finally, the assurance of *uncensored truth* seems more appropriate for religious texts than laws describing human-created technology.

By establishing a definition that explicitly promises features of immutability, auditability, and uncensored truth, Blockchain technology does not even satisfy its own legal definition in Arizona. The Arizona law has the appearance of being created to provide legislative validation, elevation,

---

[256] Arizona Revised Statutes, § 44-7061, https://www.azleg.gov/viewdocument/?docName=https://www.azleg.gov/ars/44/07061.htm
[257] Ibid

and free publicity for a technology. Laws like this may have even been partially responsible for the lofty Longfin valuation bubble. Once again, it is unclear just how much cryptocurrency (hidden money) is being funneled into our political system.

The 2017 law was incorporated into A.R.S. under Title 44 "Trade and Commerce", which defines illegal business practices and documents consequences for breaking the law. The first item in this section, A.R.S. § 44-101, is the **"Statute of frauds" which legally defines fraud in Arizona law.**

Rather than the other statues in this section, which appear to set boundaries, restrictions, and consequences, § 44-7061, if it does anything at all, seems to legally declare in Arizona statutes that blockchain "provides an uncensored truth." Additionally, by including this language, *perhaps* this law also is supposed to imply that Blockchain Technology is ***not fraud*** by legislative fiat. Arizona is not alone. *Several* states have seen Blockchain laws introduced, and many of them have passed, in the past year.[258]

Rushed Legislative Embrace

The article "Blockchain laws tend to be hasty, unnecessary and extremely thirsty" by Adrianne Jeffries offers an analysis of Blockchain laws. These laws "all share a common goal: encouraging blockchain companies to bring their high-paying jobs to the state… [Although] it's unclear if passing blockchain-themed legislation actually draws blockchain startups seeking a place to settle," says Jeffries.[259]

Another common theme is that virtually none of the legislators seem to understand the technology and what these laws truly mean. According to Jeff Weninger, the sponsor of the Arizona Blockchain law discussed above, "despite the confusion, his colleagues were eager to be at the forefront of this technology."[260] Jeffries describes the passage of the Tennessee

---

[258] Jeffries, Adrianne. "Blockchain laws tend to be hasty, unnecessary, and extremely thirsty." *The Verge.* Mar 29, 2018. https://www.theverge.com/2018/3/29/17176596/blockchain-bitcoin-cryptocurrency-state-law-legislation

[259] Ibid

[260] Fish, Nathan. "Arizona edges to front of states eyeing blockchain technology." *Cronkite News.* Aug 15, 2017. https://cronkitenews.azpbs.org/2017/08/15/arizona-edges-to-front-of-states-eyeing-blockchain-technology/

blockchain law. One member asked, "Can you just explain what we're doing here, and dumb it down for me please?" As Jeffries puts it, "Even though the explanation was inscrutable, the legislator did not ask any follow-up questions. The law passed unanimously."[261]

Extropians

One of the concepts that has some popularity in the Cypherpunk community is the concept of *extropianism*. This is also known as transhumanism or "the Singularity" where human consciousness will someday be uploaded into computer systems. The creator of Blockchain, Nick Szabo, authored an article "Smart Contracts: Building Blocks for Digital Markets" that was published in **Extropy Magazine** in 1996.[262]

Hal Finney was one of the early developers of Bitcoin. Finney received the first bitcoin ever sent (it was sent by "Satoshi"). After Finney's death in 2014, his body was frozen and is preserved by the cryopreservation company Alcor in Scottsdale, Arizona.[263] When "James A Donald" declares Bitcoin as a strike at the state from beyond the state's intellectual and *temporal* horizons[264], it is truly long-term. Crypto Anarchy began in 1988 and has been developing since that time. Extropian Cypherpunks are hoping to see it happen during their mortal life or beyond when they become one with the machine.

Contract Killings

In Chapter 11, we discussed how the "Assassination Politics" (AP) vision of Cypherpunk Jim Bell would be best, albeit frighteningly, implemented via a smart contract. The smart contract might use computer code to provide the name of the target along with parameters required to authorize payment. Software developers might be expected to work out the code to implement desired smart contract terms and conditions, such as:
- Payment Schedule: installments or "all or nothing" payment upon death

---

[261] Jeffries. "Blockchain laws tend to be hasty..."
[262] See Chapter 13
[263] Alcor. "Hal Finney Becomes Alcor's 128th Patient." Alcor Press Release Dec 16, 2014. https://www.alcor.org/blog/hal-finney-becomes-alcors-128th-patient/
[264] "Donald, James A." *The Cypherpunk Program*

- Wounds versus Death: rules handling serious wounds, but not death
- Collateral Damage: are bombs acceptable or is a "surgical strike" required?
- Force Majeure ("Acts of God"), Unexpected Delays, etc.

The paper *The Ring of Gyges: Using Smart Contracts for Crime*, coins the term "criminal smart contracts (CSC)."[265] Gyges' Ring from mythology grants the wearer the power of invisibility. In the story, the ring is used to seduce the queen, kill the king and become the new king.

Anonymity through Blockchain distinguishes smart contracts from other forms of electronic contracts. Killings can be proposed, organized, and voted on in the blockchain in an anonymous crowdfunded manner. Assassinations can be arranged in a manner where none of the parties involved will ever know any identities other than the assassination target. Funds are provided in an untraceable manner between those ordering the "hit" and the assassins.[266] Smart contracts provide the killer peace-of-mind that they will be paid upon completion of the job.

Jim Bell's *Assassination Politics* (**AP**) solved the hard problem of defending or seizing an anarchist region from a country with a centrally organized army.[267] This was crucial to making anarchy realizable. Szabo's paper on *smart contracts* was published the following year.[268] Smart contracts help make anarchy practical and provide a mechanism to help realize Bell's vision for AP.

---

[265] Juels, Kosba, & Shi. 2013. "The Ring of Gyges: Using Smart Contracts for Crime." http://www.arijuels.com/wp-content/uploads/2013/09/Gyges.pdf
[266] See Chapter 11
[267] Ibid
[268] See Chapter 13

CHAPTER 37
THE BLOCKCHAIN PREACHER

There's a sucker born every minute.
—*P.T. Barnum*

Bitcoin Evangelist Tim Draper, sporting a Bitcoin Tie
By Web Summit - https://www.flickr.com/photos/websummit/38161080176
Cd, CC BY 2.0, https://commons.wikimedia.org/w/index.php?curid=65062514

Once again, while the above quote is closely associated with P.T. Barnum, there is no evidence that he ever said those words. In January 2018, Bitcoin evangelist Tim Draper predicted: "in 5 years if you go into a Starbucks or McDonalds and try to buy a burger or a coffee with 'fiat currency' the person at the desk is going to laugh at you." At another point in the video, Draper proclaimed, "China said we shun Bitcoin… and they basically sent all the best entrepreneurs out of their country."[269]

Reality Check

As we have discussed throughout the book, cryptocurrency creates hidden money that exists outside of governments and laws. The list of engineering trade-offs that are required to make this happen is extensive. This includes slow confirmation time, potentially expensive transaction fees (especially for small transactions), and you may find out that you do not actually own the cryptocurrency that you think you own.[270] Additionally, there is the risk that the entire cryptocurrency system might even collapse overnight. While January 2023 is a ways off, it will take a "revolution" of one form or another to have cryptocurrency replace debit and credit cards.

While China has taken steps to ban Initial Coin Offerings (ICOs) and cryptocurrency exchanges[271], cryptocurrencies exist *outside* of the reach of governments and laws. Cryptocurrencies are extremely difficult to regulate. It seems a vast overstatement to say China "basically sent all the best entrepreneurs out of their country." China continues to be where the vast majority of bitcoins are mined. It appears that over 50% of *all* bitcoin mining is being done by one company (or their affiliates), the Chinese company *Bitmain*.[272]

There is a great story of decentralization that encrypts the reality. As this book is published, **the company that currently controls the Bitcoin blockchain is the Chinese company *Bitmain*.**

---

[269] Draper, Tim. "Tim Draper Q&A about Bitcoin and the Blockchain 2018" *DraperTV YouTube Channel*. Jan 11, 2018. https://youtu.be/kaLLVi_ElAw

[270] See Chapter 25

[271] Huang, Zheping. "China to block more than 120 offshore cryptocurrency exchanges as crackdown escalates." *South China Morning Post*. Aug 23, 2018. https://www.scmp.com/tech/enterprises/article/2161014/china-block-more-120-offshore-cryptocurrency-exchanges-crackdown

[272] See Chapter 27

CHAPTER 37
THE BLOCKCHAIN PREACHER

Fiat

Fiat is a fancy word that means by "by decree." Cryptocurrencies may be created by fiat (or decree) of anonymous software developers and/or Chinese companies. However, when the term "fiat currency" is used by cryptocurrency advocates like Tim Draper, this means *government currency* such as the dollar, euro, or yen.

From Secession

Draper is looking to make history by splitting up California into three separate states. He obtained enough signatures to have his proposal on the November 2018 California general election ballot. However, the California Supreme Court had it removed. The last time a state break up happened was in the 1860s during the Civil War (when part of Virginia seceded to create West Virginia).[273]

To Unwavering Commitment

While Draper seeks to break up the state of California, he is standing fast with Theranos founder Elizabeth Holmes. Tim Draper provided the **initial seed round funding that *provided validation* for Elizabeth Holmes' company, Theranos.** Holmes has been in the news following lawsuits and charges of "massive fraud" by the SEC. Draper helped launch Theranos and continued to steadfastly defend Holmes as everything fell apart. In a May 2018 interview regarding Elizabeth Holmes, Draper continued to insist, "She did a great job."[274] In a June 19 interview with Cheddar, four days after Holmes was indicted, Draper reaffirmed his support for Holmes, saying, "She was doing really good work."

---

[273] Gorman, Steve. "California high court orders proposal to split up state removed from November ballot." *Reuters*. July 18, 2018. https://www.reuters.com/article/us-california-split/california-high-court-orders-proposal-to-split-up-state-removed-from-november-ballot-idUSKBN1K8300

[274] Marinova, Polina. "Why VC Tim Draper Keeps Defending Theranos CEO Elizabeth Holmes." *Fortune Magazine*. May 11, 2018. http://fortune.com/2018/05/11/tim-draper-theranos-elizabeth-holmes/

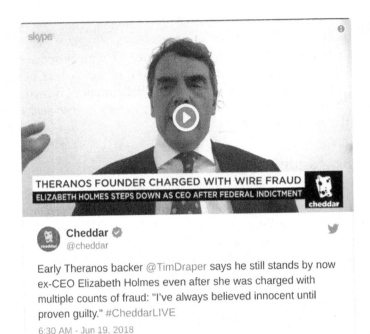

Changing Perceptions

A watershed moment in the validation of Bitcoin occurred on July 1, 2014. This was the day that the United States government officially recognized bitcoin as an asset by auctioning off nearly 30,000 bitcoins to Tim Draper. Draper's son, Adam Draper, recalls, "Up to that point our industry had a torrid history of scandal and skepticism."[275]

The FBI obtained the bitcoins for the 2014 Tim Draper sale one year earlier, in 2013. Although Bitcoin is designed to be hidden and untraceable, the feds gained access to a wallet that was owned by the operator of the Silk Road marketplace.[276] After the FBI shut down Silk Road, they auctioned off the bitcoins in the operator's wallet. Adam Draper explains, "The general masses had only heard that large sums of money had been stolen from bitcoin exchanges or that everyone buys illegal drugs with bitcoin. … For a while, it was the eBay of buying drugs, guns and hitmen,

---

[275] Draper, Adam. "Should I Do It? 30,000 Bitcoins and One Big Auction." *CoinDesk*. Apr 11, 2017. https://www.coindesk.com/bitcoin-milestones-adam-draper-silk-road-auction/

[276] See Chapter 4 for more information about Silk Road.

CHAPTER 37
THE BLOCKCHAIN PREACHER

and the currency used in this anonymous marketplace was the ever-reliable bitcoin."[277]

Adam Draper reflects:

> Now, think about what just happened. The US government successfully sold 30,000 bitcoins. Not only that, but a professional investor had won all of them... **The bitcoin community needed a catalyst to change perception, and I believe my dad created it.**[278] [*emphasis added*]

Soliciting Investors

Tim Draper led the seed round investment in Theranos with $500,000, providing crucial initial validation for investors. In the end, investors lost nearly one billion dollars.[279] Draper believes the future for Bitcoin is bright as well and encourages investors:

With the price of Bitcoin retreating from earlier highs, Draper's recommendation: "This is going to be so big so if you see a dip, jump in. Maybe it will dip further but boy, I made that prediction and I'm sticking to it. $250,000 by 2022 for Bitcoin."[280]

---

[277] Ibid

[278] Ibid

[279] Cohan, Peter. "6 Investment Lessons From Theranos's Billion-Dollar Destruction." *Inc. Magazine*. Sep 11, 2018. https://www.inc.com/peter-cohan/6-things-that-could-have-saved-theranos-investors-from-a-1-billion-wipeout-%E2%80%8B.html

[280] French, Jordan. "Tim Draper Is Not Backing Down From His Prediction of Bitcoin $250,000 by 2022." *The Street*. Sep 20, 2018. https://www.thestreet.com/investing/bitcoin/tim-draper-reiterates-250000-dollar-bitcoin-price-target-14712907

Unlike Elizabeth Holmes who is facing criminal charges, Draper is free to say whatever he wants about Bitcoin and Blockchain, likely without fear of any consequences. There is no CEO of Bitcoin who might be held accountable, so Draper and other evangelists may fill the role of the cheerleader. They may preach to the faithful, preach to those with money looking to invest, and preach, and preach, and preach.

Shaping the Future

Draper preaches to anyone who will listen, including an April 25, 2018 presentation at Stanford "How Blockchain Will Change the World."[281]

Ladies and gentlemen, children of all ages, welcome to the Greatest Show on Earth!

---

[281] "Tim Draper: How Blockchain Will Change the World." *Stanford Bitcoin Club YouTube Channel*. Apr 24, 2018. https://youtu.be/jVVvG6nZTKA

CHAPTER 38
WIKILEAKS

The most famous Cypherpunk is probably the head of the WikiLeaks organization, Julian Assange. In 2012, Assange published the book ***Cypherpunks: Freedom and the Future of the Internet***. The book was written in the form of a dialogue between Mr. Assange and three fellow Cypherpunk activists.

Cypherpunk Rising

The Assange book details the major problems of the world from the perspective of the four Cypherpunk authors. Warnings are provided regarding the potentially inevitable dystopian future the world faces at the hands of governments and large corporations. An article published by *The Verge* and authored by R. U. Sirius, "Cypherpunk rising: WikiLeaks, encryption, and the coming surveillance dystopia", offers the following insights:

> In the recent book Cypherpunks: Freedom and the Future of the Internet, Assange enlists the help of three fellow heroes of free information to set the record straight, **aligning those principles with the ideas that Tim May dreamed up in 1989** [it was actually 1988] **with "The Crypto Anarchist Manifesto."**[282][*emphasis added*]

An Enemy of Every State

In *Cypherpunks*, Assange et al. outline their viewpoint and their mission as Cypherpunk crypto-anarchists. They are an enemy of every country on

---

[282] Sirius, R.U. "Cypherpunk rising: WikiLeaks, encryption, and the coming surveillance dystopia." *The Verge*. Mar 7, 2013. https://www.theverge.com/2013/3/7/4036040/cypherpunks-julian-assange-wikileaks-encryption-surveillance-dystopia

the planet. They are not merely an enemy of the state. They are an enemy of *every* state.

According to Assange:

> While many writers have considered what the internet means for global civilization, they are wrong. They are wrong because they do not have the sense of perspective that direct experience brings. They are wrong because they have never met the enemy.
>
> No description of the world survives first contact with the enemy.
>
> **We have met the enemy.** [*emphasis added*]
>
> Over the last six years, WikiLeaks has had conflicts with **nearly every powerful state**. We know the new surveillance state from an insider's perspective, because we have plumbed its secrets. We know it from a **combatant's perspective**, because we have had to protect our people, our finances and our sources from it. We know it from a global perspective, because **we have people, assets and information in nearly every country**. We know it from the perspective of time, because we have been **fighting** this phenomenon **for years** and have seen it double and spread, again and again. It is an invasive parasite, growing fat off societies that merge with the internet. It is rolling over the planet, infecting all states and peoples before it. [*emphasis added*]
>
> What is to be done?
>
> Once upon a time in a place that was neither here nor there, we, the constructors and citizens of the young internet discussed the future of our new world.
>
> We saw the relationships between all people would be mediated by our new world, and that the nature of **states**, which are defined by how people exchange **information, economic value, and force**, would also change. [*emphasis added*]
>
> We saw that the merger between existing state structures and the internet created an opening to **change the nature of states**. [*emphasis added*]

CHAPTER 38
WIKILEAKS

> First, recall that **states are systems through which coercive force flows**. Factions within a state may compete for support, leading to democratic surface phenomena, but **the underpinnings of states are the systematic application, and avoidance, of violence**. Land ownership, property, rents, dividends, taxation, court fines, censorship, **copyrights and trademarks** are all enforced by the threatened **application of state violence**.[283] [*emphasis added*]

Tim May's Galt's Gulch in Cyberspace

As has been discussed numerous times throughout *The Blockchain Code*, Bitcoin and Smart Contracts were created to help realize Tim May's vision to create "Galt's Gulch in Cyberspace." The dream is to create a hidden corner of cyberspace using computer encryption.

Assange describes this:

> But we discovered something. Our one hope against total domination. A hope that with courage, insight and solidarity we could use to resist. A strange property of the physical universe that we live in.
>
> The universe believes in encryption.
>
> It is easier to encrypt information than to decrypt it.
>
> We saw we could use this strange property to create the laws of a new world. To abstract away our new platonic realm from its base underpinnings of satellites, undersea cables and their controllers. To fortify our space behind a cryptographic veil. To create new lands barred to those who control physical reality, because to follow us into them would require infinite resources.
>
> And in this manner to declare independence.[284]

---

[283] Assange, Julian et al. *Cypherpunks: Freedom and the Future of the Internet* (OR Books, 2012), 1-3
[284] Ibid, 4

The introduction to *Cypherpunks* then talks about the Manhattan Project and compares encryption to nuclear weapons. Assange and his fellow Cypherpunks can use the awesomely powerful weapon of encryption to:

```
create regions free from the coercive force
of the outer state. Free from mass intercep-
tion. Free from state control.
    In this way, people can oppose their will
to that of a fully mobilized superpower and
win.285
```

The Anarchist Collective

Anarchy is about the avoidance of formal societal structure and hierarchy. A *mon*archy is an organizational structure with *one* ruler. *An*archy has *no* ruler. Anarchy rejects the concept of anybody (especially a government) telling anybody what to do.

There are no rulers, but there can be organizers of anarchy. To be effective, the Cypherpunks, WikiLeaks, and Anonymous have formed together into groups with the objective of destroying *every* state, *every* government on earth. They are a sort of *anti-social* social group. Cypherpunks, WikiLeaks, and Anonymous are all manifestations of anarchy. These three groups form a sort of *anarchist collective* that share ideology and likely have shared membership.

WikiLeaks is a Cypherpunks organization. Founder Julian Assange wrote an entire book called *Cypherpunks* to try to describe the Cypherpunk ideology and the mission of WikiLeaks. WikiLeaks seeks to make the Cypherpunk vision of Cryptoanarchy and collapse of government a reality.[286]

Collapse of government does not mean collapse of just one government. It means collapse of *all* governments. The Cypherpunks, WikiLeaks, and Anonymous, this **Anarchist Collective hates the United States government, the Russian government, and every other government on earth.** As Cypherpunk Crypto-Anarchist Assange puts it, "WikiLeaks has had conflicts with nearly *every* powerful state" which is "the enemy." WikiLeaks is at war with *every* government. In Assange's words, they are a "combatant" and has "been fighting... for years."[287]

---

[285] Ibid, 5
[286] Ibid, 1-6
[287] Ibid, 2

CHAPTER 38
WIKILEAKS

WikiLeaks is a powerful combatant that is at war with the United States government and at war the Russian government as well. Assange has called **both** governments "the enemy."[288] WikiLeaks likely hates the Russian government far more than the United States government because it is even more oppressive and controlling. Anarchists seek extreme freedom, where nobody, especially governments, tell anybody what they can and cannot do. In the eyes of WikiLeaks, *every* government on earth is evil and must be destroyed!

Hillary's Emails

Controversy surrounds virtually every event involving WikiLeaks. However, no event may have been more impactful than when WikiLeaks released Hillary Clinton's emails.

According to Assange, WikiLeaks has "people, assets and information in nearly every country." WikiLeaks is a powerful combatant fighting the United States government and the Russian government. **WikiLeaks'** "people and assets"[289] were able to obtain some particularly useful information in their war to destroy the United States government and the Russian Government when they obtained Hillary Clinton's emails.

The Source

Definitively identifying the source of Hillary's emails is extremely problematic. A great deal has been written on the subject, and as of the publication of this book, the Mueller investigation is still ongoing. If the hackers are very good, like Cypherpunks, like Anonymous, and like several state actors such as Russian Intelligence, they should be experts not only in obtaining the information but also in manipulating metadata and side channel footprints. While we may be able to determine a great deal of information, understanding what actually occurred with a very high degree of confidence in the accuracy of that information seems unlikely.

---

[288] Ibid
[289] Ibid

Credible Sources

When dealing with information of a political nature, the level of information control and spin surrounding the information may make it impossible for us to ever know what truly happened. However, we have various sources of information with differing levels of credibility.

One particularly thorough reporting source for these types of matters is *The Guardian*. Perhaps this is why Edward Snowden chose *The Guardian* to tell his story when he exposed troubling surveillance activity to the world. *The Guardian* interviewed a reporter, Kevin Collier, who had apparently exchanged emails with Guccifer 2.0, the handle of an alleged hacker involved with the DNC email leak. Collier observed peculiarities in the metadata of his email interactions with Guccifer that he felt indicated Guccifer was "either an amateur, made a huge mistake, or this is part of an incredibly intricate disinformation campaign."[290]

The popular story is that "the Russians" (presumed to be the Russian *government*) hacked the DNC and pilfered the emails. Then "the Russians" provided or leaked the information to WikiLeaks. The facts involving the Russian g*overnment* are unclear and confusing.

Russian Cypherpunks and American Cypherpunks, members of Anonymous, and supporters of WikiLeaks want to take down **both** governments. So, who are these "Russians?" Russian Cypherpunks? Or is this the Russian government? These are two very different things! Russian Cypherpunks want to *destroy* the Russian government! They also want to destroy the American government. They are anarchists.

The only clear *fact* we have is that Assange, a Cypherpunk anarchist, published the emails to the world. That is the only thing that we know for sure. Releasing these emails was a successful attack advancing the cause of anarchy.

The Aftermath

In the anarchists' war against the *United States government*, this action influenced the 2016 United States presidential election and resulted in the dismissal of an FBI director. Additionally, this began a chain of events culminating an investigation into a sitting President of the United States,

---

[290] Thielman, Sam. "DNC email leak: Russian hackers Cozy Bear and Fancy Bear behind breach." *The Guardian*. July 26, 2016. https://www.theguardian.com/technology/2016/jul/26/dnc-email-leak-russian-hack-guccifer-2

CHAPTER 38
WIKILEAKS

which further increased distrust in and dysfunction of government. The anarchists must be celebrating all the damage to the United States Government and especially to both of the two major political parties.

In the anarchists' war against the *Russian government*, this resulted in a series of sanctions on Russia including expulsion of 35 Russian diplomats from the United States. The email leak also led to the passage of a 2017 "Countering America's Adversaries through Sanctions Act" in the United States which placed additional sanctions on Russia. The Russian government responded with similar sanctions back against the United States. Anarchists looking to damage the Russian government must be quite pleased.

If you are an anarchist and your enemy is *all* governments, this email leak was a spectacularly successful attack against **both** governments. This resulted in direct damage to the United States, but also managed to damage the Russian government by damaging the relationship between the two governments.

Whenever you can get two common enemies to fight amongst themselves, you win.

The Hackers

The Cypherpunk/Anonymous/WikiLeaks anarchist collective likely contains some of the most skilled hackers on the planet. Did the email leak start out with the Cypherpunks/Anonymous/WikiLeaks and then get leaked to the Russian government? Was it the other way around? Something entirely different?

It is possible that the Russian government had nothing to do with the DNC hack whatsoever. This may have been entirely the work of this global Cypherpunk anarchist collective. The only fact we know for sure is that the emails were ***published*** *by this anarchist collective*, so that would make this a far *simpler, less elaborate* story.

WikiLeaks *Powered by Bitcoin*

In December 2010, Visa, MasterCard, PayPal, and others stopped processing payments for WikiLeaks, cutting off what was then the primary means of funding. Anonymous responded by taking down the websites of

Visa, MasterCard, and PayPal in "Operation Avenge Assange."[291] Since then, Bitcoin has become a primary means of funding WikiLeaks:

Assange has crowed how the attempts at shutting off sources of funding have backfired, promoting Bitcoin's meteoric price increases:

My deepest thanks to the US government, Senator McCain and Senator Lieberman for pushing Visa, MasterCard, Payal, AmEx, Mooneybookers, et al, into erecting an illegal banking blockade against @WikiLeaks starting in 2010. It caused us to invest in Bitcoin -- with > 50000% return.

The Program

As "James A. Donald" and "Satoshi Nakamoto" were preparing to launch Bitcoin, "James" declared Bitcoin as a "strike at the state from the jungle of complexity":

```
The Cypherpunk Program

Timothy C. May summarized the plan as

"Crypto Anarchy: encryption, digital money, anony-
mous networks, digital pseudonyms, zero knowledge,
reputations, information markets, black markets,
collapse of government.

Which is intentionally obscure.  The plan is to
strike at the state from the jungle of complexity,
```

---

[291] "WikiLeaks: Banking Blockade and Donations Campaign." WikiLeaks. Oct 24, 2011. https://wikileaks.org/IMG/pdf/WikiLeaks-Banking-Blockade-Information-Pack.pdf

CHAPTER 38
WIKILEAKS

to strike at the state from beyond the state's intellectual and temporal horizons. The evil minions of the state will not be coming after cypherpunks, because they will not understand what cypherpunks are doing, and because when things start going bad for them the [sic] will not be able to link cause and effect."[292]

Collapse of Governments

Could the Cypherpunk Program, this Crypto-Anarchy Game, actually *achieve* the stated goal of "collapse of governments?" There are some very oppressive governments, where this collapse might perhaps be desired, assuming what replaces the government (anarchy?) is actually better. How about the US government?

In the United States, polls show a clear downward trend in public confidence in government:

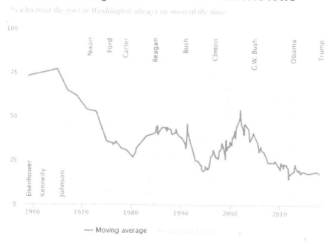

[293]

---

[292] "Donald, James A.". *The Cypherpunk Program*
[293] Pew Research Center. "Public Trust in Government: 1958-2017." Dec 14, 2017. http://www.people-press.org/2017/12/14/public-trust-in-government-1958-2017/

Public confidence in government is at or near historic lows. Is this all the work of the Cypherpunks? Of course not. However, the Cypherpunks have been doing their part, for nearly 30 years, to weaken, and hasten the demise of, all governments, everywhere.

In the early 16th century, the superior *technology* of fully armored Spanish horsemen destroyed the Inca Empire, which was then arguably the mightiest nation on earth.

In code we trust.

CHAPTER 39

NOW

If we honestly consider the *verifiable, indisputable* facts, the Republicans, the Democrats, and the Russian government finally have something that they *should* all agree on... a common enemy.

An Enemy of All States

The anarchists are equal-opportunity attackers looking to take down *all* governments, *all* politicians, and *all* political parties. Cypherpunk anarchists were without a doubt key actors, possibly the *only* actors, that triggered a series of events that resulted in a Special Counsel investigating a sitting President of the United States of America.[294] These events altered the course of the 2016 presidential election, damaged the United States government, damaged the Russian government, and damaged the relationship between these two nations.

Yet, the US national news story about the election and the Mueller investigation seems focused solely on what happened between the Trump campaign and "Russia." The popular implication appears to be that the Russian *government* was responsible for hacking into the Democratic National Committee (DNC) and pilfering Hillary's emails, not Russian members of Cypherpunks/WikiLeaks/Anonymous. I have little doubt that the Russian government attempted to influence the 2016 US presidential election. The United States government tries to influence other country's elections, too.[295]

---

[294] See Chapter 38
[295] Shane, Scott. "Russia Isn't the Only One Meddling in Elections. We Do It, Too." *The New York Times*. Feb 17, 2018. https://www.nytimes.com/2018/02/17/sunday-review/russia-isnt-the-only-one-meddling-in-elections-we-do-it-too.html

However, with respect to the **DNC email hack**, evidence of any involvement from the Russian *government* is unclear. Let's read the US government report. The "Background to" section of "Assessing Russian Activities and Intentions in Recent US Elections" from the US government states, "An assessment of attribution usually is not a simple statement of who conducted an operation, but rather a series of **judgments** [*emphasis added*] that describe… who was the **likely** [*emphasis added*] perpetrator."[296] Effectively, the official report from the US government says, "we are making our best guess."

The report discusses "press reporting that suggests more than one person claiming to be Guccifer 2.0 interacted with journalists."[297] However, the assessment directly from a journalist interacting with Guccifer 2.0 was, "It's baffling, he's either an amateur, made a huge mistake, **or this is part of an incredibly intricate disinformation campaign.**"[298] [*emphasis added*] This information was not included in the intelligence report.

The report itself says, "We assess with high confidence that the GRU [the Russian Intelligence Agency] relayed material it acquired from the DNC and senior Democratic officials to WikiLeaks." No evidence supplied in the report appears to support the "high confidence" comment, which itself seems roughly equivalent to "we believe our guess is a really good guess." The report continues to assess that, "Moscow most likely chose WikiLeaks because of its self-proclaimed reputation for authenticity." What does that even mean? Russia leaked the emails to WikiLeaks because "WikiLeaks calls themselves 'authentic'?" This assessment appears to be pure speculation.[299]

Despite the actual evidence, the anarchists, who were **the only irrefutably involved party in obtaining and publishing Clinton's emails,**[300] appear to be all but absent from the current popular news story. Imagine if when the United States was attacked at Pearl Harbor, which was clearly

---

[296] Office of the Director of National Intelligence, USA. 2017. "Background to 'Assessing Russian Activities and Intentions in Recent US Elections': The Analytic Process and Cyber Incident Attribution." Jan 6. https://www.dni.gov/files/documents/ICA_2017_01.pdf, p2

[297] Office of the Director of National Intelligence, USA. 2017. "Assessing Russian Activities and Intentions in Recent US Elections." Jan 6. https://www.dni.gov/files/documents/ICA_2017_01.pdf, p3

[298] Thielman. "DNC email leak…"

[299] Office of the Director of National Intelligence. "Assessing Russian Activities…", p3

[300] See Chapter 38

CHAPTER 39
NOW

done by Japan, we simply overlooked Japan's involvement and focused solely on Germany. Hitler was clearly the enemy, so let's not even talk about Japan??? Crypto-anarchists are hard at work, trying to realize the dream of "collapse of governments."[301]

The *Anti*-State

As we have demonstrated in detail throughout this book, the anarchist collective is busily trying to create an anonymous, hidden corner of cyberspace. This hidden "country" of sorts has its own "currency." There has been an all-out assault on the integrity of our institutions of higher learning. Bitcoins have been given away to college students on a massive scale, and this has been combined with price manipulation.[302] This has been followed by the great story of Blockchain, which will magically change everything for the better, though the reality does not match the fantasy.[303]

Cryptocurrency and Blockchain-based systems[304] are designed to live outside of the visibility and reach of governments and laws. This facilitates money laundering and investor fraud like no other system ever created. Cryptocurrencies enable ransomware and other extortion.[305] Anonymous digital money threatens the integrity of our political system, which already struggles to provide financial transparency of donors and lobbyists.[306]

Cryptocurrencies support an entire underworld economy for criminals and terrorists. This economy exists outside of the concept of national borders. Crimes such as assassinations can be funded and coordinated without any of the parties ever knowing anyone's identity by using smart contracts on a blockchain.[307]

---

[301] This has been demonstrated numerous times throughout this book and this goal has been a permanent fixture of Tim May's email signature. This is also explicitly stated in "James A. Donald's" apparent "declaration of war", *The Cypherpunk Program,* shortly before Bitcoin was announced.
[302] See Chapters 30 and 35
[303] See Chapter 31
[304] Especially *permissionless* Blockchain
[305] See Chapters 17 and 19
[306] See Chapters 29-32, 36-38 - especially Chapter 36
[307] All of this has been demonstrated repeatedly throughout the book.

The Future

Cryptocurrencies and Blockchain are truly designed to be encrypted (hidden) and exist outside of governments, so they may possibly exist regardless of any efforts to regulate them. Governments appear to have no idea what to do about cryptoanarchy, and this is by design. Cryptoanarchy has been designed by truly brilliant minds and has been under development and refinement for over thirty years. As a result, governments are being successfully manipulated into doing things that are *enabling* cryptoanarchy.[308] The first email ever sent to the Cypherpunks mailing list declared how they were smarter than every government on earth.[309] That may be true.

Lawmakers in my home state of Arizona and several other states have passed laws providing the validation that the anarchists seek.[310] Money continues to flow into cryptocurrency exchanges, into cryptocurrency businesses, into IPOs, and into hard forks.[311] These investors are at a high risk of losing their investments in the multiple ways that we have demonstrated throughout this book.

Cashing Out

If you believe you own cryptocurrency and are considering cashing out, realize that if you owned bitcoins as of August 1, 2017, the hard fork of Bitcoin that created Bitcoin Cash gave you those exact same bitcoins again as Bitcoin Cash bitcoins. The same thing goes for Bitcoin Gold, which hard forked from Bitcoin on October 24, 2017. There are several other hard forks where you may able to cash out multiple times with the same bitcoins depending on if you owned bitcoins at the time of the hard fork. In this case, there is actually a chance that you may own *more* cryptocurrency than you thought.[312] Hard forks are one example of how others can exploit investors' lack of knowledge. Knowledge is power, so now you should know.

---

[308] Discussed at various points in the book, see Chapters 32, 36, and 38, in particular for discussions of government response that actively enables crypto-anarchy

[309] See Chapter 4

[310] See Chapter 36

[311] See Chapter 34

[312] Ibid, see detailed explanation on how bitcoins and other cryptocurrency are copied through hard forks

CHAPTER 39
NOW

Possible Governmental Response

With respect to the United States, our representative democratic government is theoretically created by, for, and of The People. So, ultimately the US governmental response to some extent comes down to the will of the people. So what do you think? What do you and I want to do about this?

We could let things run its course. Perhaps governments of the world are supposed to die, as the anarchists believe. Or perhaps it is time to put an end to the now not-so-crypto madness.

Should Cryptocurrency Exchanges Be Legal?

A reasonable definition for a cryptocurrency exchange is probably "any entity exchanging traditional money for the promise of owning cryptocurrency." This would cover anybody selling any cryptocurrency (existing coins, hard forks, and ICOs). As long as cryptocurrency exchanges exist there are risks of direct fraud as well as facilitating terrorist and other criminal activity. Are cryptocurrency exchanges something that we want for our society? If there is one place where legislation is likely to make the most impact, it would be to limit or probably ban cryptocurrency exchanges altogether.

Existing Laws

Although cryptocurrency exchanges may purport to trade "currencies", a currency typically requires a recognized government that is responsible for that currency. Should "the hidden place in cyberspace created by anarchists that seek to destroy all governments" qualify as an official government? Probably not. Should cryptocurrencies such as Bitcoin ever be considered a currency?

Whether cryptocurrency is a currency or not, in the United States, money transmission laws that were enacted to deter money laundering still apply to exchanges. There are cryptocurrency exchanges that have successfully obtained such licenses, which is a highly questionable licensing decision.

An exchange may possibly perform various activities designed to comply with money transmission laws, but cryptocurrencies were created to live outside of the concept of governments and laws. If you are trying to curtail money laundering, how is it acceptable to provide a license for an exchange to convert money into a platform that is designed to circumvent all money laundering laws??? What is the logic in this?

If as a society, we are looking to relax and eventually kill all money laundering laws, continuing to license cryptocurrency exchanges seems to be a reasonable way to do this. If as a society, we want to continue to have money laundering laws, these licenses should probably be revoked from cryptocurrency exchanges, and these exchanges should be made illegal.

Blockchain Future

How will the great story of Blockchain play out? The Blockchain technology validation machine is very real, and it is everywhere. This is not just cryptocurrency-flooded colleges, it is not just IBM, and it is not just Deloitte. In November 2018, Microsoft released version 1.0 of its Azure Blockchain Development Kit for the company's cloud platform. Blockchain developers and crypto-anarchists of the world, rejoice!

If you are a Blockchain technology investor or developer, I would encourage you to take a long hard look at the reality of the technology. If you are working with private or permissioned Blockchain, time will tell how this goes. The prospects for the viability of this version of the technology is questionable at this time. There are likely simpler, more reliable, more efficient, and more secure approaches to build whatever you are creating. Be honest with yourself and with others about what you are doing.[313]

The original, permissionless (cryptocurrency-style) Blockchain may turn out to be the only effective use case in the long run. This version of the technology is great for creating ultra-anonymous, untraceable systems that exist outside of government visibility and control.[314] It is a powerful technology and "with great power comes great responsibility."[315]

Blockchain technology is creative, yet imperfect. Cryptocurrencies prove that there is potential applicability of this technology. If you are convinced that the ultra-anonymous, untraceable application you are building is a great thing for the world, go for it, but be honest about what you are building and about the technology.[316]

---

[313] See Chapters 31 and 32
[314] Ibid
[315] These are the words of Peter Parker's Uncle Ben in Marvel's *Spiderman* comics and movies, and it is a great quote. Rest in Peace, Stan Lee (1922-2018).
[316] See Chapters 31 and 32

CHAPTER 39
NOW

Decryption Complete

Our journey through the jungle of complexity is complete, and now you know the crypto-truth.

APPENDIX
THE CRYPTO-STORY OF MELTDOWN

On January 2, 2018, a news report was published about a flaw that became known as *Meltdown*. This is a problem built into Central Processing Unit (CPU) chips made **by Intel**, but not Intel rival Advanced Micro Devices (AMD).[317][318] Let's look at how the story changed over time by reviewing the details and using the Wayback Machine to understand what happened.

This story is important in its own right because:

- In August 2018, another Intel-only vulnerability was announced (Foreshadow).[319] Understanding the facts about Meltdown is helpful in understanding other CPU data breach risks.
- Several months after Intel knew about the Meltdown bug, but before it was announced, Intel's then-CEO, Brian Krzanich sold all the Intel stock he could within the constraints of the company's by-laws.[320] There has been no SEC investigation into possible illegal insider trading.

This story is important to Blockchain for several reasons:

- Regarding the Krzanich stock sale, the manner in which government regulations work and are enforced (or are not enforced) is important to the story of cryptoanarchy and Blockchain.

---

[317] Lipp, Schwarz, Gruss, et. al. Meltdown: Reading Kernel Memory from User Space. https://mlq.me/download/meltdown.pdf

[318] AMD Processor Security - Previous Updates, https://www.amd.com/en/corporate/speculative-execution-previous-updates#paragraph-337801

[319] AMD Processor Security Updates, https://www.amd.com/en/corporate/security-updates

[320] Eassa, Ashraf. "Intel's CEO Just Sold a Lot of Stock." *The Motley Fool.* Dec 19, 2017. https://www.fool.com/investing/2017/12/19/intels-ceo-just-sold-a-lot-of-stock.aspx

- Data leaks threaten to expose sensitive information, and this includes information from cryptocurrency wallets. Leaky wallets can allow others to spend your cryptocurrency.
- The Meltdown story is a story about side-channel vulnerabilities. While cryptocurrencies are designed to be anonymous and untraceable, the technology is made by imperfect human hands. There will always be potential side-channels that threaten to de-anonymize cryptocurrency actors. Gaining a better understanding of the largest side-channel exposure to date is instructive when considering Blockchain's side-channel risks.
- The full story of Meltdown has been largely encrypted (hidden) by a jungle of complexity much like the truth about Blockchain.

JUNE 1, 2017

Bug Report

Jann Horn from Google's Project Zero submitted a bug report to Intel, Arm Holdings, and AMD detailing two flaws called Spectre and Meltdown.[321] Project Zero security researchers look for *zero-day* (undiscovered) vulnerabilities. Project Zero's policy allows for 90 days for bug fixes to be created before they announce discovered flaws. This huge, complex bug that was discovered resulted in a highly unusual 7-month "information embargo"[322] that was ended **by a press release from Intel**.[323]

---

[321] Kahn, Webb, & Bernath. "How a 22-Year-Old Discovered the Worst Chip Flaws in History." *Bloomberg*. Jan 17, 2018. https://www.bloomberg.com/news/articles/2018-01-17/how-a-22-year-old-discovered-the-worst-chip-flaws-in-history

[322] Thomson, Iain. "Revealed: El Reg blew lid off Meltdown CPU bug before Intel told US govt – and how bitter tech rivals teamed up." *The Register*. Aug 8, 2018. https://www.theregister.co.uk/2018/08/09/meltdown_spectre_cert_timing/

[323] King, Ian and Cao, Jing. "Intel Confronts Potential 'PR Nightmare' With Reported Chip Flaw." *Bloomberg*. Jan 3, 2018 5:37 AM MST. https://www.bloomberg.com/news/articles/2018-01-03/amd-soars-after-rival-intel-said-to-reveal-processor-flaw

Both flaws are problems that needed to be fixed, but **Meltdown is the more serious bug.** It is easier to exploit than Spectre.[324] In addition, per the definitive paper on the subject, "Meltdown breaks all security assumptions given by address space isolation as well as paravirtualized environments... Meltdown enables an adversary to read memory of other processes or virtual machines in the cloud without any permissions or privileges, affecting millions of customers and virtually every user of a personal computer."[325]

Daniel Gruss is a co-author of *both* the definitive paper defining Meltdown and the definitive paper defining Spectre. Gruss said **Meltdown is "probably one of the worst CPU bugs ever found."**[326]

AMD is unaffected by Meltdown. Because the problem is a *data theft* problem, undetected damage may have been occurring for many years. Meltdown may *still* be exploited on some unpatched Intel servers, but not on AMD servers.

Meltdown is the result of a Design Decision

Speculative execution is a performance-enhancing feature where CPUs perform educated guesses ("speculation") regarding what instructions may need to be run in the future. This allows processors to do more work simultaneously, which significantly improves performance. Processors also play a foundational role in computer security by ensuring that rules and permissions are enforced.

To gain a performance advantage, **Intel did not strictly enforce memory access permission rules** before speculatively executing code. AMD consistently performed these checks before speculating and did not speculatively execute code that lacked proper permission.[327] [328]

---

[324] Meltdown and Spectre, https://spectreattack.com and https://meltdownattack.com

[325] Lipp, Schwarz, Gruss, et. al. *Meltdown*. https://meltdownattack.com/meltdown.pdf

[326] Gibbs, Samuel. "Meltdown and Spectre: 'worst ever' CPU bugs affect virtually all computers." *The Guardian*. Jan 4, 2018. https://www.theguardian.com/technology/2018/jan/04/meltdown-spectre-worst-cpu-bugs-ever-found-affect-computers-intel-processors-security-flaw

[327] Lipp, Schwarz, Gruss, et. al. *Meltdown: Reading Kernel Memory*

[328] AMD Processor Security Update

At the risk of speculation by this author, perhaps the thinking by Intel's engineers was that all of the speculatively executed work was "all just speculation", so they could relax the rules and only perform these checks if the results were needed "for real." If it turned out that the speculatively executed results were needed, the permissions would be checked before using the results. If the process lacked the required permissions, the results would be discarded, and it would be *as if the code never ran.* This would be reasonable thinking and a reasonable design decision to improve performance. However, the code *did* actually run, which left footprints that could be detected via side-channel analysis.

Meltdown is potentially bad for Intel from a data breach liability standpoint. Additionally, Meltdown patches introduce some unique performance penalties for Intel CPUs since systems with AMD CPUs should not require certain performance-limiting patches. Moreover, AMD can claim a certain security advantage over Intel with respect to avoiding certain avenues of speculative execution attack. All of this is terrible for Intel and great for Intel competitor AMD.

NOVEMBER 29, 2017

Intel CEO Sells Most of his Intel Stock!

The Meltdown and Spectre problems were so huge that there was an unprecedented "news blackout" surrounding the bombshell bug report that miraculously held for the better part of 2017. *In the midst of the unprecedented information blackout*, on November 29, 2017, a little over a month before Intel's massive security flaw became public, company CEO at that time Brian Krzanich executed a nearly 1 million share, $40M sale of Intel stock.[329][330]

---

[329] Eassa. "Intel's CEO Just Sold a Lot of Stock"
[330] Greenwald, Ted. *The Wall Street Journal.* "Intel CEO's Stock Sale Called Unusual by Private Securities Specialists" (Jan 8, 2018), https://www.wsj.com/articles/intel-ceos-stock-sale-called-unusual-by-private-securities-specialists-1515407400

JANUARY 2, 2018

Meltdown Uncovered & Reported

An article by John Leyden and Chris Williams titled "Kernel-memory-leaking **Intel** processor design flaw forces Linux, Windows redesign" was published by *The Register*. This ***initially*** published article provided a detailed and accurate report about **Intel's Meltdown** bug.[331]

The Register report included a quote from an AMD software engineer who effectively said (though in far more technical terms): <u>AMD CPUs do not have the Meltdown bug</u>. *The Register* correctly analyzed the actual detailed statement and produced an astute analysis that concluded that **Intel's CPUs**:

```
...would allow ring-3-level user code to read
ring-0-level kernel data. And that is not
good.332
```

This means that Intel's CPUs would violate a foundational security rule when speculatively executing code (as previously described). Nobody was ever supposed to be able to see this, but like a safecracker with a stethoscope listening to the clicks, a way to see the previously unseen information had been figured out. This is Intel's Meltdown bug, and AMD was unaffected by Meltdown. Things were looking very bad for Intel (and their then CEO).

JANUARY 3, 2018

5:37 AM MST – *Bloomberg*
"Black eye for Intel, Benefit for AMD"

A Bloomberg article highlighted how the bug reported by *The Register* is a "black eye for Intel" and that this news would benefit AMD. The article highlighted that AMD shares rose 7.2% and Intel fell 3.8% and indicated that "Intel is expected to release a statement, but hasn't yet commented on

---

[331] Leyden and Williams. *The Register*. "Kernel-memory-leaking Intel processor design flaw forces Linux, Windows redesign" (Jan 2, 2018), https://www.theregister.co.uk/2018/01/02/intel_cpu_design_flaw/
[332] Ibid

the issue." An analyst was quoted, "They need to get ahead of this and try to contain the damage to customers as well as to the brand."[333]

~3:16 PM PST[334], Intel Responds, Ending The News Blackout!

The *initial* story by *The Register* about the Meltdown bug was accurate and extremely damaging to Intel. Intel issued a press release with their spin on the story:

> **Intel Responds to Security Research Findings**
> Intel and other technology companies have been made aware of new security research describing software analysis methods that, when used for malicious purposes, have the potential to improperly gather sensitive data from computing devices that are operating as designed. Intel believes these exploits do not have the potential to corrupt, modify or delete data.
>
> Recent reports that these exploits are caused by a "bug" or a "flaw" and are **unique to Intel products** [*emphasis added*] are incorrect. Based on the analysis to date, many types of computing devices — with many different vendors' processors and operating systems — are susceptible to these exploits.
>
> Intel is committed to product and customer security and is working closely with many other technology companies, including AMD, ARM Holdings and several operating system vendors, to develop an industry-wide approach to resolve this issue promptly and constructively. Intel has begun providing software and firmware updates to mitigate these exploits. Contrary to some reports, any performance impacts are workload-dependent, and, for the average computer user, should not be significant and will be mitigated over time.
>
> Intel is committed to the industry best practice of responsible disclosure of potential

---

[333] King, Ian and Cao, Jing. "Intel Confronts Potential 'PR Nightmare'…"
[334] Per the timestamp of the first captured page in The Wayback Machine

security issues, which is why Intel and other vendors had planned to disclose this issue next week when more software and firmware updates will be available. However, Intel is making this statement today because of the current inaccurate media reports.

Check with your operating system vendor or system manufacturer and apply any available updates as soon as they are available. Following good security practices that protect against malware in general will also help protect against possible exploitation until updates can be applied.

Intel believes its products are the most secure in the world and that, with the support of its partners, the current solutions to this issue provide the best possible security for its customers.[335]

~Twelve Minutes Later, 3:28 PM[336]

Google Project Zero, the organization that was the first to discover and report the problem to Intel, officially announced problem details to the world in an article titled "Reading privileged memory with a side-channel."[337]

JANUARY 4, 2018

The next day, *The Register* responded to Intel's press release, with an article, "We translated Intel's crap attempt to spin its way out of CPU security bug PR nightmare." This article continued to focus on **Meltdown**, which it accurately describes as the more serious problem. As the article

---

[335] Intel. "Intel Responds to Security Research Findings" Company Press Release. Jan 3, 2018. https://newsroom.intel.com/news/intel-responds-to-security-research-findings/

[336] Per timestamp of the first captured page in The Wayback Machine

[337] "Reading privileged memory with a side-channel." Google Project Zero. Jan 3, 2018. https://googleprojectzero.blogspot.com/2018/01/reading-privileged-memory-with-side.html

quotes the Meltdown paper, "Meltdown breaks all security assumptions given by the CPU's memory isolation capabilities."[338]

The article includes a quote from Linux creator Linus Torvalds, "I think somebody inside of Intel needs to really take a long hard look at their CPUs, and actually admit that they have issues instead of writing PR blurbs that say that everything works as designed." *The Register* continues to report that the main problem is **Meltdown** and that AMD is unaffected by Meltdown.[339]

A second story was posted by *Quartz Media*, "Intel Insider? Intel's CEO sold off the majority of his stock after finding out about the chip flaws."[340]

JANUARY 8, 2018

Bloomberg, "Intel CEO's Stock Sales" Article

Bloomberg published an article, "Intel CEO's Stock Sales May Warrant SEC Examination." Steven Crimmins, a former SEC enforcement lawyer, indicated, "**The size of the transaction makes it inevitable that the SEC will take a look at this.** But I have to believe that the executive would have been exceptionally well advised by a good securities lawyer and everything would have been cleared. People who are CEOs of companies like Intel don't make mistakes like this."[341]

---

[338] Claburn, Thomas. "We translated Intel's crap attempt to spin its way out of CPU security bug PR nightmare." *The Register*. Jan 4, 2018. https://www.theregister.co.uk/2018/01/04/intel_meltdown_spectre_bugs_the_registers_annotations/

[339] Ibid

[340] Murphy, Mike. *Quartz Media*. "Intel Insider? Intel's CEO sold off the majority of his stock after finding out about the chip flaws." (Jan 4, 2018) https://qz.com/1171811/intel-intc-ceo-brian-krzanich-sold-off-the-majority-of-his-stock-after-finding-out-about-the-meltdown-and-spectre-security-flaws/

[341] Ritcey, Alicia & Melin, Anders. *Bloomberg*. "Intel CEO's Stock Sales May Warrant SEC Examination" (Jan 8, 2018), https://www.bloomberg.com/news/articles/2018-01-08/intel-ceo-krzanich-s-stock-sales-seen-warranting-sec-examination

The NASDAQ website publishes two years of insider stock sales. The following is a bar graph of the open market stock sales of Intel stock performed by then-CEO Brian Krzanich:

Intel CEO Krzanich - Open Market Stock Sales

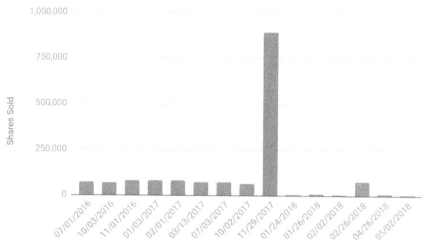

Data compiled from *www.nasdaq.com/symbol/intc/insider-trades*

The above bar graph displays the dates of all of the open market stock sales and the number of shares sold as published by the NASDAQ website. The huge bar represents the sale of all of the Intel stock that Krzanich was able to sell without violating company bylaws - one month before the Meltdown flaw became public information.[342] Despite the apparent "inevitability" of the SEC investigation, based upon Mr. Crimmins' assessment, **as of the publication of this book, nearly a year later, an SEC investigation has <u>still</u> not happened.**

Ritcey and Melin noted, "This past October [2017] he [Krzanich] issued a new set of instructions. Plus, he sold thousands more shares last year than in previous years." The trades were supposedly "pre-arranged… with the sale instructions determined at the end of October."[343] According to this article, it appears that the instructions were determined in the midst of the crisis with no public disclosure of the problems to be automatically

---

[342] Eassa, Ashraf. *The Motley Fool*. "Intel's CEO Just Sold a Lot of Stock" https://www.fool.com/investing/2017/12/19/intels-ceo-just-sold-a-lot-of-stock.aspx (Dec. 19, 2017)

[343] Ritcey and Melin. "Intel CEO's Stock Sales May Warrant SEC…"

executed one month later at the end of November. This would still be in the midst of the crisis and before public disclosure of the problems!

Is the argument that because the sale was technically "automatic" in that it was determined one month before the sale, this somehow waives obligations with respect to trading with insider information??? The Bloomberg article indicates that the sales in March, July, and October were pre-arranged in 2017.[344] That makes sense and is consistent with the bar graph above.

The problem is the **November sale which the article indicates was determined in October. This sale is large and inconsistent with the other trades.** It was a sale of every share of Intel stock that Krzanich could sell within the constraints of Intel's bylaws![345]

The article indicates that a company spokesperson said, "Brian's sale is unrelated. It was made pursuant to a pre-arranged stock plan with an automated schedule." The following graph was included in the Bloomberg article (presumably supplied by Intel/Krzanich)[346]:

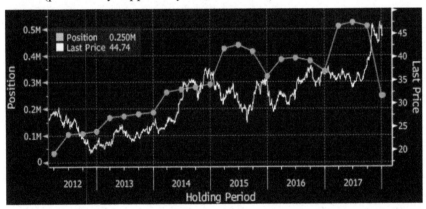

The above graph is extremely misleading in that it does not even include the 644,135 in options that Krzanich exercised and sold![347] The graph only records the 245,743 shares that he already owned and sold as a "reduction in position." When you exercise and simultaneously sell stock options, you never "own" the stock, it is not part of your "position." That

---

[344] Ibid
[345] Eassa, Ashraf. *The Motley Fool.* "Intel's CEO Just Sold a Lot of Stock"
[346] Ritcey and Melin. "Intel CEO's Stock Sales May Warrant SEC..."
[347] Ibid

is unless you define in-the-money and vested options as part of your "position", which this graph clearly did not.

When you exercise and sell, you simply cash out the option and pocket the spread between the option price and the sale price as cash. This graph would be overly complicated and misleading enough without that omission. By omitting stock options, the complicated graph ignores the majority of the November stock sale!

The simpler bar graph earlier in this chapter makes it plain. The complicated graph published in the Bloomberg article (above) appears to try to justify a massive, out of character, clearly suspicious stock sale!

Regardless, this stock trading story also seems to have been overshadowed and encrypted (hidden) by the much larger overall "Spectre/Meltdown" story, which was then dominating the news.

JANUARY 11, 2018

A Great Story Encrypts the Truth

On January 11, 2018, *The Verge* published an engaging, well-written story with a cool shadowy picture at the top called "Keeping Spectre Secret." This version of the story became the most popular rendition of what had happened. By the time this article was written, the hardcore spin had reshaped the story. <u>The story of **Meltdown** continued to fade more and more into the background.</u>

MAY 17, 2018

Intel Annual Shareholder Meeting

- Three very long-time board members (who had been on the board a combined 62 years) did not seek re-election and resigned.
- Krzanich sidestepped questions about AMD's recent market share increase in data centers at the expense of Intel.
- Responding to a shareholder question regarding his large sale of Intel stock, Krzanich said, "The sale is not at all a reflection of my confidence in the company. Intel continues to be my largest single

holding, and I continue to hold ABOVE the required level that the company has for me."[348]

JUNE 15, 2018

Motley Fool Article - Revisiting Krzanich Stock Sale and Questioning Server CPU Story

Ashraf Eassa published an article in *Motley Fool* revisiting the Krzanich stock sale indicating, "It looked bad before, but in light of recent developments, it's even worse than I thought." Eassa stands by the story he published on December 17, 2017, which contradicts Krzanich statements in the shareholder meeting saying:

> Back in December, I noticed that Intel (NASDAQ:INTC) CEO Brian Krzanich sold a *lot* of stock, effectively unloading as many shares as he could while still maintaining the minimum number of shares as required by Intel's corporate bylaws.[349]

The article goes on to highlight how Krzanich is publicly expressing confidence that Intel can "continue to deliver that leadership performance", but is telling analysts that Intel is set to lose significant market share to AMD in the data center processor market. The article concludes:

> Sorry, Krzanich, but your story doesn't add up.

Eassa was poking around the troublesome stock sale question. Even more troublesome for Intel, <u>he was asking the kind of questions that Intel does not want to have asked</u> regarding **Intel server CPUs versus AMD server CPUs**.

---

[348] Intel Annual Stockholders' Meeting 2018. May 17, 2018. Webcast Replay - https://intel.onlineshareholdermeeting.com/vsm/web?pvskey=INTEL18

[349] Eassa, Ashraf. " Revisiting Intel CEO Brian Krzanich's Huge Stock Sale." *The Motley Fool*. June 15, 2018. https://www.fool.com/investing/2018/06/15/revisiting-intel-ceo-brian-krzanichs-huge-stock-sa.aspx

JUNE 21, 2018 (ONE WEEK AFTER THE MOTLEY FOOL ARTICLE)

Intel CEO Forced to Resign

Krzanich resigned on June 21, 2018. This was one week after the Motley Fool article and nearly 7 months after the $40M stock sale. The reason provided by Intel for the apparently forced resignation was that he had a consensual affair with an Intel employee, in violation of company anti-fraternization rules. There is no mention of any potential insider trading concerns in the press release.[350]

SUMMARY

Numerous reporters have voiced concern regarding potential illegal insider trading. One such reporter is Forbes' Ken Kam who says, "Now, if Krzanich committed to sell far enough in advance that he could not have known about the coming crisis I would give him the benefit of the doubt. **But, Jan Horn, from Google Project Zero, has said on the record that he informed Intel on June 1, 2017 about their cpu's vulnerabilities. By October, when Krzanich changed his schedule of planned sales, I find it hard to believe that he did not already know of the coming crisis.**"[351] [*emphasis added*]

I share the concerns voiced by Kam, Mike Murphy, Alicia Ritcey, Melvin Anders, Ted Greenwald, and Ashraf Eassa. Many others have written about this that I have not already referenced in this chapter: Bret Kenwell, Sean Gallagher, Renae Merle, Troy Wolverton, the list goes on

---

[350] Intel. "Intel CEO Brian Krzanich Resigns, Board Appoints Bob Swan as Interim CEO." Company Press Release. June 21, 2018. https://newsroom.intel.com/news-releases/intel-ceo-brian-krzanich-resigns-board-appoints-bob-swan-interim-ceo/

[351] Kam, Ken. "Does It Matter That Intel And Facebook CEOs Sold Stock During A Crisis?" *Forbes Magazine*. Mar 31, 2018. https://www.forbes.com/sites/kenkam/2018/03/31/does-it-matter-that-intel-and-facebook-ceos-sold-stock-during-a-crisis/#7088a5fd5295

and on and on. Intel was in the midst of what should have arguably been the largest crisis in the company's history. In a stressful interaction with Linus Torvalds, one Intel Engineer even raised the spectre of "a two-decade product recall and giving everyone free CPUs."[352]

Krzanich likely knew that Intel's marketing machine was good, but it seems unlikely he could have expected the spin to be as successful as it was. In addition, as the Foreshadow bug demonstrates, Intel is *still* contending with speculative execution architectural problems that does not impact AMD. Foreshadow was discovered in January 2018 and disclosed to the public on August 14, 2018.[353]

Intel was able to realize a performance *advantage* over AMD for many years with a design that did not strictly check permissions before speculatively executing code. This competitive advantage has now flipped around, and Intel's speculative execution design has become a *liability* for Intel that they must now resolve. AMD's design, which appears to strictly check permissions before speculatively executing code should pay dividends for the company some time to come. As CEO, it seems likely that Krzanich would have been aware of not just the short-term impact, but also the long-term impacts that Meltdown represented to Intel.

In January 2018, Bloomberg's expert advised that an SEC investigation into the Krzanich stock sale was "inevitable." Nearly a year later, as this book is published, this investigation has <u>still</u> not occurred.

A Great Story Encrypts

The scandal of a consensual sexual affair and the resignation of Krzanich gave Motley Fool and others plenty of other things to write about, so we could all move on from **Intel's data center CPU market share losses and the Krzanich stock sale**.

The Meltdown story is recent, yet the truth has already been heavily spun and become largely encrypted (hidden). The spin surrounding Blockchain far exceeds the spin surrounding Meltdown and has been spun for many years.

---

[352] Email discussion between Linus Torvalds and Intel Engineer, David Woodhouse. "Re: [RFC 09/10] x86/enter: Create macros to restrict/unrestrict Indirect Branch Speculation." Jan 21, 2018. https://lkml.org/lkml/2018/1/21/192

[353] Foreshadow - Breaking the Virtual Memory Abstraction. https://foreshadowattack.eu/

ACKNOWLEDGMENTS

Stephanie, you are my partner in life and truly my better half. Thank you for your patience and love. I would not be the man I am without you and this book would not be the book it is, without your candid, detailed feedback.

David Rice, thank you for diving in on my earliest raw drafts and challenging me in all the right places.

Mom and Dad, thanks for your review, suggestions, and questions. Your feedback challenged me to improve the structure of the book to make it more accessible to the non-technical reader. This encouraged me to further simplify, clarify, and provide additional history of Crypto-Anarchy.

Nelson, you are the best father-in-law I could ask for in so many ways. Thank you for sticking it out and reading one of my earlier very rough drafts all the way through. Your direct, candid feedback encouraged me to strengthen my conclusion and ensure that I could prove all of my assertions. You are partially responsible for this book having 350 footnotes.

Peter Myers, thank you for your review and comments on early drafts. As a cryptocurrency and Blockchain advocate, your feedback was enormously helpful.

Bill Fox and Cory Young thanks for your thoughtful review and feedback.

Janelle and Sarah, thank you for your support and understanding. I love you and I am so proud of both of you.

Lisa Bormaster Fontes, thank you for insisting that I write about Blockchain in the first place. Neither of us could have had any idea what you were getting me into.

Made in the USA
Middletown, DE
27 February 2019